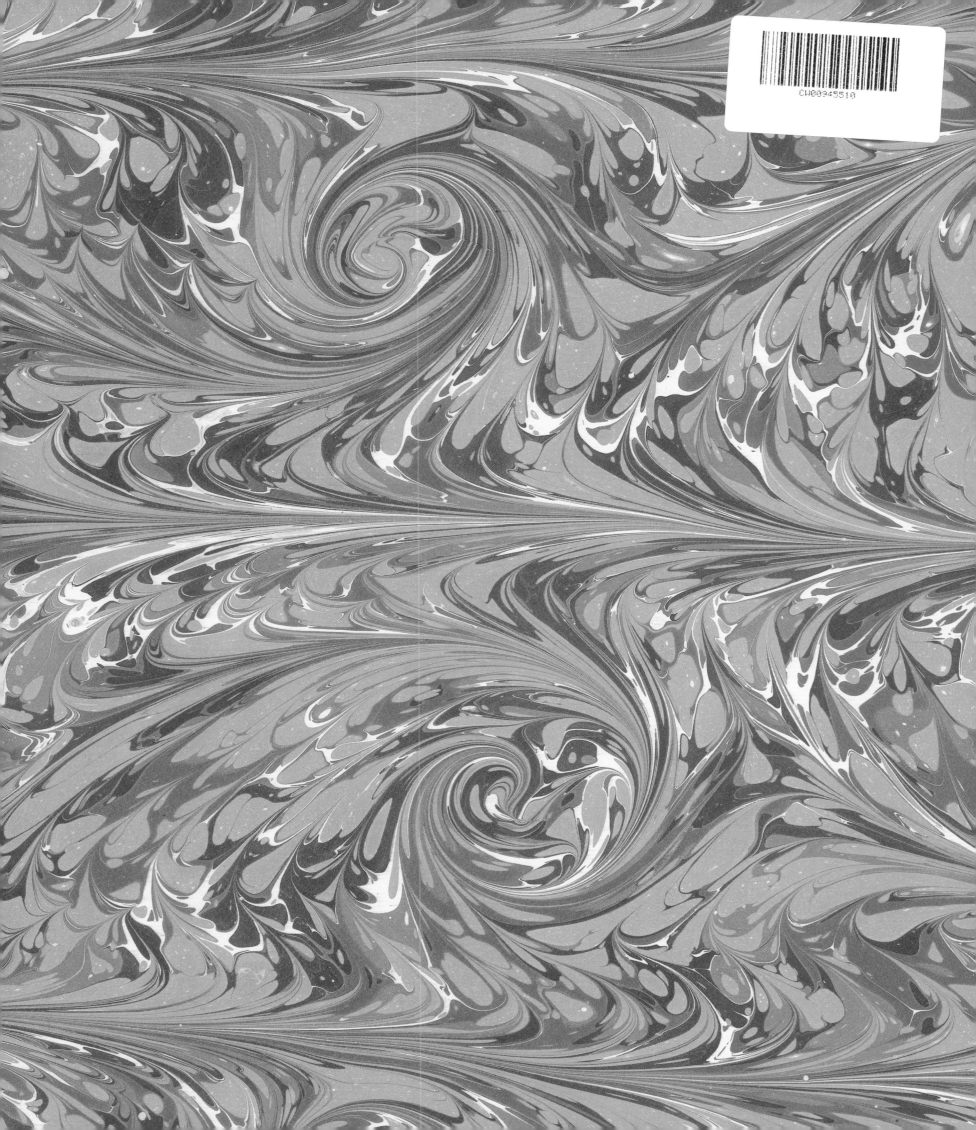

GREAT HOUSES
OF ENGLAND & WALES

GREAT HOUSES
OF ENGLAND & WALES

HUGH MONTGOMERY-MASSINGBERD
CHRISTOPHER SIMON SYKES

LAURENCE KING

HALF TITLE The fanfare on the road to Castle Howard.

FRONTISPIECE The south front of Blickling Hall.

Published in 1994 by
Laurence King Publishing Ltd
361–373 City Road
London EC1V 1LR
United Kingdom
Tel: +44 (0)20 7841 6900
Fax: +44 (0)20 7841 6910
e-mail: enquiries@laurenceking.com
www.laurenceking.com

Reprinted in 2014

This book was designed and produced by Laurence King Publishing Ltd, London

A catalogue record for this book is available from the British Library.
ISBN: 978-178067402-5

Designed and typeset by Karen Stafford, DQP
Printed in China

CONTENTS

Introduction 6

ALNWICK CASTLE 16

HADDON HALL 26

POWIS CASTLE 42

PENSHURST PLACE 56

SYON HOUSE 70

KNOLE 82

COMPTON WYNYATES 96

GRIMSTHORPE CASTLE 106

WILTON HOUSE 116

BURGHLEY HOUSE 132

BURTON CONSTABLE 144

LONGLEAT 154

HARDWICK HALL 166

BLICKLING HALL 180

WOBURN ABBEY 190

TREDEGAR HOUSE 204

BADMINTON HOUSE 218

RAGLEY HALL 232

CHATSWORTH 244

PETWORTH HOUSE 260

BOUGHTON HOUSE 276

CASTLE HOWARD 292

BLENHEIM PALACE 304

HOUGHTON HALL 316

HOLKHAM HALL 330

SLEDMERE HOUSE 342

HAREWOOD HOUSE 350

KEDLESTON HALL 362

BELVOIR CASTLE 372

HIGHCLERE CASTLE 384

CARLTON TOWERS 396

WADDESDON MANOR 408

Acknowledgements 418
Bibliography 419
Index 421

INTRODUCTION

Let us see these handsome houses
Where the wealthy nobles dwell

TENNYSON, *The Lord of Burleigh*

I N HIS stories about the adventures of the eccentric Earl of Emsworth, P.G. Wodehouse painted a beguiling picture of surely the *beau ideal* of a great house of England and Wales (indeed, conveniently situated around the border between the two countries), Blandings Castle, which dates from a time, as the author tells us, when the landed gentry 'believed in building their little nests solid'. The understatement is, of course, deliberate, for the 'huge, grey and majestic' Blandings, family seat of the Threepwoods, 'unquestionably takes the eye'.

We are told of its turrets, battlements and stone terrace with its curved balustrade; the celebrated library (with, among other treasures, the Mazarin Bible attributed to Johann Gutenberg); the Picture Gallery, hung with Threepwood portraits (one notably improved by the present Earl's revolver); and the Amber Drawing Room, with its remarkably early landscape of the Vale of Blandings by Pourbus (Franz the Younger?). We are led up to the tapestried bedrooms (slept in by Tudor monarchs on their progresses) and down to the butler's pantry. Outside, on a sultry summer afternoon, we see the famous rose garden, the lake, the deer park and, in the corner of a buttercup meadow, the sty of Lord Emsworth's beloved sow, the Empress of Blandings, the Noblest of her Species.

It all sounds like paradise. As Evelyn Waugh observed, 'The gardens of Blandings Castle are that original garden from which we are all exiled.' Waugh himself created an irresistible vision of a later, baroque, great house in *Brideshead Revisited*, the seat of the Flytes, Marquesses of Marchmain, with its classical lodges, picturesque landscape, dome and columns, fountain, temple and obelisk.

Were these figments of the Wodehousian and Wavian imaginations merely idyllic fantasies, or were they approximations of the truth? Waugh wrote *Brideshead* during the Second World War, when it seemed, as he put it in the

A view across the baroque magnificence of the Great Hall at Castle Howard.

preface to the revised edition of 1959, 'that the ancestral seats which were our chief national artistic achievement were doomed to decay and spoliation like the monasteries in the 16th century'. So, as he said, he 'piled it on rather, with passionate sincerity'.

Yet, after going round the 32 great houses of England and Wales featured in this book, and looking at the illustrations laid out on the pages that follow, one can only conclude that the Garden of Eden represented by Blandings and Brideshead is far from an illusion. Indeed, there are evocative whiffs of Blandings at Powis Castle and Penshurst Place, and of Brideshead at Castle Howard.

As Waugh observed, it was impossible to foresee in the 1940s – that drearily utilitarian and egalitarian decade – the 'present cult of the country house'. The war and its austere aftermath led to the destruction of many houses. Yet, as Sir Osbert Sitwell noted, 'Alas! how curious it is that these works of art only begin to obtain a wide appreciation when they are on the verge of being destroyed.'

By the end of the 1950s Waugh considered that 'Brideshead today would be open to trippers, its treasures rearranged by expert hands and the fabric better maintained than it was by Lord Marchmain'. Certainly the 'cult of the

PRECEDING PAGES 'Brideshead', *alias* Castle Howard, across the lake.

country house' and the ubiquitous 'expert hands' have done a great deal of good in focusing attention on the artistic importance of these buildings and their collections. Previous pictorial surveys of the subject (not all that numerous, let alone recent), however, have tended to view great houses purely in terms of arts and crafts, as if they were merely museums dumped in the middle of a field and belonging to an ancient and long-vanished civilization.

We have preferred to look at them as they are today, at the end of the 20th century, in their present ownership. While the text gives due credit to the architects, artists and craftsmen employed on their creation, greater emphasis is laid on the social history of the families who commissioned and directed the work and who actually lived – in most cases, still live – in them. For while the principal rooms of many great houses in England and Wales were built primarily for 'state and parade', they were (are) still essentially family homes.

It is this combination of architectural splendour, social status and domestic comfort that gives the great houses of the British Isles their special quality. As Christopher Hussey (whose essays in *Country Life* probably did more than anything else to open people's eyes to the riches of the home-grown architectural heritage) pointed out, 'country houses are England's most characteristic visible contribution to the riches of European civilization'. The key factor is the atmosphere of being lived in for generations; the varied contents of different periods and the matured bosky setting should form an homogeneous whole that represents a somehow artless design for living *à la Anglais*.

On the continent a 'great house' would tend to signify a town palace, in England and Wales one automatically assumes it to be a country house. Naturally, the great English families maintained great houses in London – few of them, alas, still standing – but they have always regarded their country houses as their true homes. On the other hand, the aristocrats of some continental countries, such as Italy, tend to prefer their town residences to their country estates. Historically, some of the grander continental aristocrats might perhaps have spent only a fortnight or so a year on their estates in the country. While they were there, they frequently lived as strangers to the surrounding district – like a late 19th-century Princess Batthyany, who surprised an English guest at her castle in Hungary by her almost total lack of knowledge of any of the neighbouring castles, and of the other aristocratic families who lived in them.

The British aristocrat's love of the country, however, has been an essential part of his nature all through the ages. He knows that the bedrock of his existence is land, land and more land. However much he might be preoccupied by affairs of state in the metropolis, he never forgets that the ownership and acquisition of land is his *raison d'être*; the estate is his territorial base and the family seat what Mark Girouard has aptly called 'the power house'.

The size and splendour of the great house tends to be in proportion to the extent of the estate. The income for the former depends upon the latter. Nonetheless there have been several cases – Blickling, Houghton, Kedleston and Carlton Towers, for instance – where the principal builder's grandiose ideas have galloped beyond the confines of the estate's rent-roll, leaving his successors a difficult inheritance to maintain.

When dividing the greater aristocracy from the lesser, land-holdings are of paramount importance. In the late 19th century there were about a hundred English territorial magnates each owning more than 20,000 acres and a few,

A statue in the sunken parterre at Penshurst.

including the Duke of Northumberland, of Alnwick and Syon, and the Duke of Devonshire, of Chatsworth, owned 100,000 or more English acres. So, on the whole, 'great houses' tend to be the seats of great landowners.

Besides Alnwick and Syon, the great Percy inheritance included Petworth, also featured here. That inveterate builder Bess of Hardwick's legacy accounts for Hardwick as well as Chatsworth; and the landowning dynasty of Herbert and its descendants are represented by no less than four seats in this small selection – Powis, Wilton, Badminton and Highclere. The Manners family weigh in with two – Haddon and Belvoir – and the illustrious House of Howard is represented by Castle Howard and Carlton Towers.

Whereas the extent of the estate supporting the house has been one factor in assessing its 'greatness', its architecture – both in terms of quality and quantity – has been another. The architectural history of great houses in England and Wales stretches back to the feudal fortress of the Middle Ages, built for purposes of defence rather than aesthetics. As this book is essentially about houses rather than castles, however, we have restricted ourselves to only a couple of medieval castles by way of example – Alnwick and Powis – and even they are most notable for later remodellings: Tudor and 17th-century at Powis and 18th- and 19th-century at Alnwick.

'An academie as well as a palace': the east front of Wilton.

The Jacobean arcade at Knole, one of the most 'English' of all the great houses of England.

On the roof at Knole, with its quintessentially English park beyond.

The next stage in the development of the great house was the medieval manor house, with their Great Halls used for eating and business, their solars for retiring and, often, their gatehouses and moats for defence. Haddon, which was actually never fortified, and Penshurst are outstanding examples of this type.

Syon recalls the pre-eminence of the monasteries in the Middle Ages. Monastic architecture was considerably superior to that of country houses which tended, as at Compton Wynyates, to grow in rather a haphazard fashion. The result is an endearing jumble. 'Its beauty', as James Lees-Milne has written, 'is accidental, approximating to the beauty of oaks and elms which have grown laboriously out of the English soil.'

From the end of the 15th century, the Tudor monarchy gave England an internal peace and security such as she had never previously enjoyed, and the great houses of this period were, for the first time, universally unfortified. Instead of sheltering behind castle walls, the Tudor landowners lived in pleasant and civilized houses with large windows overlooking garden and park and the surrounding countryside. Many of the old magnates had disappeared during the cataclysmic Wars of the Roses and the new agrarian revolution under the Tudors was to see the break-up of the old feudal system, enclosures of common land and, after the Dissolution of the Monasteries, the distribution of former monastic estates. It is, though, a myth that the new class of magnates who benefited from this revolution were all upstarts. The majority of them actually sprang from medieval knightly families.

Being so prosperous, the Tudor landowners built themselves many new country houses. These were influenced by the splendours of the Renaissance, which, broadly speaking, reached England from Italy by way of northern Europe. Although the Gothic tradition remained powerful, the new style of architecture took note of symmetry and ornament, even – as the 16th century proceeded – of 'classical' touches. Brick took the place of timber and supplemented masonry; the use of glass for windows flourished. The English Renaissance came into full bloom during the reign of Queen Elizabeth.

Romance, in its most extravagant and ostentatious form, now took the upper hand. Longleat, Burghley, Burton Constable and Hardwick are outstanding examples included in this book.

The early 17th century saw the aristocracy achieve a high pitch of civilization, epitomized by Van Dyck's portraits in the Double Cube Room at Wilton of the family of the 4th Earl of Pembroke, the patron of Inigo Jones, who was chiefly responsible for introducing the classical style of the Italian Andrea Palladio into English architecture. However, it was to take nearly a century to really catch on; the style of the two great Jacobean houses in this book, Knole and Blickling, harks back more to the Elizabethan age.

Blickling is an instance of where we have sought to highlight a lesser-known great house in favour of what might be called 'an old chestnut'. It is in fact designed by Robert Lyminge, the same architect as the better-known Hatfield House, and we opted for the romantic Norfolk pile of the Hobarts rather than the familiar Hertfordshire palace of the Cecils – who are, in any event, represented here by the spectacular Burghley, further up the Great North Road.

The late Stuart age was notable for a Dutch style of classicism, and this is reflected in the architecture of another lesser-known great house, Tredegar, in Wales. The splendid Restoration seat of Ham House by the Thames in Surrey would have been another strong candidate, but for the fact that it was undergoing a thorough overhaul at the time we were preparing this book.

Towards the end of the 17th century, the flamboyant baroque style was in the ascendant in great English houses. Ragley, Chatsworth, Petworth and Boughton are examples from this period.

The early 18th century was the golden age of the great house, not only in architectural terms but in patronage of the arts and the perfection of country house life. First came Sir John Vanbrugh's baroque magnificence at Castle Howard, Blenheim and Grimsthorpe. Then, in the age of Whig supremacy, came a series of great Palladian houses including Houghton, Holkham, Badminton and Woburn.

These 18th-century palaces, which acquired the nature of local courts, were filled with works of art collected on their owners' Grand Tours, furnished and decorated by the likes of William Kent, and set in picturesque landscapes by 'Capability' Brown (which almost invariably involved sweeping away the old formal gardens). The apotheosis of the Whig oligarchy was Wentworth Woodhouse in Yorkshire, where the architect Henry Flitcroft designed the longest front in England for the 2nd Marquess of Rockingham. It was tempting to include this staggering pile in the book, but most of the contents were removed after the Second World War, when the 8th Earl Fitzwilliam decided that Wentworth Woodhouse would never be lived in again, and there was open-cast mining in the park. However, at the time of writing, Wentworth Woodhouse has acquired a new private occupant.

The great houses featured here tend to have retained their collections and their atmospheres as what Gervase Jackson-Stops, organizer of the magnificent 'Treasure Houses of Britain' exhibition in Washington in 1985, has called 'temples of the arts'. In that respect the great houses of England contrast with, say, the châteaux of the Loire, which are often empty due to the dispersal of family inheritance under French estate law, which operates on different principles to the English 'primogeniture'.

In the second half of the 18th century, the grandiose and austere Roman manner of the great house gave way to a more restrained and delicate interpretation of the classical ideal. Inspired by the refreshingly feminine

A doorcase at Wilton House, seat of the Earls of Pembroke and Montgomery.

detail exposed in the archaeological excavations of the time at Pompeii and elsewhere, the brilliant young Scot, Robert Adam, brought a new elegance to English architecture on the grand scale. Adam's genius is well represented in the pages that follow by such great Georgian houses as Syon, Kedleston and Harewood, where the decoration and furniture are all of a piece, forming exquisite ensembles.

The late Georgian age also saw the stirrings of a Gothic revival. James Wyatt, formerly a neo-classicist (his work in this manner can be seen at Heveningham Hall in Suffolk – another regrettable absentee in this book, due to its present sorry state, the result of disastrous mismanagement by the Government), switched enthusiastically to this style. He was initially responsible for Belvoir Castle, which developed into an example of the romantic Regency vision of medievalism.

Not far from Belvoir – indeed it was built by the eccentric George de Ligne Gregory in the 1830s with a view to outdoing it – is surely the most extraordinary 19th-century great house in England, Harlaxton Manor, a fantastic mixture of the Vanbrughian and 'Jacobethan' styles. The theatrical interiors are a riot of baroque exuberance but, alas, now largely empty – which accounts for its nonappearance in the main text of this book. This curiously little-known palace is now the European campus of the American University of Evansville, who care for the fabric most sympathetically.

Baroque splendour at Chatsworth: the gold of the west front's windows glows on a spring evening.

Another spectacular early 19th-century great house we are sorry that it has not been possible to include is the vast Norman Revival castle of Penrhyn in North Wales, designed by Thomas Hopper for the Pennant family (and now owned by the National Trust). From the Victorian age we have featured a characteristically eclectic and heavily ornamented trio: Highclere, Carlton Towers and, finally, Waddesdon Manor.

It would have been pleasing to have included some examples from the 20th century to illustrate that the country house tradition is far from exhausted. Certainly there have been plenty of buildings on the grand scale – such as Luton Hoo in Bedfordshire, Castle Drogo in Devon (by Sir Edwin Lutyens), and more recently the new Eaton and Henbury Halls, both in Cheshire – but perhaps none that could truly merit the appellation 'great'.

The decline of the great house as a power base can be traced back to the Reform Bill of 1832, which deprived the territorial magnates of their political power. Their supporting estates were diminished by first the repeal of the Corn Laws in the 1840s and then, later in the 19th century, by a succession of agricultural slumps. Some of the great art collections began to be dispersed, but it was not until the First World War that there was a flood in the breaking-up of country houses and their estates, as capital taxation began to bite large chunks out of the great families' fortunes.

The gallery of Hawksmoor's chapel at Grimsthorpe Castle.

By the Second World War, the position seemed bleak indeed. In many cases country houses were requisitioned by the military (and sometimes damaged beyond repair); the families moved out, often never to return. In the austere aftermath of hostilities there was a prevailing pessimism that great houses had become 'white elephants', social anachronisms, doomed to extinction. The 1950s witnessed a constant and depressing series of demolitions.

The National Trust, a charity originally founded in the 1890s to protect threatened areas of landscape, stepped in to save a number of houses for posterity, including several featured in this book – Blickling, Knole, Hardwick, Petworth, Powis, and more recently, Kedleston. Yet successive British governments failed to take the necessary fiscal steps to safeguard what became known as 'the National Heritage', and by the 1970s the crisis was so acute that private owners banded together to form the Historic Houses Association to lobby for better conditions.

Some reliefs from taxation were achieved (though not on the vital costs of repairs and maintenance), and various forms of charitable trusts were set up to secure the future of great houses, but lesser houses continued to be alienated from their long-established families at an alarming rate – indeed a fifth of the total have been sold up by their traditional families in the last 20 years. Overall, it may be difficult not to take a gloomy view about the survival of the English country house.

Yet this is a celebration of *great* houses and, on the contemporary evidence before us, there is still much to encourage. Previous studies of the subject have tended to stop the social history *circa* 1914 or, at a pinch, 1939, and to mourn the great days in the distance enchanted. The feeling was that country houses could never survive the passing of the resident domestic servant. The present generation of owners, however, have shown this to be all a nonsense, and much fresh air has been blown into frowsty old corridors.

We have looked at the great house from a contemporary viewpoint, and it has been invigorating to see how the post-war owners have courageously bucked the trend that such places are 'out of date'. As Evelyn Waugh observed in his preface to the revised edition of *Brideshead Revisited*, 'the English aristocracy has maintained its identity to a degree that then [1944] seemed impossible.... Much of this book therefore is a panegyric preached over an empty coffin.'

We pay due tribute to the efforts of the 'stately home industry', pioneered by such showmen as the late Marquess of Bath of Longleat, the present Duke of Bedford at Woburn and the present Marquess of Hertford at Ragley; as well as to the heritage lobby, in which the late Lord Howard of Henderskelfe at Castle Howard was such an expansive force. George Howard was only one of numerous modern owners not content merely to preserve or restore their great houses, but who continued to embellish and beautify them in the grand tradition of patronage and taste.

Chatsworth, for example, has never looked better than in the confident hands of the present Duke and Duchess of Devonshire. Nor has Penshurst, with the present Viscount and Viscountess De L'Isle; or Burghley, thanks to Lady Victoria Leatham; or Badminton, in the floruit of the present Duke and Duchess of Beaufort. The same must be said of Holkham, after the efforts of Viscount and Viscountess Coke; of Sledmere, during the stylish stewardship of Sir Tatton Sykes, Bt.; of Harewood, after its rejuvenation by the present Earl and Countess of Harewood, and indeed of several other great houses in the 1990s, not least the last in the book, Waddesdon Manor, now being given a superlative face-lift by the present Lord Rothschild.

Praiseworthy as the conservationist efforts of the National Trust have been, their properties inevitably have a museumified atmosphere, as if pickled in aspic. It is the living families *in situ* that make the great houses of England and Wales so full of character and incident, of anecdote and humour in the Wodehousian tradition. Long may they remain there to give a human dimension to the visual glory.

Adam's library at Harewood.

1

ALNWICK
CASTLE

F ROM A distance Alnwick Castle in Northumberland is everything one expects from the great Border fortress of the Percys, who succeeded the de Vescy family as hereditary Wardens of the Scottish Marches early in the 14th century. Best seen from across the River Alne, the castle, with its spectacular fortifications, commands a natural defensive position on a rocky precipice above the river. Like Windsor, it seems a fairy-tale ideal of a medieval stronghold – even if, on closer inspection, some of the baronial flourishes date from the 19th century.

The rugged setting is enhanced by a fine park, in which the rocky crags were reduced, in the mid-18th century, to green slopes by the great landscape architect Lancelot 'Capability' Brown. The castle still dominates the old town of Alnwick and one experiences a frisson of feudalism as one negotiates the medieval arch of Hotspur Tower – named after Harry 'Hotspur' Percy, the celebrated medieval warrior-son of the 1st Earl of Northumberland – to be confronted with the menacing defile of the barbican.

Although traces of the original Norman castle of the de Vescys remain, Alnwick was substantially rebuilt by the Percys in the early 14th century. The keep (the main castle) was remodelled with semicircular bastions and given an uncompromising entrance with twin octagonal towers. The Percys were to the fore in the long drawn-out Border warfare, but by the time of the 'Wizard Earl' of Northumberland (so called because of his devotion to scientific experiments) in the early 17th century, their influence in the north of England was on the wane.

Later in the 17th century the male line of the Percys died out, and in 1670 Alnwick was inherited by Elizabeth, the four-year-old daughter of the 11th and last Earl of Northumberland. After brief unions with Lord Ogle and the scapegrace Thomas Thynne of Longleat (see pages 154-65), Elizabeth married, in 1682, the 6th 'Proud Duke' of Somerset. By this time Alnwick

LEFT The Guard Chamber, a vestibule to the state rooms of the castle, leads off from the Grand Staircase. The pavement of Venetian mosaic was made in Rome; the circular gaming table in the centre has decorative swags; and the frieze incorporates scenes by Francis Goltzenberg from *The Ballad of Chevy Chase*, in which Harry Hotspur features prominently. The marble figures represent Justice and Britannia.

BELOW A smiling Ceres, herself flanked by the fruits of the earth, beside one of Alnwick's magnificent fireplaces.

had fallen into decay, but parts of the castle were fitted-up for habitation and during the tenure of the 7th Duke of Somerset it again became a family seat.

The 7th Duke of Somerset had an only daughter, another Elizabeth, who became the heir to the great Northumbrian estates of the Percys. We are given a revealing portrait of Lady Elizabeth, who was to play such a notable role in the history of Alnwick, in the racy letters of the 18th-century observer, Horace Walpole. He described her as 'a jovial heap of contradictions... the blood of all the Percys and the Seymours swelled in her veins and in her fancy, her person was more vulgar than anything but her conversation, which was loaded indiscriminately with stories of her ancestors and her footmen... she was familiar with the mob, while stifled with diamonds.'

In 1740 Lady Elizabeth married a handsome Yorkshire baronet called Sir Hugh Smithson. The ambitious Smithson provoked much hilarity by exchanging his homely surname for the historic handle of Percy. Feeling that his new position deserved appropriate recognition, he also solicited (and was given) the Most Noble Order of the Garter – 'the first Smithson to have it', as King George II is said to have unkindly remarked – and, eventually, in 1766 he was created Duke of Northumberland.

It is a nice irony that Smithson, the name of which Sir Hugh was so keen to divest himself, became famous through the scholarship and munificence of his bastard son. For James Smithson, the scientist after whom the

PRECEDING PAGES Alnwick Castle: the great Border fortress of the Percys from across the River Alne.

'Smithsonite' carbonite of zinc is named, was a by-blow of this new Duke of Northumberland. A radical of republican persuasion, Smithson left a sizeable part of his considerable fortune 'to the United States of America, to be formed at Washington, under the name of the Smithsonian Institution, an establishment for the increase and diffusion of knowledge among men'.

Although it is easy enough to make fun of Duke Hugh and Duchess Elizabeth – whose full-length portraits by Sir Joshua Reynolds still dominate the dining room at Alnwick – they did have the taste and confidence to commission the brilliant Scots architect Robert Adam to remodel the castle. The Duchess had a passion for Gothic, and Adam interpreted his clients' wishes with a free treatment of 'Georgian Gothic' that was to be largely swept away in the 19th century in favour of a more 'baronial' style.

In their heyday, though, Adam's rooms witnessed much state and parade. In 1770, for example, the 1st Duke and Duchess of Northumberland entertained the Duke of Cumberland (King George III's brother) in regal style: His Royal Highness was accorded a 21-gun salute and the banquet comprised 177 dishes exclusive of dessert. The Duchess was well pleased with the jollifications. 'In short,' she noted in her diary, 'the magnificence and hospitality display'd on this occasion at Alnwick Castle by its present illustrious possessors gave a striking picture of the state and splendour of our ancient barons.'

Horace Walpole was less impressed. He considered that 'the pipers and drummers and obsolete minstrels of her family and her own buxom countenance at the tail of such a procession' were more like 'an antiquated pageant or mummery'.

BELOW The Red Drawing Room, intended to be the most splendidly decorated interior at Alnwick, is hung with red damask, ornamented in gold. The Carrara marble chimneypiece, supported by two caryatids by Nucci, was executed in Rome; the frieze, by Mantovani, was suggested by Giulio Romano's friezes at Castel Sant'Angelo, Rome; and the ebony cabinet on the right is one of a pair in the room made for Louis XIV by Domenico Cucci at the Gobelin factory in 1683. The landscape painting, further to the right, is J.M.W. Turner's *The Temple of Jupiter Panhellenios, Aegina*.

Similarly, the Duchess's critics were not over-enamoured of her architectural improvements to the castle. While Adam's furniture – much of it still *in situ* – and the splendid fan-shaped staircase found favour, the large windows (some pointed, some quatrefoil in shape) were regarded as out of keeping with a medieval castle. Such embellishments as picturesque little turrets on the towers of the curtain walls and dinky stone figures dotted on the roofs and battlements, in poor imitation of the medieval figures on the octagonal towers, only added to the bizarre effect.

When Sir Walter Scott visited Alnwick early in the 19th century that great burnisher of medievalism observed that what the castle lacked was a central feature in the shape of a high tower to dominate the others. The 2nd Duke of Northumberland, a general, was too preoccupied with military matters (he raised 1,500 of his tenantry into a regiment based at the castle at the time of one of the threatened Napoleonic invasions) and his son, the 3rd Duke (described by the diarist Charles Greville as 'an eternal talker and prodigious bore'), too entranced by the sound of his own voice to do anything about it. On the 3rd Duke's death in 1847, however, Alnwick passed to the 'Building Duke'.

The 4th ('Building') Duke, a former naval officer, was a scholar, traveller and perfectionist. Yet, according to the poet Frederick Locker-Lampson, he also had a 'playful disposition', was 'tall and fair, and wore his hat just a little

RIGHT The Music Room (originally Robert Adam's saloon), as done over in the Italian taste by Salvin in the 1850s, with the help of Commendatore Luigi Canina and teams of Italian craftsmen. The chimneypiece was carved by Nucci in Rome.

LEFT Detail of the carving on the Music Room door by Bulletti of Florence, who had been recommended by Cardinal Antonelli, Secretary to the Vatican.

ABOVE The library, which occupies the whole of one floor of the Prudhoe Tower at Alnwick, built by the 4th Duke of Northumberland in 1854. The two tiers of bookcases (oak, inlaid with maple) were designed by Commendatore Canina's assistant, Giovanni Montiroli.

RIGHT View from the courtyard of the castle.

bit on one side'. He followed the late Sir Walter Scott's suggestion, but went a great deal further, to create what must rank as one of the most remarkable Victorian interiors in England.

As his architect the Building Duke employed Anthony Salvin, originally a pupil of John Nash. Salvin added a chapel, the Prudhoe Tower, the north terrace (which gives a majestic view of Adam's bridge across the Alne) and a massive arcade that more than holds its own against the genuine medieval architecture.

Nonetheless, close up, the exterior of the domestic quarters of Alnwick Castle may strike the modern visitor as slightly disappointing after the nobility of the distant prospect. Somehow it seems a little compact for a ducal seat. This, though, is to reckon without the wonders Salvin ingeniously contrived within the cramped shell.

The sensational surprise at Alnwick is that the interior of the castle resembles a High Renaissance palace. This contrast between a feudal exterior and a sophisticated treasure house inside was a deliberate policy of the Building Duke. He wanted Alnwick to emulate the palaces he had seen in Italy: ruggedness without, polish within. To those who complained about the insertion of such lavish interiors within a medieval fortress the playful Duke replied: 'Would you wish us only to sit on benches upon a floor strewn with rushes?'

The Duke employed Italian decorators to supervise the local craftsmen who carried out the work. With their exotically coffered ceilings, damask wall-hangings and monumental chimneypieces, the series of sumptuous rooms provide a fitting background for the Northumberland art collection.

The anteroom, for instance, contains three parts of *The Visitation* (a fresco by Sebastian del Piombo), an *Ecce Homo* by Tintoretto and no fewer than three Titians, including *The Bishop of Armagnac and his Secretary*. In the Music Room are views by Canaletto of Alnwick and Northumberland House, the last of the great palaces that used to line the banks of the River Thames upstream from Westminster. It was demolished in the late 19th century, when some of its contents were brought up to Alnwick and the rest removed to the family's other Thameside seat, Syon House (see pages 70-81).

In the Red Drawing Room at Alnwick can be found an amazing pair of French ebony cabinets, made by Domenico Cucci at the Gobelin factory in 1683 and incorporating Florentine *pietre dure*. These cabinets had belonged to Louis XIV but at the time of the French Revolution they were looted from the Tuileries, and later bought by the talkative 3rd Duke of Northumberland. In the dining room a special treat is provided by two Meissen dinner services – one (1740) painted with wild beasts, including a sturdy rhinoceros, the other (1780) with more restful scenes from Aesop's *Fables*. The family portraits extend from works by Sir Anthony Van Dyck to those of the present day.

ABOVE An unusual view of the castle, looking down from the town of Alnwick.

LEFT The chapel and the Prudhoe Tower.

The 10th Duke of Northumberland, who died in 1988, is depicted appropriately in fox-hunting attire with Alnwick in the background. 'Hughie' Northumberland was Master of the Percy Foxhounds for nearly 50 seasons and a most public-spirited peer, who served as Lord Steward of the Queen's Household, president of the Royal Agricultural Society of England and chairman of the Agricultural Research Council and of the Medical Research Council. He also happened to have more ducal connections than any of his contemporaries – when it had become much less usual for dukes to marry the daughters of dukes than in days of yore. He himself married a duke's daughter; both his sisters married dukes; his mother was the daughter of a duke and so was his paternal grandmother.

Elizabeth Duchess of Northumberland, Hughie's widow, was the former Lady Elizabeth Montagu Douglas Scott, elder daughter of the 8th Duke of Buccleuch, the great Scottish magnate. Her marriage in 1946 to the 10th Duke of Northumberland united the Percys and the Douglases who had, for so long in the Border warfare of the Middle Ages, been hereditary enemies. Their son, Harry, a bachelor film producer born in 1953, is now the 11th Duke of Northumberland and still lives at Alnwick. Part of the castle is let as municipal offices and one of the towers is devoted to the museum of the Northumberland Fusiliers; there is also a museum of Stone-, Bronze- and Iron-Age antiquities. The state rooms are open regularly to the public and deservedly attract many visitors, drawn to this 'Windsor of the North'.

2

HADDON HALL

DERBYSHIRE

NOTHING could have been so sensitively done as the scholarly renovation of Haddon Hall in Derbyshire, carried out by the 9th Duke of Rutland between 1912 and 1927. Yet however careful or authentic a restoration may be, somehow a contemporary flavour is added to that of the past. This is not a complaint but a celebration. The early 20th-century reverence for old manor houses, tapestries, simple wooden furniture and carving, not to mention old-fashioned roses in terraced gardens, infuses Haddon with a significant part of its charm.

Nothing captures the mood so well as Rex Whistler's idealized picture of Haddon, painted in 1933 and hung above the fireplace in the Long Gallery. The 9th Duke stands, gun over his shoulder, dogs and his eldest son (the present Duke) at his feet, and surveys – from a mythical vantage point high above the landscape – what appears to be a little Gothic city set in a medieval tapestry. What could be more romantic than this vision of grey walls, battlements, towers and courtyards, perched on a spur above the River Wye?

For was it not in this very room, the Long Gallery, that Dorothy Vernon, daughter of Sir George Vernon of Haddon (the 'King of the Peak'), slipped away from her sister's wedding to a younger son of the Earl of Derby, to elope with her lover? This swain, Sir John Manners, was, so the story goes, waiting with horses on the bridge below, at the bottom of the 76 dry-stone steps.

Well, possibly; or rather possibly not. The steps, for instance, down which Dorothy is supposed to have fled, were not actually built until about a century after the alleged elopement. Moreover, a cynic might observe that there could hardly have been any need for such an elaborate 'elopement'. After all, why should Sir George have objected to his daughter (not a raving beauty, judging from a portrait in the Great Chamber) marrying a son of the 1st Earl of Rutland? The only possible explanation seems to be that Sir

George, who was notorious for his choleric nature (being prone to hang suspected felons without due process of law), was not an admirer of his daughter's in-laws, having already had a Manners for a stepfather.

The elopement yarn appears to be a 19th-century fabrication to add to Haddon's air of romance. In any event, it was this marriage that brought Haddon into the Manners family in the 1560s, and they own it to this day.

For their part, the Vernons had been at Haddon since the 12th century, having inherited the property from one William Avenel, a steward. Originally it was held by William the Conqueror's bastard son, Peverel of the Peak.

You can still see stonework of the 12th century at the base of Peverel's Tower, in the chapel and in some of the boundary walls at Haddon; but the battlements are actually a picturesque feature of the late Middle Ages, for the house was never fortified. Indeed, it is one of the best examples of the great medieval houses in England and Wales that were never castles.

Haddon assumed its present form in the late 14th century, when its two courts were bisected by the Great Hall. Building work continued off and on until the early generations of the Manners ownership. Sir John Manners, Dorothy Vernon's husband, gave the Long Gallery its haunting, silvery-grey panelling. Sir George Manners, their son, altered and re-roofed the chapel; and his son, John, who inherited the earldom of Rutland in 1641, laid out much of the gardens.

Subsequently, though, the Earls and (from 1703) Dukes of Rutland principally based themselves at their Leicestershire seat of Belvoir (see pages 372-83), a spectacular Regency castle by James Wyatt (later restored after a fire). Haddon fell into a long sleep.

'A gloomy and solemn silence pervades its neglected apartments', noted Rhodes in his *Peak Scenery* (1819), 'and the bat and the owl are alone among the inmates of its remaining splendour.' Thirty years earlier, the diarist and traveller John Byng (later 5th Viscount Torrington) was impressed by this 'poor abandon'd place', and recorded how the local farmer who acted as his guide told him that many gentlemen thought Haddon more worth seeing than the neighbouring Chatsworth. The farmer gave Byng a 'sword hilt, with part of the blade, said to be worn by the Vernons in the wars of France'.

Having duly looted this treasure, Byng fell to wondering why the Dukes of Rutland did not restore Haddon. In all fairness, it should be said that Haddon was not altogether neglected and it can only be regarded as a blessing that the medieval house avoided the unwelcome attentions of 18th- and 19th-century 'improvers'. The happy consequence is that today, following the efforts of the 9th Duke of Rutland and his expert craftsmen, Haddon seems untouched by time since the 17th century.

From the moment one passes under the gateway at the top of the very steep uphill drive, it is difficult not to be utterly bewitched by Haddon's spell. The sight of the deeply concave steps, worn away by generation after generation of feet, is enough to give the visitor a flavour of the extraordinary atmosphere of antiquity. As the heavy gatehouse door shuts behind you, you feel trapped in a time warp.

There, up some more eroded steps, is the enclosed lower courtyard: an apparently drunken assortment of buildings and levels held together by a labyrinthine network of squinches. It might look as if the masons botched their job, but in fact they were finding an ingenious solution to a difficult problem – how to squeeze the gatehouse into the corner of two ranges. The rainwater heads are decorated with intricate pierced designs and medieval gargoyles catch the eye.

PRECEDING PAGES Haddon: looking up to a corner of the south front.

RIGHT 'Childe Roland to the Dark Tower came...': the entrance in the north-west tower.

BELOW The weathered grey stone paving, worn by time, in the lower courtyard.

BELOW The chapel, with its medieval wall paintings, 17th-century woodwork and poignant marble effigy of Lord Haddon, carved from a model made by his mother, Violet Duchess of Rutland, in the 1890s.

RIGHT The three skeletons on the west wall of the chapel (part of an incomplete group which would once have included kings as well) point, in the uncompromising medieval manner, to the moral that all earthly things are merely vanity.

The chapel is adorned with medieval wall-paintings and a 'three-decker' pulpit in mellow early 17th-century woodwork. The west wall features three enjoyably ghoulish skeletons, pointing the medieval moral that all earthly possessions are mere vanity. The most haunting item in the chapel, however, is the 1890s effigy, in luscious white marble, of Lord Haddon, the 9th Duke of Rutland's elder brother, who died aged nine. It was carved from a model by his mother, Violet Duchess of Rutland.

Violet and her husband, the 8th Duke of Rutland, took to spending the summer months away from Belvoir in a house near Haddon. Their youngest daughter, Lady Diana Cooper, recalled how the family would go over to 'empty Haddon Hall most afternoons for water-colour sketching and gardening.' It was these visits that kindled a passionate love of Haddon in her surviving brother, John, who resolved to restore the sleeping beauty.

The achievement of that worthy ambition was his life's work. So successful were his efforts that today it is difficult, if not impossible, to tell which part of Haddon is original and which is a 20th-century restoration.

The Banqueting Hall is the oldest room in the house where the original structure is still substantially intact. The walls, the doorways at either end, the windows and possibly also the stone floor are as Sir Richard Vernon built them *circa* 1370, though the oak screen is mid-15th century. No less impressive is the oak ceiling, which was erected in the 1920s to the design of Sir Harold Brakespeare. Forty tons of carefully selected timber from oaks grown on the Haddon and Belvoir estates of the 9th Duke of Rutland went into the new roof.

Off the Banqueting Hall, in the old kitchens, you are transported back lustily to the Middle Ages. There are collections of early bread- or 'dole' cupboards and a nostalgic butcher's kitchen, complete with bench, salting trough, hanging rack and much-hacked-upon chopping block.

The dining room was Sir Henry Vernon's parlour and owes its present dimensions to his rearrangements of *circa* 1500. Sir Henry was treasurer to Arthur, Prince of Wales (elder brother of the future King Henry VIII and chiefly known to history for his laddish brag of having been 'in Spain' on the

BELOW The perfect 'English' vision of a manor house: the terrace at Haddon, overlooked by the bulging leaded lights of the Long Gallery.

LEFT A gargoyle pulls a disgusting face in the lower courtyard.

BELOW RIGHT 'Dorothy Vernon's Steps', down which the Haddon heiress is traditionally supposed to have eloped.

ABOVE Stairs from the Banqueting Hall to the Long Gallery.

RIGHT The alcove of the dining room, with its carved medallions, variously said to depict Henry VII and his Queen, Elizabeth of York, or Sir George and Lady Vernon.

LEFT The Banqueting Hall, erected *circa* 1370 by Sir Richard de Vernon. The screen (left foreground) is *circa* 1450; the gallery and panelling *circa* 1600; the roof-timbering is a splendid reconstruction of the 1920s for the 9th Duke of Rutland by Sir Harold Brakespeare.

night of his wedding to Catherine of Aragon), and decorated the room in a riot of Tudor heraldry, both in the panelling of the walls and on the painted ceiling. Two carved medallions in the alcove are variously said to depict King Henry VII and his Queen, Elizabeth of York, or Dorothy Vernon's parents, Sir George and Lady Vernon.

Unlike many great houses, Haddon can boast little in the way of fabulous artistic treasures – the house itself is the treasure – though the tapestries are exceptionally fine. They include a French tapestry of *circa* 1460 and an early 17th-century set from Mortlake depicting the five senses – 'Seeing', 'Hearing', 'Tasting', 'Feeling', 'Smelling' – with scenes from Aesop's *Fables*. These amused the 13-year-old Princess Victoria when she visited Haddon in 1832 with her formidable mother, the Duchess of Kent, for the costumes in the tapestries bore a remarkable resemblance to those worn by some of the ladies in the royal suite.

It is a cruel irony that this notable collection of tapestries had hung on the walls during the centuries of neglect, and survived the even more dangerous

looting tendencies of tourists, yet when some 60 pieces were in store above the stables during the building's restoration in 1925 they were destroyed by a fire. Notable survivors of the fire include the tapestries in the State Bedroom (16th-century Brussels hunting scenes) and the Earl's Bedroom (Flemish woodland scenes).

The State Bedroom also contains an endearingly naive late 16th-century plaster relief above the fireplace, depicting Orpheus charming the beasts. The local craftsman who executed the work appears to have over-reached himself in trying to squeeze too many creatures into this strange menagerie. One of the deer, for instance, looks as if he is giving another a good kicking.

This craftman's style is similar to some of the carving to be found at Hardwick Hall in the same county (see pages 166-79), and there is another echo of the mighty Hardwick ('more glass than wall') in Haddon's most delectable interior, the Long Gallery. This wonderfully airy room (bitterly cold in winter) is 110 feet long by 17 feet broad and lit by a wall of windows. Even that inveterate grumbler Horace Walpole was impressed: he pronounced the Long Gallery 'the only good room'.

When the 9th Duke of Rutland came to restore the Long Gallery he found that it needed less work than most of the other rooms. He was careful to preserve the curious bulging of the leaded windows, which produces such a magical effect when viewed from the terraced gardens outside.

ABOVE The steps up to the Long Gallery, which are reputed to have been made from the roots of a single Haddon oak (and the floor of the Long Gallery from the rest of the tree).

RIGHT The elaborately carved doorway from the Long Gallery to the anteroom of the State Bedroom.

The Long Gallery at Haddon: one of the great English interiors, a silvery-grey vision 110 feet long by 17 feet broad.

Indeed, it is when wandering in the gardens above the River Wye that you can best savour Haddon's tranquil spirit. The house and gardens are opened regularly to the public by the present (10th) Duke of Rutland, now the senior duke in Britain (having inherited the title on the death of his father in 1940), who still spends part of the year at Haddon.

The serene beauty of the long, low, south front can be seen at its best from the gardens, with their yews, bowling alleys, balustrading and abundance of

A distant view of the most romantic house in England: like a little Gothic city set in a medieval tapestry.

roses and clematis. The trickle of the fountain and the distant chuckle of the Wye far below conjure up an irresistible image of the golden age of the English country house at the beginning of the 20th century, paying tribute to the *beau ideal* of an historic medieval manor. Here, in short, is the most romantic house in England.

3

POWIS
CASTLE

POWYS

HE ROSE-RED castle of Powis on the Welsh side of the Marches, perched high above spectacular terrace gardens, is the closest approximation you could hope to find in reality to match the fiction of P.G. Wodehouse's idyllic Blandings Castle. Seen on a balmy summer's day, Powis, with its magnificent gardens, seems positively paradisial.

Yet its history has been turbulent. Its position on top of a rocky limestone outcrop above the Severn Valley was clearly chosen for strategic purposes; rock provided a natural defence and on the other three sides a moat was dug and earthworks raised. The castle was originally constructed by Welsh princes, the descendants of a chieftain called Bleddyn ap Cynfyn, who founded the principality of Powys in the 11th century.

The present building dates back to at least *circa* 1200, though most of the work would seem to have been carried out between 1275 and 1320. It follows the Norman plan of a strong keep, and a large inner bailey (the entrance courtyard), hedged by a massive curtain wall.

In the Middle Ages Powis – or Poole Castle as it was then known – was something of a shuttlecock in the Border warfare of the Welsh Marches. In 1286 Owain ap Gruffydd ap Gwenwynwyn, last Prince of Powys, was obliged to pay homage to King Edward I of England; subsequently his plucky young daughter, Hawys, who defended the castle from a siege laid by her uncle, was confirmed as owner of Powis by royal charter. She married Sir John Cherleton who became Lord Cherleton of Powis and a Marcher magnate. The estate remained in the Cherleton family until a descendant of the 5th and last feudal Lord of Powis sold it to Sir Edward Herbert in 1587.

Herbert was the second son of William Herbert, 1st Earl of Pembroke, a powerful figure under the Tudors to whom King Henry VIII – William Herbert's brother-in-law through his wife, a sister of Henry's sixth and last Queen, Catherine Parr – granted the Abbey of Wilton in Wiltshire (see pages

PRECEDING PAGES Powis Castle, above its magnificent terraces.

LEFT The west front, with its forecourt dominated by the lead statue of Fame borne aloft by the winged horse Pegasus. The sculpture was signed by Andries Carpentière (*alias* Andrew Carpenter), a pupil of John van Nost, *circa* 1705; it was derived from the marble group made by Antoine Coysevox for Louis XIV's palace at Marly.

116-131). The story of Powis as a great house really begins with Sir Edward Herbert as it was he who extensively remodelled the interior of the old Marcher castle between 1587 and 1595. Only one of his interiors survives, the Long Gallery (completed in 1593), but it is surely the finest in the house – and indeed one of the most enchanting rooms anywhere.

Unusually, it is shaped in the form of the letter *T*, which causes a divertingly irregular play of light. Whereas the gorgeously elaborate plasterwork, the colourful heraldry, the chimneypieces, the elm floor and the delightfully dotty doorcase are all contemporary with Sir Edward's remodelling, the *trompe-l'oeil* painted wainscot presumably dates from the early 17th century.

During the Civil War Powis was captured by Parliamentary troops, who destroyed the western gateway. Later in the 17th century, however, the castle enjoyed a brief golden age under the flamboyant Marquess of Powis, whose chequered career ended in exile in France. His Catholicism (a religion pursued by the Herberts since Sir Edward's marriage to Mary Stanley) proved his undoing. First, he was fingered by the odious Titus Oates in the illusory 'Popish Plot' to kill King Charles II and had to languish in the Tower of London for five years; and then, despite his urging moderation on King James II, he felt obliged to follow his royal master into exile. James created him a duke (an honour not recognized by his successors), but this was small consolation for being banished from his beloved Powis.

He had transformed the old castle into the seat of a great nobleman. In the 1660s he created an astonishing gilt-encrusted State Bedroom, the only one of its kind in Britain, where a balustrade rails off the bed alcove from the rest of the room. The reason for this was rooted in a Versailles-style ritual, whereby only the highest of the high were allowed into the vicinity of the bed.

BELOW Looking through to the inner courtyard.

LEFT Detail of the crisply carved and beautifully inlaid staircase.

RIGHT The Grand Staircase, attributed to Captain William Winde. The walls 'painted in the pompous stile of King William's time' (as one later critic put it), were decorated in 1705 by Verrio's pupil, Gerard Lanscroon.

How often this courtly etiquette was practised remains a little hazy. There is a tradition (undocumented) that King Charles II came to stay, and the Duke of Beaufort, Lord President of Wales, enjoyed 'noble Enterteinments' at Powis in 1684. In any event, the State Bedroom is a remarkable survival of Restoration splendour – thanks to the wise advice of the Georgian architect T.F. Pritchard of Shrewsbury (designer of the first cast-iron bridge in England, at Coalbrookdale) who, when improvements were under discussion in 1772, recommended that the 'whole appartment should be preserved to keep up the stile and dignity of the Old Castle'.

Another of the Marquess of Powis's interiors which certainly added to that 'stile and dignity' was the Grand Staircase leading up to the state rooms on the first floor. The staircase has crisply carved woodwork and a painted ceiling by Antonio Verrio, the mural artist who inspired Alexander Pope's lines:

On painted ceilings you devoutly stare
Where sprawl the Saints of *Verrio* and *Laguerre*,
On gilded clouds in fair expansion lie,
And bring all Paradise before your Eye.

LEFT *Trompe-l'oeil* columns and floral flourishes add to the drama of the scrolled pediment at the head of the stairs.

RIGHT The State Bedroom at Powis: a remarkable survival from the 1660s and the only one left in Britain where a balustrade still rails off the bed from the rest of the room. The Marquess of Powis was very fond of state ceremonial, a taste fully shared by his brother-in-law the 1st Duke of Beaufort, Lord President of Wales, who prided himself on his Plantagenet descent.

The ceiling, adapted from Veronese's *Apotheosis of Venice*, is thought to represent the coronation of King Charles II's Queen, Catherine of Braganza. The wall-paintings, dating from 30 years later, are the work of Verrio's pupil, Gerard Lanscroon, who also painted the ceiling of the Blue Drawing Room at Powis.

The Marquess of Powis's architect at Powis is generally thought to have been Captain William Winde (of Buckingham House fame), a gentleman-practitioner who is on record as having designed Lord Powis's London house in Lincoln's Inn Fields. Winde's hand also appears evident in the layout of the terraces at Powis (he is known to have constructed similar features at Cliveden on the River Thames), though a Frenchman called Adrian Duval has some significant entries in the Powis archives.

After the death in exile of Lord Powis, the castle suffered further vicissitudes – King William III granted the income from the estate to a Dutch cousin, the Earl of Rochford – though oddly enough, the 2nd Marquess of Powis was apparently able to continue building the terraces until the estates were returned to him in 1722. Later in the 18th century Powis passed to a Protestant kinsman, Henry Herbert, who was given a new earldom of Powis.

The Long Gallery, where the Caesars which the diarist John Byng complained about have lately been exchanged for some little boys which, while chubby, are not of such 'great size and weight' as to precipitate them through the floor – as the National Trust feared would happen to the Caesars. The Long Gallery (completed in 1593) is the only room to have been decorated by Sir Edward Herbert that has survived intact, and a most romantic interior.

Initially he preferred to stay on at his place in Shropshire, Oakly Park. However, under aesthetic bullying from Lord Lyttelton (who reckoned that 'about £3,000 laid out upon Powis Castle would make it the most august place in the Kingdom') and financial pressure caused by the gambling of his wife (who was addicted to the game known as 'Loo'), Henry settled at Powis Castle and sold Oakly to his friend, Clive of India.

Henry's bachelor son, who seems to have taken after his mother, was happiest, according to the acidulous diarist John Byng, indulging 'in the prodigalities of London and in driving high phaetons up St James's Street'. Byng also called this Lord Powis 'a mean silly man, the bubble of his mistress (and of his Steward consequently)', who rarely went to Powis Castle other than 'to sneak about for a day or two'.

In fairness to the extravagant Lord Powis, it should be mentioned that he commissioned Pritchard to design a new ballroom and brought back the classical marbles and vast Florentine table in the Long Gallery from his Grand

Tour, when he also sat to Pompeo Batoni, that peerless portrait painter, in Rome. Byng, though, was not won over. Such treasures, he observed sarcastically in *A Tour to North Wales* (1793), 'must add much to the comforts of the castle, in which there is not one carpet, not one bed fit to sleep in, nor, probably one hogshead of wine!! What abominable folly is all this? I should exchange the Caesars for some comforts; and the inlaid Roman table should go towards the purchase of a good English dining table.'

On the death of the bachelor Lord Powis, the castle went to his nephew, Edward Clive, a grandson of Clive of India. (Clive's son, the 2nd Lord Clive, had married Lady Henrietta Herbert, the bachelor Earl's sister.) Clive of India's biographer, Mark Bence-Jones, has pointed out that the reason why the bachelor Earl left the castle and estates to his nephew rather than to his sister and brother-in-law was because the 2nd Lord Clive had unwisely remarked that the castle would make a beautiful ruin, which could be admired for its picturesque qualities from a new house on a different site.

Be that as it may, the 2nd Lord Clive was himself created Earl of Powis (the third creation) on the strength of his son's inheritance, and his son changed the family name from Clive to Herbert (as well as repairing the castle with the help of the architect Sir Robert Smirke). The Clive connection with Powis is, however, far from forgotten, and there is an imaginative Clive Museum at the castle in the old billiard room (next to Pritchard's ballroom in the detached wing of the castle), devoted to Indian treasures. These include

The Clive Museum at Powis, ingeniously devised by the designer Alec Cobbe in the 'Hindoo' or 'Indo-Gothic' style of the 19th century to show off the family's exotic treasures of the Raj.

LEFT The Aviary Terrace, with its figures by Henry Cheere or John van Nost, which were added to the balustrade at the end of the 18th century. The terraces were probably commissioned by the 1st Marquess of Powis in the 1680s, and continued in the early 18th century during the tenure of the Earls of Rochford.

RIGHT The elephantine hedges in the gardens.

objects picked up not only by the effective founder of the British Raj, but also by his son, the 2nd Lord Clive and 1st Earl of Powis, who was himself Governor of Madras.

The display cases, cleverly tricked up by the brilliant designer Alec Cobbe in an amusing evocation of the early 19th-century architectural style known as 'Hindoo' or 'Indo-Gothic', contain such items as a solid gold tiger's head encrusted with emeralds and rubies from the throne of Tipu Sahib, bejewelled hookahs and weapons, ivory, jades and silks. You can thrill to the Nawab of Bengal's palanquin (abandoned on the battlefield of Plassey) and the jolly reconstruction of a corner of Tipu Sahib's State Tent. Only the suit of elephant's armour, once at Powis but now in the Royal Armouries Museum in the Tower of London, is absent on parade.

These exotica add greatly to the treasures of Powis, which are in themselves by no means negligible. They include a noble view of the River Adige by Bellotto; Isaac Oliver's exquisite miniature of the philosopher Lord Herbert of Cherbury in repose; and numerous other portraits, among them Nathaniel Dance's study of Clive of India.

Sadly, many of the best books in Clive of India's grandson's collection, including several rare Welsh volumes and the esoteric *A Delicate Diet for Daintie-Mouthed Drunkardes* (Gascoigne, 1576) were sold in the 1920s. The bibliophile 2nd Earl of Powis himself met an unfortunate end: in 1848, during a shoot, he was mistaken for a woodcock by one of his sons, who was thenceforth nicknamed 'Bag-Dad'.

The figure of Pan on the Aviary Terrace, looking
out across the Welsh Marches.

The 3rd Earl of Powis, a minor politician, was offered the Viceroyalty of India by Disraeli but, with aristocratic insouciance, merely scrawled on the envelope of the Prime Minister's letter: 'Not worth considering – Powis.' His successor at Powis, the 4th Earl, brought in the architect G.F. Bodley in the early years of the 20th century to carry out various improvements in the 'Jacobethan' style.

The 4th Earl lost a son in the First World War, and another in the Second, after which he bequeathed the castle and its gardens to the National Trust (with private apartments for his successors). In 1929 he had also lost his wife Violet, otherwise Lady Darcy de Knayth in her own right, in a motorcar accident.

Before her death Violet had set about transforming 'a poor and meagre garden', as she put it in her journal, into 'one of the most beautiful if not the most beautiful in England and Wales'. Her greatest achievement was to lay out the new formal garden at the foot of the terraces. 'In my mind's eye (shall I ever see it in any other?) I see all ugliness removed. The wall removed – the grape house level with the earth: I see velvet lawns and wide paths: rose gardens – fountains – clipped yews – marble seats – herbaceous borders.'

As visitors to this superb National Trust showplace in Wales will confirm, Lady Powis's vision was joyfully realized.

4

PENSHURST PLACE

KENT

THE FIRST sight of Penshurst, as one breasts a wooded hill plunging down into a seemingly untouched English village, is almost overpowering. There it is, a vision of warm, mellow browns, reds and greens, weathered sandstone, brick and yew, nestling unassertively in the still-rural Kent countryside.

It is hard to think of a great house in England and Wales that has a more potent aura than Penshurst, the seat of the Sidney family from 1552 to the present day. 'Thou are not Penshurst, built to envious show', wrote Ben Jonson in 1620, 'but standst an ancient pile.' This 'ancient pile', you feel, encapsulates the history of England.

The precise, and complex, architectural chronicle of the assorted towers, halls and galleries, and the catalogue of the house's treasures – splendid as they undoubtedly are – signify little. It is the *genius loci* of Penshurst which is so overwhelming.

The gardens are as old and as remarkable as the house. They date from the 14th century and retain the formal Elizabethan framework now so seldom found at other great houses, where 18th-century 'improvers' such as 'Capability' Brown have swept away the old structures. Today some 11 acres of gardens are criss-crossed by a mile of yew hedge so as to form an enchanting series of small 'rooms' out of doors.

Penshurst must surely rate as the best cared-for formal garden in Britain. Much of the credit should go to the late Viscount De L'Isle, a former Governor-General of Australia, who won the Victoria Cross at Anzio during the Second World War. 'Bill' De L'Isle carried out a thoroughgoing restoration of Penshurst and its gardens over 45 years until his death in 1991. He added such attractive new features as the Nut Garden, the Magnolia Garden and the Grey Garden (all designed by John Codrington), as well as the ingeniously coloured Union Flag Garden.

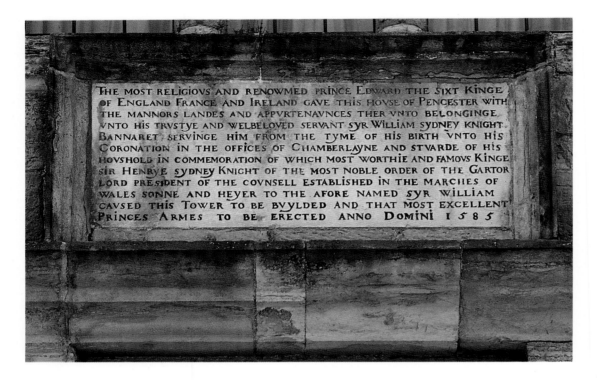

LEFT Inscription commemorating Edward VI's gift of Penshurst to Sir William Sidney in 1552.

Lord De L'Isle's son Philip, the present Viscount, and his wife Isobel are carrying on the good work and have already restored three of the garden ponds, including the Prince of Wales Feathers' Fountain. The live-wire Lady De L'Isle has taken special responsibility for the gardens and contents of Penshurst; her knowledgeable enthusiasm for the place as a living entity, and above all as a family home (her children are to be seen charging around the yew alleys on their bicycles), rather than as a museum, is most engaging.

A tour of the house has to begin in the Great or Barons Hall, a breathtaking 14th-century structure in a perfect state of preservation, with a massive, 60-foot-high chestnut roof, pinkish tiled floor, original hearth and 20-foot-long trestle tables. This is, quite simply, one of the great interiors of the world.

It was built in the late 1330s by Sir John Pulteney, a prominent merchant in the City of London who was four times Lord Mayor. Subsequently, King Henry V's brother, John Duke of Bedford, added a second hall in the 15th century – a somewhat awkwardly angled addition. Yet to criticize the architectural composition of Penshurst is beside the point: the way it has grown in a distinctly haphazard fashion is an essential part of its charm.

In the early 16th century Penshurst passed to the Staffords, Dukes of Buckingham, the third of whom, the 'Proud Duke' of Buckingham, entertained King Henry VIII here in 1519. The jollifications laid on for the King cost some £2,500 (a staggering sum, worth almost a million pounds in today's money), and aroused uneasy suspicions in the piggy eyes of Henry who saw the Proud Duke as a threat. Buckingham was arrested on a trumped-up charge of treason and beheaded; his forfeited estates duly came to the Crown. The King subsequently came to stay at Penshurst while he courted Anne Boleyn in the nearby castle of Hever, and Anne's brother was put in charge of the Penshurst estate.

Penshurst remained Crown property until 1552 when the boy-king Edward VI decided to reward Sir William Sidney, his tutor and the steward of his household, with the gift of the house and estate. Sir William's son, Henry, was the young King's closest friend – legend has it that Edward died in Henry Sidney's arms.

BELOW A frosty view of the north front.

Sir Henry Sidney, having astutely avoided involvement in the Lady Jane Grey fiasco even though his wife, Mary, was a sister-in-law of the 'Nine Days' Queen', went on to become a faithful servant of Queen Elizabeth I. Mary Sidney wore a mask in public to hide the scars of smallpox, which she contracted while nursing Queen Elizabeth.

Although Sir Henry, who was Lord Deputy in Ireland, did not enjoy great riches – in 1583 he was complaining that he had not 'so much land as would graze a mutton' – he managed to make some important improvements to Penshurst without upsetting its medieval character. Among his remodelling work, he linked the Great Hall with a new range and gatehouse to the north and introduced an arcade with Tuscan columns – a remarkable novelty for 1579 and perhaps the earliest classical loggia in England.

Sir Henry's eldest son was the legendary Sir Philip Sidney, praised by the antiquary William Camden as 'the great glory of his family, the great hope of mankind, the most lively pattern of virtue, and the glory of the world'. In view of the fact that Philip Sidney was not a particularly distinguished politician or soldier, and that his literary works were not published in his lifetime, this encomium might strike some as a little high-flown. Yet to his contemporaries Sir Philip was the prototype of the perfect gentleman, the personification of the aristocratic ideal, combining virtue, chivalry and nobility.

LEFT The well-worn steps leading up from the Barons Hall.

RIGHT Tucked around a corner: an oak dresser-cum-china cabinet, with a fine selection of pottery and porcelain.

His apotheosis came, aged 31, on the battlefield of Zutphen in Holland. Lying mortally wounded and about to take a swig from his hip-flask, he noticed a dying soldier looking longingly at the bottle. 'Thy necessity', quoth Sidney, as he passed the drink to his comrade-in-arms, 'is yet greater than mine.'

As well as poetry, Sir Philip Sidney wrote the prose romance *Arcadia*, dedicated to his sister Mary Countess of Pembroke, who helped make Wilton 'an academie as well as a palace'. Sidney's description of the great house in *Arcadia*, though, is thought to have been based on Penshurst; certainly it captures the spirit of the 'ancient pile':

> The house itself was built of fair and strong stone not,
> affecting so much any extraordinary kind of fineness as
> an honourable representing of a firm stateliness...
> the consideration of the exceeding lastingness made the
> eyes believe it was exceedingly beautiful.

On Sir Philip's death, Penshurst was inherited by his younger brother Robert, who was created Earl of Leicester early in the 17th century. Robert added the Long Gallery at Penshurst. Lit by mullioned windows and elaborately panelled in oak, it makes a fine setting for the Sidney family portraits – from Sir Henry, possibly by Hans Eworth, and Sir Philip, to the black sheep of the Sidneys, the republican Algernon (tried by Judge Jeffreys and beheaded on Tower Hill) by J. van Egmont.

Robert brought some much-needed cash into the Sidney family by marrying a Welsh coal-mining heiress, Barbara Gamage. There is a striking portrait by Gheeraerts of Barbara and six of her children in the State Dining Room. With the help of her fortune Robert embarked on an ambitious venture to build a house in London (subsequently demolished and commemorated by Leicester Square) and collected a celebrated library – sold in the 18th century by the erratic 7th (and last) Earl of Leicester, whose wife was notorious, as the Penshurst guidebook tells us, for 'entertaining young men in rustic snuggeries and attending country dances'.

The 7th Earl's niece, Elizabeth, married William Perry and there is a hilarious conversation piece of them and their brood in the Queen Elizabeth Room at Penshurst. Perry looks a prize ass: smug, stout and supremely self-satisfied. In the scramble for Penshurst following the death of his wife's uncle in 1737, he managed to get his chubby paws on the place and set about a disastrous programme of 'Georgianization'. His scheme was inspired by 'the great window in ye baths of Pisa in Italy'. 'This is ye actual plan,' he proudly declared, 'given me by ye architect himself on the spot. I intend it for the upper hall at Penshurst.'

Soon the great medieval house was covered in a rash of sash and Venetian windows. Although some of Perry's acquisitions in the way of *objets d'art* were welcome enough – such as the harpsichord from Queen Christina of Sweden in the Queen Elizabeth Room – his architectural changes were having a deleterious effect on the personality of the house. Fortunately, before he could wreck Penshurst altogether, Perry was certified a lunatic and clapped in an asylum.

His legacy to the house greatly exercised the compiler of the 1838 guidebook to Penshurst. Employing heavy sarcasm, the writer noted that 'Some of the windows show tracery of a superior order and others have huge common sashes, introduced by the tasteful Mr Perry...'. As for the gables of the Great Hall, 'On the point of each gable is an old stone figure – the one a tortoise, the other a lion couchant, – and upon the back of each of these old figures... good Mr Perry clapped a huge leaden vase which had probably crowned aforetime the pillars of a gateway, or the roof of a garden house.' The guidebook writer pleaded that: 'It is to be hoped that Lord De L'Isle will not long delay his intention of having these monstrosities pitched from their undeserved elevation.'

The peer to whom he was addressing his plea was Perry's great-grandson, the 1st Lord De L'Isle and Dudley, who had married Lady Sophia FitzClarence, the favourite bastard daughter of King William IV by the actress Mrs Jordan (a liaison described by the Court wags as 'bathing in the River Jordan'). The splendid Rockingham dinner service on show at Penshurst came to the house through this marriage.

The 1st Lord De L'Isle's grandmother, Elizabeth Perry, had married Sir Bysshe Shelley, Bt. (himself the grandfather, through his first marriage, of the poet Percy Bysshe Shelley). The Shelley's son, Sir John, added the name of Sidney and began a sympathetic restoration of Penshurst. This was carried on

The panelled Long Gallery, lit from three sides by mullioned windows, dates from 1599 to 1607.

5

SYON
HOUSE

NE OF the joys of a walk in the Royal Botanical Gardens at Kew in Surrey is the climax of the central avenue, where the gardens meet the River Thames. There you can stop and sit on a bench to survey the prospect across the river to Middlesex. It is a most unexpected sight amid the urban sprawl of Greater London: a nobleman's park adorned by the stately pile of Syon House, still the seat – or one of them – of the Duke of Northumberland.

Yet for all its air of castellated grandeur and its Percy lion in pride of place, the exterior of Syon, on closer inspection, is not all that remarkable. Similarly, while a case can be made for its historical importance – this is the place where Caesar's legionaries crossed the Thames in 54 BC; where Henry V founded a Bridgettine monastery; where Henry VIII's coffin burst open and his rotting corpse was worried by dogs; where Lady Jane Grey unwisely decided to accept her father-in-law the Duke of Northumberland's offer of the crown – Syon does not demand inclusion in a survey of great houses on association alone. No, it ranks among the most illustrious buildings in England and Wales on account of its superb interiors, created by Robert Adam in the 1760s. As Sir John Betjeman observed, 'You'd never guess that battlemented house contained such wonders as there are inside it.'

Adam's patrons were the Earl and Countess of Northumberland (the former Sir Hugh Smithson and Lady Elizabeth Seymour, who took the name of Percy and ended up as Duke and Duchess of Northumberland), for whom Adam had also worked at Alnwick Castle in Northumberland (see pages 16-25). The grandiloquent Hugh and Elizabeth found Syon 'ruinous and inconvenient', and commissioned 'Capability' Brown to landscape the rather flat riverside park while Adam set about transforming the interiors of the old rectangular building.

The original monastery had been rebuilt in the late 1540s by the Duke of Somerset, Protector of the Realm during the short reign of the boy-king

PRECEDING PAGES The river front of Syon House, refaced in Bath stone in the early 19th century by the 3rd Duke of Northumberland.

RIGHT The bronze of *The Dying Gaul* faces Apollo, in the apse, down Adam's Great Hall, with its noble stucco work by Joseph Rose.

LEFT Marble Roman figures in togas stand sentinel on either side of the front door in the Great Hall. The pedestals were designed by Adam and executed by Rose.

BELOW The Percy lion (after a model by Michelangelo), formerly upstream at Northumberland House, now facing the right way on the east front at Syon.

Edward VI. 'Protector' Somerset's personal physician, Dr Turner, also laid out what was probably England's first botanic garden here; the old mulberry trees in the Nun's Orchard, which still bear fruit, are believed to have been planted by him.

Later in the 16th century Syon passed to the Percys, Earls of Northumberland, the 9th of whom, Henry (the 'Wizard Earl'), carried out another rebuilding early in the 17th century. He earned his nickname whilst languishing in the Tower of London on suspicion (quite unjustified) of being involved in the Gunpowder Plot. Henry was a keen scientist and enjoyed dabbling in alchemy and chemistry; the Syon archives record numerous purchases by him of retorts, crucibles, globes and even a crystal ball. His library at Syon was celebrated.

Further alterations and improvements were made to Syon by the 'Proud' 6th Duke of Somerset at the end of the 17th century. He had come into the Percy property by marrying the heiress of the 11th Earl of Northumberland, Lady Elizabeth Percy, widow of the murdered Thomas Thynne of Longleat. The Proud Duke was well named: when his second wife (a much younger

ABOVE 'The clash of cymbals...'. Detail of a gilded classical musician atop one of the Ionic columns in the anteroom.

LEFT The opulently imperial anteroom, with its columns of either ancient verd-antique (transported from the bed of the River Tiber) or scagliola. The polished floor is a remarkable example of 18th-century scagliola work. The gilded trophies were executed by Joseph Rose.

woman, Lady Charlotte Finch) once ventured to tap him on the shoulder with her fan, the Duke drew himself up haughtily and said: 'Madam, my first Duchess was a Percy, and *she* never took such a liberty!'

In addition to improving Syon House, the Proud Duke planted the avenue of limes that forms the approach to the main entrance. On the whole, though, he preferred to spend his time at his palatial country seat of Petworth in Sussex (see pages 260-75) rather than at Syon.

Even so, it is hard to imagine that Syon was quite so 'ruinous' as his granddaughter, Elizabeth Duchess of Northumberland, made out. From the ducal viewpoint of her and her husband Hugh, however, it was clearly 'inconvenient', being built round a courtyard.

When Adam arrived in 1762, still fresh from his Grand Tour, the south range contained state rooms, the north family rooms, the west a Long Gallery and the east a Great Hall. The plan was for Adam to remodel and redecorate the entire interior, and, for good measure, to put a ballroom in the courtyard.

In the event, funds only permitted the brilliant young Scotsman to reach about halfway round. Nonetheless, many judges would consider that the rooms Adam did complete at Syon rank among his very finest.

The Great Hall, furnished with statues like a Roman *atrium*, is two storeys high with a black and white marble floor and a subtle combination of colours on the walls. The decorative stucco work is by Joseph Rose. Adam was faced with the problem of uneven floor levels, but cleverly overcame it by devising steps and a screen of Doric columns. In front of the steps leading to the anteroom broods a bronze of *The Dying Gaul,* cast in Rome by Valodier and acquired by the Duchess of Northumberland in 1773 for £300.

By contrast with the cool grandeur of the Great Hall, the anteroom is a riot of gold and marble – including some genuine Roman marble columns dredged up from the River Tiber and brought to Syon in 1765. Adam took a special interest in contemporary archaeological discoveries and drew on the latest scholarship to show that classical decoration could be warm and colourful rather than merely cold and monumental. The result is a glorious feeling of lavish luxury.

Here again Adam's genius for architecture as well as decoration is evident. He has contrived to make an irregularly shaped room (in fact it is 36 feet 6 inches by 30 feet with a height of 21 feet) seem perfectly square by his arrangement of columns and statues.

The dining room, in cream and gold, is quintessential Adam with its arched recesses, apses, half-domes and columnar screens. The chiaroscuro frieze panels are the work of Andrea Casali.

The Red Drawing Room takes its name from the original and still-sumptuous Spitalfields silk with which it is decorated. It is furnished with pieces mostly designed by Adam, who liked to have a hand in everything the eye could see. The ceiling medallions are by G.B. Cipriani.

Adam effectively designed the Red Drawing Room only as a prelude to what he saw as the real withdrawing, or ladies' room – the Long Gallery. This he rearranged, as he put it, 'in a style to afford variety and amusement'. It was originally the 16th-century gallery, and a long, low room – 136 feet by just 14 feet high and 14 feet wide – which must have presented Adam with considerable problems.

He skilfully disguised the length by breaking the room up into sections: units of four pilasters are grouped with wide intervals, centred upon the three doors and two fireplaces. The eye is diverted by gilded cornices, lunettes and medallions by Francisco Zuccarelli and landscapes by Thomas Marlow. The

ABOVE Looking back from the Long Gallery through the
Red Drawing Room along the south range at Syon.

ceiling has cross-lines which somehow expand the width of the room. Last but not least the furniture in the Long Gallery is an absorbing mixture of Adam's own designs and items from old Northumberland House, the family's principal town house, high upstream on the bank of the Thames at Charing Cross.

Among the more unusual portraits in the Print Room at Syon is one by the American artist Gilbert Stuart of Thayadneega, a Red Indian chieftain of the Mohawk tribe who was head of the Iroquois Confederacy or 'Six Nations' in the State of New York. Thayadneega – also known, more prosaically, as Joseph Brant – rendered useful assistance to Earl Percy, heir to Adam's patron and a general in the British Army, during the American War of Independence. Stuart's portrait of the 2nd Duke of Northumberland, as he became, also hangs in the Print Room. He spent much time at Syon on his retirement from the army and built the pavilion boathouse, to the designs of another Scots architect, Robert Mylne, as a surprise for his wife.

RIGHT The Red Drawing Room, hung with crimson Spitalfields silk and Stuart portraits and adorned with ceiling medallions by G.B.Cipriani. The carpet, designed by Adam for the room, was executed by Thomas Moor of Moorfields, London, in 1769.

His son, the 3rd Duke of Northumberland, used to enjoy swimming from Richmond Bridge to this boathouse – a fair stretch of the Thames. The 3rd Duke was ambassador-extraordinary at the coronation of Charles X of France in 1825, and the stupendous Sèvres vase, which stands in the well of the staircase at Syon, was made especially for him according to the French King's command.

The 3rd Duke, who entertained at Syon on a princely scale, rebuilt the north side of the quadrangle of the house and refaced all the exterior in Bath stone. He also built the riding school and added one of Syon's most notable features, the conservatory.

This amazing Roman temple in glass was designed in the 1820s by Charles Fowler, the architect responsible for the old flower market at Covent Garden. Built of gunmetal and Bath stone, it has an extraordinarily ethereal quality, as if it was constructed of spun sugar. It is said that Joseph Paxton, once the head gardener at Chatsworth (see pages 244-59), made a detailed study of this pioneering building before designing the Crystal Palace for the Great Exhibition of 1850, and that the Syon conservatory was also the inspiration for the Palm House at Kew, across the river.

During the tenure of the 4th Duke of Northumberland, who succeeded his brother in 1847, the ceilings in the north range at Syon – notably that of the Print Room – were remodelled to their present form by Monteroli. In 1874, when the Metropolitan Board of Works demolished Northumberland House to make way for the thoroughfare now known as Northumberland Avenue, the stone statue of a lion (which is after a model by Michelangelo and which had surmounted the street front at Charing Cross) was removed to Syon by

RIGHT Detail of a chimneypiece from Northumberland House, now in the private drawing room.

BELOW The Long Gallery, which stretches down the length of the river front at Syon. Ingeniously converted by Adam from an Elizabethan or Jacobean-style Long Gallery to a library-cum-withdrawing room, it was 'finished in a style to afford variety and amusement'. The criss-cross lines of the ceiling have the effect of expanding the narrow room's width. Much of the furniture was made especially for the room by Adam.

the 6th Duke of Northumberland. The 6th Duke, a pious man who was the
largest landowner in England a century ago (with 186,000 acres bringing in
an income of £176,000 per annum), re-erected the lion on the east front of
Syon House.

According to family tradition, when the lion was first at Northumberland
House it had faced towards St James's Palace, but one of the Dukes of Northumberland, displeased by a slight from the reigning sovereign, turned it to
face the other way. At Syon the lion's loyal position has been restored, which
seems fitting not only because of the Percy's leonine emblem but also because
an heraldic coat of augmentation, featuring the three lions of England, was
granted to the Seymour family, Dukes of Somerset, by King Henry VIII.

That king's own undignified sojourn at Syon, after his death *en route* from
Westminster to Windsor in 1547, fulfilled a strange prophecy. A dozen years
earlier, a Franciscan friar had predicted 'that God's judgements were ready to
fall upon his head... and that the dogs would lick his blood as they had done
Ahab's'. The disagreeable sight of the Syon dogs lapping up various remains
of Henry VIII struck some observers as a divine retribution for the
desecration of the Syon monastery.

Today, though, Syon seems a majestic oasis in the metropolis. Although
office blocks litter the neighbouring Great North Road, no modern building
can be seen from the house itself. It even survived a turbulent spell during the

Welcoming opulence: one of Syon's bedrooms, with splendid canopied bed.

Second World War when 69 bombs fell in the grounds, 2 firebombs penetrated the roof and a pair of 'doodlebugs' caused extensive blast damage. During the war the house quartered officers of the 9th Battalion Grenadier Guards – serving with which the 9th Duke of Northumberland was killed in France in May 1940 – and later served as a home for nurses from the West Middlesex Hospital.

The 10th Duke of Northumberland, who succeeded his brother in 1940, carried out restoration work at Syon after the war, notably of the great conservatory. The house was opened regularly to the public and has developed a wide range of attractions, including a garden centre, craft exhibitions, a butterfly house, a National Trust gift shop and a banqueting and conference centre. Some of the structures in which these various commercial enterprises are housed do not entirely, it must be said, chime with their surroundings, but there is still plenty of space in the gardens and 'Capability' Brown's park in which to escape.

Syon has also proved popular as a film location – most memorably in the 1960s film *Accident,* starring Dirk Bogarde and Michael York – a calling particularly sympathetic to the house's present owner, the 11th Duke of Northumberland, who is a film producer.

6

KNOLE

KENT

I T IS characteristic of the unassertively English quality of Knole that it has no grand lodge gates, no trumpets or fanfares. Indeed it is easy to miss the narrow opening between buildings on the main road in the middle of Sevenoaks which leads, unpromisingly, down a narrow hill, to a park of deep valleys, magnificent old trees and grazing deer.

It is only when you breast another steep rise that you catch a glimpse, in the distance, of an astonishing jumble of red-tiled roofs, chimney stacks and battlements. This apparition, covering some four acres in all, strikes one not so much as a house but as a medieval village or small town.

Although owned by the National Trust, Knole is still the family home of the Sackville-Wests, Lords Sackville, and no-one has expressed its potent charm better than Vita Sackville-West, only child of the 3rd Lord Sackville. She loved Knole with all the passion of one, so to speak, disinherited by her sex. If she had been a boy – as, of course, she longed to be – it would have been hers. As it was, Knole ceased to be her home on her father's death in 1928.

In that year her great friend Virginia Woolf published her novel *Orlando* (recently filmed, using Knole as a location) in which Vita is clearly the model for the hero-cum-heroine transmigrating down the line of her Sackville ancestors. Knole and its singular character resonates through the story: 'Indeed, when Orlando came to reckon up the matter of furnishing with rosewood chairs and cedar-wood cabinets, with silver basins, china bowls and Persian carpets, every one of the three hundred and sixty-five bedrooms which the house contained, he saw it would be no light one.'

Three hundred years later the modern Orlando/Vita returns home in a motorcar: 'She drew up in the courtyard where, for so many hundred years she had come, on horseback or in coach and six, with men riding before or coming after. She strode into the dining room where her old friends Dryden, Pope, Swift, Addison regarded her demurely.'

Vita Sackville-West herself also featured Knole in one of her own novels, *The Edwardians*, as the family seat of 'Chevron'. One balmy summer's afternoon Sebastian, the young duke in the novel, escapes from having to play host for his mother by going on the roof. Country house roofs are supremely evocative vantage points, as Evelyn Waugh showed in *Brideshead Revisited* and Alan Bennett in his spoof Great War memoir ('We climbed out on to the leads among the turrets and towers and the green copper cupola. I remember the weather vane's shrill singing in the breeze...') in *Forty Years On*; but what could be more nostalgic than:

> Acres of red-brown roof surrounded him, heraldic beasts
> carved in stone sitting at each corner of the gables.
> Across the great courtyard the flag floated red and blue
> and languid from a tower. Down in the garden, on a lawn
> of brilliant green, he could see the sprinkled figures of
> his mother's guests, some sitting under the trees, some
> strolling about; he could hear their laughter and the
> tap of the croquet mallets.

The Sackvilles were granted Knole in 1566 by Queen Elizabeth I, a cousin of the family. The Queen's father, King Henry VIII, had appropriated the property from the Archbishop of Canterbury and greatly enlarged it. The original house had been built by Thomas Bourchier, Archbishop of Canterbury, between 1456, when he acquired the estate, and his death in 1486, when he bequeathed it to the See of Canterbury.

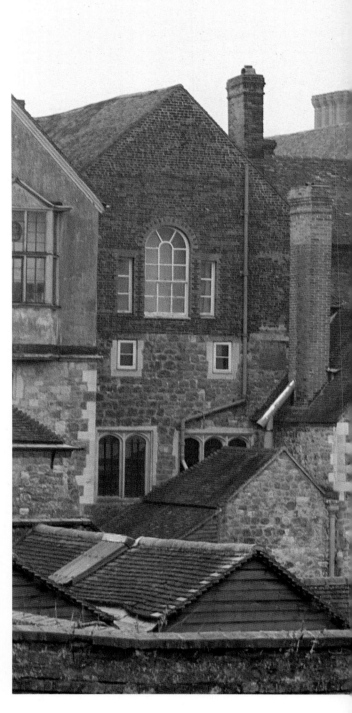

ABOVE Acres of architectural jumble form a homogeneous whole.

LEFT Gables, chimneys and yews: 'No other country but England could have produced it...'

PRECEDING PAGES Looming out of the early morning mist, Knole looks like a medieval village or small town.

The first Sackville owner, Thomas, later Lord Buckhurst and the 1st Earl of Dorset, was a poet and statesman who carried out a splendid remodelling between 1603 and 1608, probably to the designs of the surveyor John Thorpe. The consequence was that Knole, with its series of enclosed court-yards, grew to be less like a house and more like a university college.

The work was carried out on a lavish scale, with craftsmen imported from Italy and even musicians brought in to form Lord Dorset's private orchestra. Many original plasterwork ceilings (by the King's plasterer, Richard Dungan), marble chimneypieces (by Cornelius Cuer), the carved wooden screen in the hall (probably by the King's carpenter, William Portinton) and the painted decorations of staircase and Cartoon Gallery (by Paul Isaacson) survive from Lord Dorset's time.

ABOVE Detail of the gloriously grotesque wooden screen in the Great
Hall, probably carved by William Portinton in the early 1600s.

Luxurious as it all sounds, it is worth bearing in mind that, judging from a letter of Lord Dorset's, he only had a single basin and ewer in which to perform his ablutions. Similarly, during the legendarily extravagant tenure of the 3rd Earl of Dorset, we learn from the diary of his heiress-wife, Lady Anne Clifford, that she cut up her husband's shirting to make cloths, or 'clouts'. A list dated 1623 of the Dorsets' household at Knole shows that 111 persons were then employed – ranging from such figures as 'Mr Matthew Caldicott, my Lord's favourite' and 'Widow Ben' to 'Solomon, the Bird-Catcher', 'Lowry, a French boy', 'Men to carry wood' and a couple of 'Blackamoors'.

The spendthrift 3rd Earl mortgaged Knole and died in debt to the tune of £60,000. His brother, a loyal Cavalier, lost the house to the Parliamentarians during the Civil War, when most of the original pictures and furniture were dispersed. Fortunately the 6th Earl of Dorset was able to make good these losses when he inherited the contents of Copt Hall in Essex (seat of his maternal grandfather, the Earl of Middlesex) and also through his position as Lord Chamberlain to King William III. Thanks to this Lord Dorset, Knole can now boast one of the best collections anywhere of 17th-century furniture and textiles.

The 6th Earl was, by all accounts, a most genial fellow: poet, patron, lover of Nell Gwyn and a generous host at Knole. 'A freedom reigned at his table', wrote Matthew Prior, the poet and diplomatist, 'which made every one of his guests think himself at home.' Once, when entertaining a party of friends, Lord Dorset suggested that each guest should write an impromptu note and

RIGHT A sturdy wooden soldier guards the doorway from the Great Hall to the Great Staircase.

LEFT The Great Staircase, remodelled by Thomas Sackville, 1st Earl of Dorset, between 1605 and 1608 in an innovative architectural manner. It is adorned with grisaille decoration and an unusually early example of *trompe-l'oeil*.

that John Dryden, the poet, should act as judge. Dryden, having solemnly studied all the entries, declared Dorset the winner for his contribution, which read: 'I promise to pay Mr John Dryden five hundred pounds on demand. Signed, Dorset.'

The 6th Earl's son, Lionel, who was created Duke of Dorset in 1720, added some delicious pieces of furniture by William Kent to Knole's already outstanding collections, and commissioned the Huguenot artist Mark Antony Hauduroy to decorate several of the rooms. Later in the 18th century, the dashing 3rd Duke of Dorset made further important acquisitions, principally through his friendships with such artists as Sir Joshua Reynolds and Thomas Gainsborough. The Crimson Drawing Room at Knole is almost entirely devoted to the works of Sir Joshua; his subjects include the 3rd Duke himself and the 3rd Duke's Chinese page, one Wang-y-Tong (known at Knole as 'Warnoton'), whom the Duke had educated at the local grammar school.

BELOW Detail of a *trompe-l'oeil* newel post on the staircase, showing a Sackville leopard holding an heraldic shield.

RIGHT Looking into the ballroom from the upper landing of the Great Staircase. Originally the solar, or chief living room, of Archbishop Bourchier's late medieval house, this great room was panelled in the early 17th-century remodelling of Knole by the 1st Earl of Dorset, who would have dined here. The elaborate carving was probably by William Portinton, and the plasterwork ceiling was by Richard Dungan. The superb Renaissance chimneypiece and overmantel, incorporating marbles and alabaster in an exuberant design, has been attributed to Cornelius Cuer.

ABOVE The Brown Gallery, part of Archbishop Bourchier's original building, was remodelled in the Jacobean style by the 1st Earl of Dorset and given a ribbed ceiling, 88 feet in length. The room is sometimes called 'the Reformers' Gallery' because of the portraits of Luther, Melanchthon and Pomeranus among the historical array. The collection of English furniture on show here is without peer.

RIGHT The Cartoon Gallery, with its copies of Raphael's cartoons, serpentine plasterwork ceiling by Dungan and spectacular marble and alabaster chimneypiece and overmantel. The full-length portrait in the centre of the back wall shows the Earl of Surrey, in a rare 16th- or early 17th-century frame.

The 3rd Duke's chief interests seem to have been games and women. In *The Prophecies of Delphos* (1791) he is described as 'a most admirable cricket-player – more cannot be said of him as he is not in possession of any brains'. An even less kind account in *The Jockey Club* (1792) considered him 'arrogant and haughty, ignorant and illiterate... under his roof fiddlers and buffoons, w––res and parasites, sharpers and knaves were always welcome... Billiards and hazard engrossed almost the whole time... unless when he relaxed from the fatigues of gaming in the arms of beauty'.

Among the arms in which he is said to have relaxed are those of Marie Antoinette, Elisabeth Countess of Derby, the notorious courtesan Nancy Parsons and the dancer Giannette Bacelli, whom he installed in a tower at Knole. The plump nude plaster statue of Madame Bacelli, reclining invitingly on her stomach at the foot of the grisaille-decorated Great Staircase, is one of the most memorable sights at Knole.

During the minority of the 4th Duke of Dorset (who was a schoolfriend of the poet Lord Byron at Harrow), his stepfather, Earl Whitworth, made some minor structural changes to Knole in the Gothick manner. The dukedom died out later in the 19th century and Knole passed to the West family who became Sackville-Wests and Lords Sackville.

Finally, in 1946, the 4th Lord Sackville made Knole over to the National Trust. 'It was the only thing to do', wrote Vita Sackville-West, his niece, 'and as a potential inheritor of Knole I had to sign documents giving Knole away. It nearly broke my heart, putting my signature to what I couldn't help regarding as a betrayal of all the traditions of my ancestors and the house I loved.'

LEFT The sensational late 17th-century silver furnishings of the King's Room at Knole, only rivalled by the set at Windsor Castle which were presented to Charles II by the City of London. The Knole set was supplied by Gerrit Jensen in the early 1680s, though the candlestands and mirror probably date from a few years earlier.

RIGHT Detail of the state bed in the Venetian Ambassador's Room, made for James II in 1688, with hangings of Genoa velvet. Its rich carving and gilding was probably by Thomas Roberts. The bed came to Knole from Whitehall via Copt Hall as one of the 6th Earl of Dorset's 'perquisites' after Queen Mary's death in 1695.

Yet, though Vita Sackville-West could not bear to return to Knole – she wrote the guidebook from memory – she had a deep respect and admiration for the National Trust and all it did for the salvation of country houses. Indeed it was she who was largely instrumental in finding the ideal visionary for the first appointment of a secretary to the Trust's 'country house scheme': James Lees-Milne. Lees-Milne has aptly described Knole as 'having a perenially romantic history and seeming to be immortal'.

Curiously, notwithstanding the inevitable 'museumization' necessary for conservation purposes, Knole retains its magical atmosphere under National Trust ownership. The ruggedness of the exterior, in its rough Kent rag stone, in no way prepares one for the fabulous riches within.

One stands in awe before its Jacobean panelling and plasterwork, the state beds and tapestries, the luscious 17th-century furniture. There is a cornucopia of historical portraits in the Brown Gallery, while the Cartoon Gallery takes its name from the copies of Raphael's cartoons, probably done in the workshop of Franz Cleyn, of scenes from the lives of Saints Peter and Paul (some of the treasures inherited from the Earl of Middlesex). The greatest thrill is to see, *in situ*, in the King's Room, the set of silver looking glass, table

and stands of 1676–81 which stole the show at the great 'Treasure Houses of Britain' exhibition in Washington in 1985. As the exhibition's organizer, Gervase Jackson-Stops, architectural adviser to the National Trust, noted in the catalogue: 'The silver furniture at Knole still evokes the unrivalled splendour of English country house life in the baroque period.'

It is its unchanged quality that gives Knole part of its unrivalled charm. That, and the sheer size of it: 365 rooms (one, as legend has it, for every day of the year), 52 staircases, 7 courtyards. Only the arch-cynic Horace Walpole, in the 18th century, could have been disappointed. 'The house not near so extensive,' he noted, 'as I expected...'.

Walpole found:

> The furniture throughout, ancient magnificence; loads of
> portraits, not good nor curious; ebony cabinets,
> embossed silver in vases, dishes, etc; embroidered beds,
> stiff chairs, and sweet bags lying on velvet tables, richly
> worked in silk and gold... There is never a good staircase...
> sundry portraits of the times; but they seem to have been
> bespoke by the yard, and drawn all by the same painter.
> In the chapel is a piece of ancient tapestry; Saint Luke in
> his first profession is holding an urinal.

Knole: 'these irregular roofs, this easy straying up the contours of the hill, these cool coloured walls, these calm gables, and dark windows mirroring the sun'.

ABOVE Stag at bay... or rather, underneath the mullions.

After such a negative chronicle it is a relief to turn to the diary of the 20th-century poet Denton Welch, for whom Knole epitomized English history, autumnal-like, an evanescent dream of the past, yet –

> an eternal moment always dissolving which will yet
> re-occur a thousand times to a thousand other people when
> we are dead, who will look out in the same way through
> the windows in their heads & see the falling rain, the
> bracken, the pattern of the oak bark, and wonder
> and go on wondering for years.

For the last word on Knole, though, we must leave the stage to Vita Sackville-West, whose history of Knole and the Sackvilles (now reprinted in paperback by the National Trust) is a classic of the country house genre. Knole, she pointed out, is:

> no mere excresence, no alien fabrication, no startling
> stranger seen between the beeches and the oaks. No other
> country but England could have produced it, and into no
> other country would it settle with such harmony and such
> quiet. The very trees have not been banished from the
> courtyards, but spread their green against the stone.
> From the top of a tower one looks down upon the acreage
> of roofs, and the effect is less that of a palace than of
> a jumbled village upon the hillside... . It is not an
> incongruity like Blenheim or Chatsworth, foreign to the
> spirit of England. It is, rather, the greater relation
> of those small manor houses which hide themselves away so
> innumerably among the counties... . The great Palladian
> houses of the eighteenth century are in England, they are
> not of England, as are these irregular roofs, this easy
> straying up the contours of the hill, these cool coloured
> walls, these calm gables, and dark windows mirroring the sun.

7

COMPTON WYNYATES

WARWICKSHIRE

MANY OF the sentiments expressed about Knole in the last chapter by Vita Sackville-West, such as it being true to the spirit of England and a greater relation of the traditional small manor house, could equally well be applied to Compton Wynyates, hidden away in a valley in Warwickshire. Families naturally tend to be passionately partizan about their beloved seats, but just as Vita Sackville-West was indubitably right about Knole, so the 5th Marquess of Northampton spoke nothing but the truth about Compton Wynyates when he claimed, at the beginning of the 20th century:

> No-one can see it and remain unmoved. One is carried
> away from this world and into some other where the
> supernatural would be quite at home, and where anything
> trivial or modern or practical would be out of place.

Certainly Compton Wynyates, cradled in a hollow, at the foot of gently wooded, grassy hills which rise away from it on all sides, is so beautiful that the first glimpse takes the breath away. The vision of red brick against the green background is the epitome of romance.

The colour of the old bricks dazzles the senses. The constant variation of shading – from pink to plum, from russet to rose – makes it difficult to focus the eyes. Then you notice the bluish diaper pattern on the walls, caused by using bricks fumed in the kiln.

Faced with this lovable, asymmetrical hotchpotch of crenellated towers, gables (some half-timbered), moulded chimneys, oriel windows and mullioned windows, it is difficult to discern much in the way of pattern or plan. Architecture, though, is hardly the point of Compton Wynyates. Its very irregularity, the apparently haphazard nature of its construction, is what allows the imagination to take flight. Here, one feels, is the essence of England.

It has been the home of the Compton family since 1209. Indeed they take their surname from the place-name, which means 'the settlement in the coombe'. 'Wynyates' alludes to the vineyards which once flourished on the slopes surrounding the house.

The original moated manor house was pulled down by Edmund Compton in the second half of the 15th century. Edmund constructed a new squarish structure on the same spot, probably similar in style to the moated manor house at Ightham Mote in Kent (now, unlike Compton Wynyates, a property of the National Trust).

In 1493 Edmund Compton died and was succeeded as squire of Compton Wynyates by his son William, who raised the family from minor county gentry to 'great commoner' status. William was appointed page to the young Prince Henry, Duke of York, in the Tudor household and became an indispensable companion to the bluff Prince 'Hal' who grew up to be King Henry VIII.

Once Henry acceded to the throne in 1509, Sir William Compton's star was in the ascendant. He became Chief Gentleman of the Bedchamber (presumably an active job with such a lusty master), Usher of the Black Rod and Keeper of the Privy Purse. After distinguishing himself at the Battle of Tournai in 1512, Compton was given the post of Chancellor of Ireland, though he never troubled to set foot there. He preferred to remain at the King's side – accompanying him to the expensive spectacle of the 'Field of the Cloth of Gold' near Calais in 1520 – although he did give staunch support to the Earl of Surrey during his skirmishes against the Scots.

Compton's reward for all this loyal service to the House of Tudor was the commodity that underpinned the aspirations of all upwardly mobile aristocrats – land. As Sir Bernard Burke, the genealogist, recorded, 'This great man, one of the most eminent of his time, had estates in 20 counties in England.'

These estates included Castle Ashby in Northamptonshire, which the Comptons were later to make their principal seat, but Compton Wynyates remained their root. Sir William determined to aggrandize the old family home, and he was largely responsible for the rambling house built round a courtyard that we see today.

The house used to have a moat, but that was drained during the Civil War when the Comptons were to the fore on the Royalist side. The yawning, embattled porch was once the entrance for horsemen who would have crossed the moat by means of a drawbridge, the chains of which have left deep grooves above the arch. Above the entrance Sir William Compton proclaimed his loyalty to his monarch with an inset Royal Arms, supported by a dragon and a greyhound and surmounted by a crown bearing the legend '*DOM REX HENRICUS OCTAV.*'

Each side of the porch incorporates a stone bench with upcurved ends, where retainers used to sit looking out across the moat. Through the arch lies a delightful courtyard, dominated by the great oriel window of the Big Hall, as it is known. This window – and several other of the cusped and arched window surrounds in the house, as well as the Big Hall's moulded timber ceiling – are all said to have been brought to Compton Wynyates from the ruined 15th-century castle of Fulbroke, or Fulbrooke, near Warwick, also granted to Sir William Compton by Henry VIII. That the ceiling at least was originally made for somewhere larger is evident from the fact that the wall-posts are cut off in irregular lengths and do not rest on corbels as they normally would.

PRECEDING PAGES Compton Wynyates, or 'Compton-in-the-Hole', lying in its hollow in the heart of England. As John Loveday, the 18th-century sightseer, observed; 'tis situate in a bottom almost surrounded with Hills... a most retired Place'.

RIGHT The Big Hall, which rises to the full height of the house. The panel set at mid-height in the carved wooden screen depicts the Battle of Tournai of 1512, when Sir William Compton fought alongside Henry VIII.

BELOW Purl and plain: chimneystacks at Compton.

The Big Hall also boasts a finely carved screen. The central panel depicts the Battle of Tournai in 1512, in which Sir William Compton fought alongside Henry VIII. There is handsome linenfold panelling and, above, half-timbered walls featuring a minstrel's gallery.

There is an impressive variety of ceilings in the dining room, drawing room and Council Chamber. The Council Chamber, in the south-west tower, is a particularly atmospheric room, reached by a substantial circular oak staircase. It has no fewer than six doors and the walls are covered with wainscot boards of split oak.

Two of the doors in the Council Chamber give access to newel staircases, one of which leads past a priest's hole to a room hidden away in the roof and known as 'the Priest's Room'. According to tradition, this was used as a Romish chapel in the days of anti-Catholic persecution. Sloping timbers, with plaster between them, form the walls, and beneath the south-west window is a large slab of elm thought to have been used as an altar. The Priest's Room

The ancient fishponds in the grounds.

itself has three more doors, with newel staircases leading away from them, through which one might easily make a daring escape, if the need arose.

Sir William Compton, who was eventually granted a licence to wear his hat in the King's presence, died in 1528 before the family could benefit still further from Henry VIII's largesse in the form of the Dissolution of the Monasteries. Gradually they stepped up the ladder of the peerage. In 1572 Sir William's grandson, Sir Henry Compton, described by the antiquary Sir William Camden as 'a person of fine wit and solid judgement', was created a Baron by Writ.

This 1st Lord Compton was given permission by Queen Elizabeth I in 1574 to demolish the derelict 13th-century castle at Castle Ashby on the family estate near Northampton and to build a new house on the site. As loyal to Good Queen Bess as his grandfather had been to Bluff King Hal, Lord Compton (who was one of the peers to try Mary Queen of Scots) constructed a new seat in the shape of the letter *E*.

ABOVE The Council Chamber, with its plaster ceiling, six doors and walls covered with wainscot boards of split oak.

RIGHT Three of the doors in the Council Chamber. The one in the centre leads up, past a priest's hole, to 'the Priest's Room'.

ABOVE The Priest's Room: the slab of elm beneath the window is thought to have been used as an altar.

As the Comptons went up in the world, so Compton Wynyates drifted into the wings of their glittering stage. Nonetheless, the 1st Earl of Northampton (as Lord Compton's son William became in 1618) appears to have inserted some pleasing Jacobean panelling at Compton Wynyates during his tenure.

For the most part though, he and his fabulously rich wife, Elizabeth (only child of Sir John Spencer, Lord Mayor of London and owner of the Canonbury and Islington estates north of the City), preferred to live at Castle Ashby. 'The Rich Spencer' (as Lord Northampton's father-in-law was known) had been violently opposed to the match but Elizabeth herself, despite savage paternal beatings, kept a cool head. At the time of their marriage, having set out her expensive requirements in the way of allowances and attendant gentlemen and gentlewomen ('it is an indecent thing for a gentlewoman to stand mumping alone, when God hath blessed their Lord and Lady with a great estate'), she advised William 'to pay your debts, build Ashby House, and purchase lands; and lend no money, as you love God, to the Lord Chamberlain' (the spendthrift Earl of Suffolk).

Although Lord Northampton had failed to impress King James I with his 'mean' entertainment at Castle Ashby, he seems to have become rather carried away by his new fortune. As Sir Bernard Burke enthusiastically recorded, after being made a Knight of the Garter, 'the Earl rode to his installation from Salisbury House, in the Strand, to Windsor Castle, with such splendour and gallantry, and exhibited so brilliant a cortège, being attended by nearly a hundred persons, that a vote of thanks was decreed to him by the Chapter of the Most Noble Order'.

During the Civil War the Comptons were gallant Cavaliers and their old home of Compton Wynyates suffered accordingly at the hands of the Parliamentarians. Among the indignities was the demolition by the rebels of the church there, where generations of Comptons had been buried. The 3rd Earl of Northampton (who had been fighting alongside his father, the 2nd Earl, when the latter was killed at the Battle of Hopton Heath in 1643) rebuilt the church before being buried there himself at Christmas, 1681.

The vivid colours of the west front take on an extra magic at dusk.

In the 18th century various 'improvements' were made at Compton Wynyates, including the installation of early Georgian fireplaces in the Big Hall and dining room, and some distinctly incongruous sash windows in the east wing. Yet its timeless character remained little changed, as that inveterate sightseer John Loveday of Caversham noted in the spring of 1737:

> Not far out of the way to Oxford, is Compton Wynyate, the
> Earl of Northampton's ancient brick Seat, (from which place
> he also borrowed his Name;) 'tis situate in a bottom almost
> surrounded with Hills; it is a most retired Place, Fishponds
> about it and a Rookery; the Garden rises from the house; the
> Church just by is small but very neat... Here are some very
> mutilated recumbent Effigies in Alabaster; also a Mural
> Monument of later date for one of this family; for in this
> Vault this family bury.

Some 30 years later Compton Wynyates itself was nearly buried. By this time the Compton fortunes had declined alarmingly, thanks to the gambling and ruinous political expenses of the 8th Earl of Northampton, who was obliged to decamp to Switzerland. From there he issued orders for the demolition of Compton Wynyates as he could no longer afford to keep it up.

Fortunately his faithful steward, John Birrell, who loved the old house as if it were his own, chose to ignore these desperate instructions. Instead he blocked up most of the windows to avoid the window tax, disposed of the contents by sale, and kept the place painted up for posterity as best he could.

And so Compton Wynyates became enveloped in somnolence. As often happens, such comparative neglect proved a blessing in disguise, for the house thereby avoided further unnecessary changes to its Tudor character. There it lay in its hollow in the heart of England, until the Victorian antiquarians, suckers for ancient romance, rediscovered its charms and fell upon Compton Wynyates with a passion. In 1867 the scholarly 3rd Marquess of Northampton brought in Sir Matthew Digby Wyatt, one of the prolific architectural dynasty who had also worked at Castle Ashby, to restore Compton Wynyates to its true self.

The silly sash windows of the east wing were removed; the south facade given a more Tudorish feel; the main staircase installed behind a Gothic bay. Into the dining room Wyatt inserted the sumptuous Elizabethan panelling from the old Spencer seat of Canonbury. The wooden chimneypiece in the drawing room also came from there.

Doubtless Wyatt was also responsible for some of the 'Tudor' ceilings at Compton Wynyates, though the fine one in 'Henry VIII's Bedroom' is definitely original. The contents, too, are a sympathetic blend of oak furniture, tapestries and family portraits. The splendid topiary garden dates from the 1890s.

A narrow-minded pedant might complain that, owing to its 19th-century restoration, Compton Wynyates is all too good to be true. Yet such purism is really quite irrelevant when confronted by this irresistibly picturesque farrago.

And the best news is that it is now very much a family home again. Although the present Marquess runs Castle Ashby as a successful showplace and conference centre, he and his family actually live at Compton Wynyates, which he has recently closed to the public. The accompanying photographs show how wise he was to retreat to this 'retired Place' in the hollow from which his family took their name nearly 800 years ago.

8

GRIMSTHORPE CASTLE

LINCOLNSHIRE

ALTHOUGH unquestionably one of the great houses of England and Wales, Grimsthorpe Castle in Lincolnshire is surprisingly little known. This may partly be because it has only recently been opened regularly to the public, but is more likely to be on account of its situation in England's second largest, yet least appreciated county – as the eminent local historian, the Reverend Henry Thorold, has put it, with withering sarcasm, 'dull, flat, boring Lincolnshire, so no-one comes, thank God'.

They do not know what they are missing. For Grimsthorpe is the last great country house to have benefited from the genius of Sir John Vanbrugh, architect of Castle Howard and Blenheim (see pages 292-303 and 304-15). Having been originally commissioned by the 1st Duke of Ancaster and Kesteven (described by Bishop Burnet as 'a fine gentleman, hath both wit and learning', though Dean Swift 'never observed a grain of either') in 1715, 'Van' finally began work on the north front nine years later for the 2nd Duke. The plan was for Vanbrugh to rebuild the whole of the old castle, but in the event only this front was completed.

It is more than enough to make Grimsthorpe very special indeed: a serene and gracious facade, with corner towers and Doric columns, which gloriously expresses the joys of architecture. Behind the facade is Vanbrugh's masterpiece, the supremely noble, arcaded, two-storey Great Hall – 'the Vanbrugh Hall', as it is called by the present chatelaine, Lady Willoughby de Eresby, a Maid of Honour at the Queen's Coronation and 27th holder of the title.

This ancient Barony by Writ dates back to 1313, but it was not until two centuries later that the family acquired the Grimsthorpe estate. In 1516 the 10th Lord Willoughby de Eresby married Maria de Salinas, who was also Maid of Honour to a queen – in this instance, her cousin Catherine of Aragon, first wife of King Henry VIII, who granted 'the reversion of the

Manors of Grimsthorpe, Southorpe and Edenham, Lincolnshire, and also of Grimsthorpe Park' to the bridegroom.

The history of the old castle goes back to the early 13th century when Grimsthorpe was owned by the de Gant family, Earls of Lincoln. King John's Tower, at the south-east corner of the present house, was probably built by Gilbert de Gant in the reign of that ill-fated monarch; its seven-foot-thick walls and two stone-vaulted rooms with their groined roofs proclaim the tower's medieval origins.

Later in the 16th century the Willoughbys' daughter, Katherine (named after Henry's barren Queen), married the ambitious Charles Brandon, Duke of Suffolk, widower of the Dowager Queen of France (who had herself been a sister of Henry VIII) and some 35 years older than his new bride. With an eye to the main chance Brandon decided to provide his brother-in-law, the King, with a convenient stopping-place on his way north, and proceeded to pull down the nearby Vaudey Abbey, which he had been granted at the Dissolution of the Monasteries, and to use the materials to rebuild Grimsthorpe.

Brandon converted the medieval castle into a commodious quadrangular house round an open courtyard, with a second courtyard to the north. Henry VIII and his new queen, Catherine Howard, duly came to stay in 1541 but the occasion could hardly be deemed a success as it later transpired that Catherine was unfaithful to the King during their stay, with fatal consequences for Queen no. 5.

After Brandon's death in 1545, Katherine married Richard Bertie. As staunch Protestants they were obliged to flee to the continent during 'Bloody Mary's' reign, and Grimsthorpe subsequently suffered from further neglect during the tenure of their son, Peregrine (so named on account of his parents' wanderings), a busy military campaigner immortalized in the traditional 16th-century *Ballad of the Brave Lord Willoughby*.

It was through Peregrine's marriage to Lady Mary Vere, daughter of the 16th Earl of Oxford that the family became entitled to a share in the office of Lord Great Chamberlain. This hereditary office – not to be confused with the Royal Household post of Lord Chamberlain – involves responsibility for the Palace of Westminster and helps explain the presence at Grimsthorpe of various items, such as the chairs of state in the dining room and regal canopies over some of the beds.

Peregrine's son Robert, who was created Earl of Lindsey, entertained King James I and his Queen, Anne of Denmark, at Grimsthorpe in 1611, so the castle must have been in reasonable shape again by this date. The next significant architectural improvement, however, came much later in the 17th century, during the time of the 3rd Earl of Lindsey who married, as his first wife, Mary Massingberd, a co-heiress of John Massingberd, treasurer of the East India Company (and, incidentally, a kinsman of the present writer). This Lord Lindsey commissioned a new north front in a mature classical style; the architect is unrecorded but some architectural historians think it might have been Captain William Winde (for whom see the chapter on Powis Castle, pages 42-55). Winde is also thought to have had a hand in Belton, one of Lincolnshire's other great houses.

This elegant facade, recorded in an engraving by Johannes Kip, was to have a short life, being replaced only a generation or so later by Vanbrugh's north front. John Harris, the architectural historian, has described this as 'out of Seaton Delaval in Northumberland by Lumley Castle in County Durham' (both previous Vanbrugh designs).

ABOVE Vanbrugh's north front at Grimsthorpe: 'out of Seaton Delaval in Northumberland by Lumley Castle in County Durham'.

RIGHT The Willoughby family coat of arms above the gates on the north front, which were probably designed by Edward Knutt.

PRECEDING PAGES The old south front of Grimsthorpe Castle, which Vanbrugh never got around to rebuilding.

Vanbrugh's Great Hall within contains seven paintings in grisaille by Sir James Thornhill (who also worked with 'Van' at Blenheim) depicting the seven English kings – as one sees them, from left to right, William I, Edward III, Henry V, George I, William III, Henry VIII, Henry VII – from whom the family received titles or land through the ages. The spectacular overmantel is an enlarged version of the chimneypiece in the Duchess of Marlborough's bedchamber at Blenheim.

Vanbrugh died in 1726, well before his main designs for Grimsthorpe were fully executed, and it is not clear what part his right-hand man Nicholas Hawksmoor played in the proceedings. The authorship of the chapel – one of the most ravishing interiors in England, with a ceiling in the manner of Inigo Jones – is something of a mystery, though designs are recorded in the sale of Hawksmoor's effects after his death in 1736.

Among the other great names of 18th-century craftsmanship associated with Grimsthorpe are Sir Henry Cheere (the rococo chimneypiece in the dining room); Thomas Warren (possibly responsible for the iron balustrading on the stairs); Francesco Sleter (to whom are attributed the painted ceilings); and the stuccoist William Perritt, whose work can, in all probability, be seen in King James's Drawing Room and the exotic Chinese Drawing Room.

Early in the 19th century Grimsthorpe passed to the 2nd Lord Gwydir, who, in 1828, succeeded his mother to become the 21st Lord Willoughby de Eresby. An ingeniously practical character, Lord Gwydir set up a railway on the estate and introduced a novel form of steam ploughing-tackle. Indoors, he turned his hand to embroidery. In the best Nancy Mitford tradition, this masculine talent for needlework was inherited by his descendant, the 3rd (and last) Earl of Ancaster, father of the present chatelaine.

ABOVE 'The Vanbrugh Hall', a majestic, arcaded two-storey Great Hall, with its grisaille paintings of seven English kings by Sir James Thornhill.

RIGHT A lobby of the Great Hall. The iron balustrade of the staircase in the foreground was the work of Bell of Sheffield.

RIGHT The chapel, magnificently restored and redecorated by the late Countess of Ancaster and John Fowler. The original design is attributed to Hawksmoor, though the ceiling and pulpit show the influence of Inigo Jones.

BELOW A corner of the State Drawing Room, showing portraits of the 18th-century 3rd Duke of Ancaster and his second wife, the former Mary Panton. Their daughter, Priscilla, inherited the barony of Willoughby de Eresby.

Edwardian architect Detmar Blow to install plenty of panelling; and then her daughter-in-law, 'Wissy' Astor, wife of the 3rd Earl, who was determined to bring a lighter, lived-in touch to Grimsthorpe.

After the Second World War the 3rd Earl and his wife commissioned the architect R.J. Page and the venerable stonemason A.S. Ireson of Stamford (founder of the internationally respected 'Men of Stone') to carry out a thorough overhaul and modernization of Grimsthorpe. Mr Page proved a good deal more industrious than his 19th-century predecessor and namesake; among his many sympathetic touches was the Vanbrughian facade to the stables.

In redecorating the interior of the house the late Lady Ancaster longed for off-white simplicity – the so-called 'English Look', an ironical name for a style that actually had its roots in her mother Nancy Astor's native Virginia, and was later evangelized by Lady Ancaster's cousin, the redoubtable Nancy Lancaster. Mrs Lancaster, proprietor of the fashionable interior decorators Colefax & Fowler, introduced her cousin to the brilliant designer John Fowler.

So began the perfectly matched double act of 'Wissy' and 'Folly' (the nickname Lady Ancaster coined for him) that transformed the stately but unfocused Grimsthorpe into one of the most stylish, cheerful and understated great houses of the late 20th century. Fowler and Lady Ancaster sparked each other off; as so often in creative matters, an element of tension produced the right result.

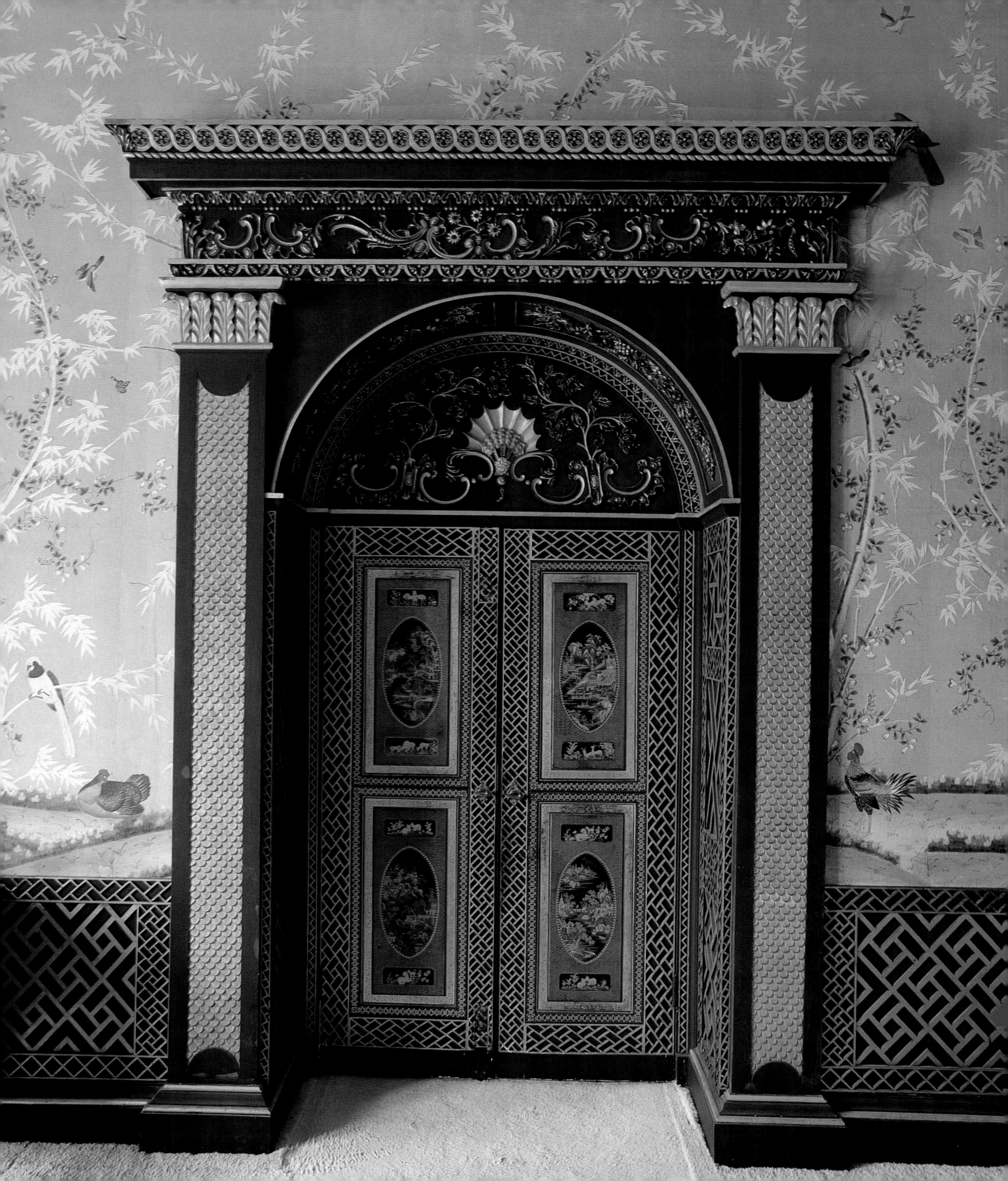

For example, in the Chinese Drawing Room, Fowler wanted to repaint the ceiling in its authentically garish bright Georgian blue. Lady Ancaster preferred something more faded. 'It takes 200 years for the right colours to fade', Fowler said. 'I don't have 200 years', Lady Ancaster replied.

On many other points – such as 'never put too much good furniture in a room', the swagged pelmets, the fringes and the ubiquitous flowers – the pair were happily at one. The 'Bess of Hardwick' rush matting from Suffolk introduced by Lady Ancaster into the state rooms started a tidal wave that engulfs not just National Trust properties but many other country houses to this day.

Fowler and Lady Ancaster must have had particular fun in restoring the enchanting Birdcage Room in King John's Tower, where the early Chinese wallpaper of the 18th century was painstakingly repaired. The partnership extended to creating the new kitchen garden and continued to Lady Ancaster's death in 1974. A memorial underneath the gallery in the chapel – the *pièce de résistance* of the new work, with its subtle shades of stone wash on the woodwork – stresses that 'The restoration of this Chapel and much of this house was accomplished by her enthusiasm and generosity.'

In 1978 her widower, the 3rd Earl of Ancaster, set up the Grimsthorpe and Drummond Castle Trust to secure the future of the Heathcote-Drummond-Willoughby heritage for the nation. The earldom expired with his own death five years later – his heir, Timothy, had disappeared at sea in the Mediterranean in 1963 – but the ancient Barony of Willoughby de Eresby was inherited by his daughter, Jane.

She and the trustees open Grimsthorpe to the public on a fairly regular basis in the summer months. It is worth going a long way, even to the depths of Lincolnshire, to see.

LEFT The doorway, with its lavish gold fish scales, in the exotic Chinese Drawing Room.

BELOW The Tudorish west front from across the lake.

9

WILTON HOUSE

WILTSHIRE

ANY would claim that Wilton House near Salisbury, seat of the Earls of Pembroke and Montgomery, is the most beautiful great house in England and Wales. Bearing in mind its ravishing south front with corner pavilions and a noble Venetian window, its gloriously opulent interiors such as the celebrated Double Cube Room and its exquisite Palladian bridge set in an Arcadian landscape, few could disagree.

Wilton's greatest claim to fame is its long association with the peerless English architect and pioneer of classicism, Inigo Jones. Born in 1573, the son of a London clothworker, Jones was a protégé of the 3rd Earl of Pembroke, at whose expense the budding designer travelled on the continent as a young man. The 3rd Earl – one of 'the incomparable pair of brethren', together with his brother, the 4th Earl, to whom William Shakespeare dedicated the First Folio of his plays – was a notable patron of the arts and at one stage was supposed to be the 'Mr W.H.' (William Herbert) to whom Shakespeare's Sonnets were addressed. Similarly, his mistress Mary Fitton was once thought to be the 'Dark Lady' of the Sonnets. The 3rd Earl was also Chancellor of Oxford University and Pembroke College, Oxford, is named after him.

Even before Jones's time, Wilton enjoyed a reputation as the nursery of the English Renaissance. The old abbey of Wilton had been granted by King Henry VIII, after the Dissolution of the Monasteries, to Sir William Herbert, 1st Earl of Pembroke, in 1542. The Pembrokes were a bastard scion of the illustrious Norman-Welsh family of Herbert, which is also represented at several other great houses – in the female line by the Dukes of Beaufort at Badminton (see pages 218-31) and the Earls of Powis at Powis, and in a cadet branch by the Earls of Carnarvon at Highclere (see pages 384-95).

The 1st Earl, a shrewd operator who managed to enjoy favour under four Tudor sovereigns (his first wife, Anne Parr, was a sister of Henry VIII's sixth and last queen), transformed the monastic buildings into a Tudor seat, built

round a courtyard. According to tradition, Lord Pembroke consulted Hans Holbein, the court painter, about the design of his new house; he would have had to be quick about it as Holbein died in 1543. In any event, the original entrance porch (now ornamenting the garden) is still called 'the Holbein Porch'.

In the Elizabethan heyday of the 2nd Earl of Pembroke and his Countess, Mary, sister of Sir Philip Sidney of Penshurst (see pages 56-69), Wilton, in the words of the local antiquary John Aubrey became 'an academie as well as a palace'. Mary, who Aubrey described as 'the greatest patronesse of wit and learning of any lady of her time', was celebrated in verse by Edmund Spenser and the dedicatee of her brother Philip's romance *Arcadia*, which was written at Wilton. Another Wilton tradition is that Shakespeare's *As You Like It* was first performed under her roof.

ABOVE A view of the east front (originally the entrance), looking across to the Palladian bridge, which is on the left of the picture.

PRECEDING PAGES Inigo Jones's Double Cube Room at Wilton House: one of the most deservedly celebrated interiors in England. It takes its name from the fact that it is double the length (60 feet long; but 30 feet wide and high) of the adjoining room which is a perfect 'cube'. Now, as in earlier days, it is used as a dining room, though in the 19th and 20th centuries it has been both a drawing room and ballroom. The portraits of the Herberts are by Van Dyck, the gilt furniture by William Kent.

It was the second of the Bard's 'incomparable pair of brethren', the 4th Earl of Pembroke, who carried out the Renaissance remodelling of Wilton in the 1630s. According to Aubrey again, it was King Charles I (who visited Wilton every summer) that 'did put Philipp Earl of Pembroke upon making this magnificent garden and grotto, and to new build that side of the house that fronts the garden, with two stately pavilions at each end, all *al Italiano*'. Work was in progress on a vast new formal garden (1,000 feet long and 400 feet wide) by 1632 and on the south front by 1636. The executant responsible for both was Isaac de Caus, but, as Aubrey mentions, he had 'the advice and approbation' of Inigo Jones.

By this time the 3rd Earl of Pembroke's old protégé had risen to be the King's Surveyor-General of Works and had recently completed the Queen's House at Greenwich, the most elegant and sophisticated building of its time. Jones was an advocate of external restraint and interior flamboyance: 'Outwardly', he wrote, 'every wise man carries a gravity, yet inwardly has his imagination set on fire and sometimes licentiously flies out.'

Nowhere is this sound principle better expressed than at Wilton. The outside of the south front is soothingly serene in its nobility; the inside a feast of magnificence that gives us some inkling of what Whitehall Palace might have looked like if King Charles I and Inigo Jones had ever achieved their ambition of building a great Carolean royal palace. The series of state rooms rivals the best decoration of the mid-17th century in France – a part classical, part baroque extravaganza of white and gold.

Jones liked simple geometrical measurements in his designs. For example, the principal room at the Queen's House at Greenwich is a single cube (40 by 40 by 40 feet) and the Banqueting House at Whitehall (the only part of the palace constructed) a double cube – 110 by 55 by 55 feet. Wilton boasts both a Single Cube Room (30 by 30 by 30) and a Double Cube Room (60 by 30 by 30), two of the most celebrated interiors in England and Wales.

The Double Cube Room is adorned with carved swags of fruit, flowers and classical masks, and its panelling was designed to show off a series of portraits of the Herberts by Sir Anthony Van Dyck. The splendid gilt furniture by

RIGHT The Palladian bridge across the River Nadder, which runs through the park at Wilton. The bridge was built by Roger Morris and the 9th 'Architect Earl' of Pembroke in 1737.

William Kent, added a century later, is perfectly in keeping. In the Single Cube Room, which has a coved ceiling of arabesques, there are dado paintings of scenes from Sir Philip Sidney's *Arcadia*.

While no-one doubts Jones's vital influence on the south front and state rooms at Wilton, his precise role remains unclear. Matters are complicated by the fact that the south front suffered a bad fire in 1647–8. The necessary rebuilding work and reconstruction of the interior was undertaken by John Webb, a pupil and nephew-by-marriage of Inigo Jones. By this stage Jones was an old man, but the faithful Aubrey insists that he still had a hand in the proceedings and one is inclined to believe him. By way of documentary evidence, drawings for the interior survive, dated 1649, and some of them are indeed annotated by Jones and Webb.

Jones's long connection with the Herberts and Wilton finally came to an end with his death in 1652, a couple of years after the 4th Earl's demise. Of the subsequent Lords Pembroke, the 7th Earl stands out as a black sheep amid the worthy family chronicle of patronage and public service. By all accounts, he seems to have been a homicidal maniac; as Aubrey noted, he was 'chiefly known for deeds of drunkenness and manslaughter'. In his short life (he died at 30) he was guilty of foul play in a duel, languished in the Tower of London for blasphemy 'and other misdemeanours', and was convicted first of manslaughter and then of murder (numerous other offences not being taken into account), only to receive an ill-deserved royal pardon from King Charles II.

LEFT Fishy door furniture.

ABOVE A statue of Shakespeare by Scheemakers (1743) dominates the Front Hall. The Bard dedicated the First Folio of his plays to the 4th Earl of Pembroke; tradition has it that *As You Like It* was first performed at Wilton.

The 8th and 9th Earls of Pembroke restored the Herberts' reputation. The 8th Earl was a connoisseur on the grand scale, collecting antique sculpture, books, drawings and paintings – most notably the 'Wilton Diptych' now in the National Gallery. The Old Master pictures that remain at Wilton – Andrea del Sarto, Lucas van Leyden, Rembrandt, Rubens *et al* – were mainly acquired by this Lord Pembroke, who was president of the Royal Society and founded the Wilton Royal Carpet Factory in the village.

LEFT The Gothic vaulted cloister-corridor, inserted by James Wyatt for the 11th Earl of Pembroke. It serves as a fine gallery for the sculpture collection.

RIGHT, ABOVE AND BELOW During house parties at Wilton, single ladies and gentlemen were strictly segregated along appropriately named corridors – 'Bachelors' Row' and 'Maiden Lane'.

The 9th Earl of Pembroke, known as the 'Architect Earl', was to the fore in the Palladian movement with the Earl of Burlington and William Kent. It was this Lord Pembroke who built the beautiful bridge across the River Nadder in the park, and in the process swept away de Caus's formal garden of a century before. The Architect Earl, with the assistance of the professional designer Roger Morris, designed the bridge in 1737 on the pattern of a drawing by Andrea Palladio. It sets off Inigo Jones's south front to wonderful effect.

The 10th Earl of Pembroke, a military man, was primarily interested in horses and wrote a masterly work on the *Method of Breaking Horses*. As well as building a riding school at Wilton, he brought in the architect Sir William Chambers to build an arch surmounted by an equestrian statue of Marcus Aurelius.

Initially, this arch was erected on top of the hill south of Wilton as an eyecatcher, but in the time of the 11th Earl of Pembroke, the architect James Wyatt brought it down so as to close the new forecourt of the house, and the Holbein Porch was banished to the garden. Chambers's triumphal arch certainly provides a handsome introduction to the splendours of Wilton.

Wyatt played a significant part in Wilton's architectural history. He rebuilt both the west range and the north front, which became the main entrance. He created the present forecourt by giving it embattled walls and raising the

ABOVE Classical undress: detail of one of the carved figures flanking the doorway of Lord Pembroke's private drawing room.

LEFT The Earl of Pembroke's private drawing room.

The 15th Earl's elder son and successor, Sidney, the 16th Earl, repainted the Upper Cloisters in terracotta and grey, changing them from Wyatt's dreary grey stucco of 1814, and also replaced Wyatt's painted wood and slate clock turret, or cupola. The new cupola, installed in 1962, was inspired by the one shown in a drawing of the Tudor Wilton, dated 1566.

Sidney Pembroke had a hand in the design of this cupola and was a scholarly connoisseur in the tradition of his family. He devoted himself to cataloguing and publishing *The Pembroke Papers* and produced a detailed catalogue of the remarkable collection of paintings and drawings at Wilton – which besides the Old Masters and Van Dycks includes works by Sir Peter Lely, Sir Joshua Reynolds and the topographical genius Richard Wilson.

Sidney's younger brother, David Herbert, author of an amusing memoir *Second Son*, also had aesthetic tastes and in the brothers' younger days, before the Second World War, Wilton once more became a fashionable haunt of artists and writers. One of them, Cecil Beaton, left a vivid account of Sidney's coming-of-age in 1927: 'In the gloaming the Inigo Jones facade looked its most noble with the long range of tall lighted windows... It was a grand occasion... How beautiful the night scene was! How calm and visionary.'

RIGHT Sir William Chambers's triumphal arch, designed in 1755 for the expert horse-breaker, the 10th Earl of Pembroke. Surmounting the structure is the equestrian statue of Marcus Aurelius.

BELOW 'Blow, Gabriel, blow...'. A rare roof-top view of an idyllic landscape, set off by the Palladian bridge.

10

BURGHLEY HOUSE

THE PRE-EMINENCE of Burghley House in Northamptonshire (now arbitrarily dumped in Cambridgeshire by the odious boundary changes of the 1970s) as the greatest treasure house in England and Wales was illustrated by the fact that the landmark 'Treasure Houses of Britain' exhibition, held in Washington in 1985, featured no less than 38 items – far more than from any other family seat – from the Elizabethan stronghold of the Cecils.

Indeed there is so much to see at Burghley, a fairy-tale structure of towers and turrets set in one of 'Capability' Brown's finest parks, that the visitor can feel somewhat overwhelmed. There is almost too much for the visitor to take in – the furniture and fabrics; the carvings in the manner of Grinling Gibbons; the staggering series of painted rooms by Antonio Verrio; and Old Master paintings by artists such as Ludovico Carracci, Guido Reni, Orazio Gentileschi, Carlo Dolci, Luca Giordano and many more. The family portraits are by Van Dyck, Lely, Kneller, Gainsborough and Lawrence. The collection of state beds is of unrivalled grandeur and there is a Queen Anne wine cooler reputed to be the largest in the world.

Where does one begin? Fortunately the present chatelaine, Lady Victoria Leatham, youngest daughter of the 6th Marquess of Exeter, is the very model of a modern historic house curator and has rationalized the presentation of Burghley in a most impressive manner. To help focus attention on detailed aspects of the house's extraordinarily rich collections, 'Vicky' Leatham has arranged a series of exhibitions in the courtyard gallery highlighting such subjects as silver, jewels, miniatures, scientific instruments, clocks, books and oriental porcelain.

Engagingly humorous and down-to-earth, Vicky Leatham is celebrated for her breezy performances on such television programmes as *The Antiques Road Show* and *Heirs and Graces*. Beneath the delightfully unstuffy manner, though, is considerable expertise: Lady Victoria is a director of Sotheby's and has a special passion for what she calls 'old pots'.

ABOVE Verrio's ceiling for the tiny Jewel Closet, which leads off the First George Room.

LEFT The Hell Staircase, where the Italian Antonio Verrio portrayed, in the early 18th century, the mouth of Hades as the gaping mouth of a cat. The walls were painted a century later by Thomas Stothard. The cantilever staircase is 1786 and of local Ketton stone. Against the wall at the bottom of the well of the staircase is an elaborate musical box by Samuel Troll *et fils* of Switzerland, *circa* 1870.

PRECEDING PAGES A fairy-tale vision reflected in the lake: Burghley House, treasure house of the Cecils.

Her father set up a charitable preservation trust to own and manage Burghley before his death in 1981, and the trust appointed Lady Victoria as its curator. She has brought enormous enthusiasm and energy to the task of revitalizing a place that had rather gone to sleep, and to doing justice to the scope of its treasures.

Lady Victoria has also been a pioneer in procuring commercial sponsorship for restoration work, such as from Remy Martin, who also sponsor the well-known three-day equestrian event in the park. A subtle difference has been wrought by the introduction of halogen lighting, which brings out the artistry of the objects on view in sharp relief – for example in the minutely observed study of a dead bird in the Marquetry Room, carved by Jean Demontreuil in the mid-18th century from one solid piece of pearwood.

Among the many other improvements in the showing of Burghley, the formerly cluttered Great Hall has been dramatically cleared to provide a fitting climax to the house tour.

The Great Hall, together with the kitchen, is one of the few surviving interiors of the original Elizabethan house. The Gothic hall, more than 60 feet in height, has a steep double hammer-beam roof and a soaring, classical chimneypiece; the kitchen has a lofty stone vault rising to a lantern (only recently rediscovered and restored), which would have served to extract smoke.

The old kitchen in particular evokes the world of the Tudors in which the Cecil family, perhaps the best known of the so-called 'New Men' – being descended from modest gentry called Sysilt (hence the correct pronunciation of the surname as Sissel) in the Welsh Marches – flourished so spectacularly. William Cecil, the builder of Burghley, rose to become the most powerful man in England as Queen Elizabeth I's chief minister. At his death in 1598 he was described by Lord Essex in a letter to the Queen as 'The greatest, gravest and most esteemed Councillor that ever Your Majesty had.'

Cecil began building Burghley of the durable local Barnack rag stone in about 1555, when there is evidence that the east and south ranges were going up. Cecil appears to have been his own architect, with a little help from an

LEFT A pyramid of pots around the fireplace in the Blue Silk Dressing Room.

RIGHT Verrio's masterpiece, the Heaven Room, painted with remarkably lifelike scenes from ancient mythology. The artist himself is depicted sitting at the forge of Cyclops (right), without his wig. The carpet is an English copy of a Savonnerie.

ABOVE Burghley as portrayed on Chinese porcelain.

LEFT The newly restored state bed in the Second George Room. Originally supplied by the London firm of Fell & Newton in 1795 for £3,000 (a vast sum of money in those days), it was reduced in size and decorated with the royal arms for Queen Victoria's visit to the house in 1844.

RIGHT Rabbits' skulls, old copper and His Lordship's injunction in the old Tudor kitchen.

Antwerp mason called Henryk. His correspondence shows that he could supply a 'tryke' (drawing) of some detail when required.

The west front, with its gatehouse, was finished in 1577; the north ten years later. The style was an intriguing combination of sophisticated Elizabethan splendour and a homely, old-fashioned quality which harks back to Cecil's Henrician youth. Indeed, Cecil kept up the old custom of dining in the Great Hall with his entire household.

William Cecil's devoted service to the Queen brought him great riches but no higher rank than baron as Lord Burghley. His younger son, the ambitious hunchback Robert Cecil, who succeeded his father as the Queen's minister and later served King James I, acquired the Hatfield estate in Hertfordshire at the other end of the Great North Road, and was raised to the peerage as Earl of Salisbury on the same day as his elder brother, William, was created Earl of Exeter.

As the *Dictionary of National Biography* notes with some asperity, this William was 'a person of very ordinary abilities, and that if he had been born of *other* parentage, we should have heard nothing of him'. Much the same could be said of many of his successors, though the 5th and 9th Earls of Exeter were to make significant contributions to the appearance of Burghley.

The inner courtyard and clock tower at Burghley.

The Complete Peerage notes sniffily that the bloom is rubbed from the romance when it is realized that 'the Lord of Burleigh', having made a false declaration that he was a bachelor, led 'the maiden' to 'the village altar' with a view to bigamy. When they finally did marry, the wretched Sarah Hoggins was heavily pregnant.

In 1801 the new Marquess celebrated his elevation in the peerage by building the dramatic Bottle Lodges, the main entrance gates to Burghley, to the designs of W.D. Legg of Stamford – the handsome Georgian stone-built town which abuts the park – and by commissioning Thomas Stothard to complete the Hell Staircase. Stothard successfully covered the walls with more dark doom and gloom: 'War', 'Intemperance' and 'Orpheus Descending to the Underworld'.

The 2nd Marquess of Exeter employed the architect J.P. Gandy to construct a two-storey corridor around the inner courtyard, and proceeded to entertain on a lavish scale. He spent a fortune on having Queen Victoria and the Prince Consort to stay at Burghley in 1844 and further encumbered his estates by heavy expenditure on the Turf.

The 3rd Marquess was of a more agricultural turn of mind and devoted himself to pisciculture and the breeding of shorthorn cattle. He did not make a good impression on the gossipy country house crawler Augustus Hare, who found him only interested in the memory of his prize bull Telemachus. As for Burghley itself, Hare wrote: 'There is a series of state rooms, dull and oppressive, and a multitude of pictures with very fine names, almost all misnamed.'

That is not altogether an unfair description of this great house, up to its present renaissance under Lady Victoria Leatham. Today it is bursting with life and full of absorbing objects to admire – from silver fireplaces, needle-work and copper utensils to the now carefully attributed art and antiques.

Particularly evocative are the memorabilia connected with Lady Victoria's father, the 6th Marquess of Exeter, who as Lord Burghley carried all before him on the athletics track in the 1920s and early 1930s. Visitors can see the Olympic Gold Medal he won for the 400-metre hurdles at Amsterdam in 1928, the Silver Medal from Los Angeles in 1932 and a nostalgic portrait, resplendent in Cambridge blue, by Sir Oswald Birley.

These mementoes conjure up the golden age of amateur sport and the Olympic movement, and put one in mind of the Oscar-winning film *Chariots of Fire*. The fictional character 'Lord Lindsay' (played by Nigel Havers) in the film obviously owed something to the then Lord Burghley – though understandably, the late Marquess was not best pleased at the way the scriptwriter, presumably in an attempt to make a 'class' point, had the dashing peer coming second. In real life, of course, he came first – and as a soldier, politician, businessman and colonial governor, as well as an athlete, surely ranks as the most prominent public figure among the owners of Burghley after its builder, the Great Cecil.

11

BURTON CONSTABLE

YORKSHIRE

A FAMILIAR complaint about the Humber Bridge – that magnificent folly of the Harold Wilson era – is that 'it does not lead anywhere'. Setting aside the doubtlessly worthy claims of Hull on the one side and Grimsby on the other, an historic house fancier could counter that, in fact, it leads to one of the great treasure houses of England and Wales, Burton Constable, family seat of the Chichester-Constables.

Certainly the house is in an isolated position, north of the Humber, out on a strangely deserted limb of the old East Riding of Yorkshire (or 'Humberside', as nobody in the area has ever bothered to call the obnoxious and anti-historical 'new county'). Its far-flung situation has had much to do with Burton Constable's troubled modern history.

For when John Chichester-Constable opened the house regularly to the public in the mid-1970s – as he was obliged to do, having received an exceptionally generous 75 per cent grant to renew the roofs from the then Historic Buildings Council (now subsumed by the Historic Buildings and Monuments Commission, or 'English Heritage', as it was called by its first chairman, Lord Montagu of Beaulieu) – the operation did not prove a commercial success. Indeed, by the end of the 1980s it was actually making a loss as a heritage attraction; several of the treasures specifically made for the house (such as two sarcophagus wine cisterns by Jeremiah Hargrave and two Italian marble and giltwood tables) had to be sold; and the future of Burton Constable was looking extremely bleak.

Fortunately, in the early 1990s, the National Heritage Memorial Fund, which had largely paid to buy back the tables and the wine cisterns, stepped in and began to negotiate a rescue operation. In 1992 John Chichester-Constable generously gave the contents of the house to Leeds City Council, which, in turn, placed them on permanent loan to the Burton Constable Foundation, a new charitable trust. To complete the rescue package, the

Foundation – endowed to the tune of £5.4 million by the National Heritage Memorial Fund – also acquired the house and immediately adjoining lands. The upshot of this unusual and innovative arrangement was that Mr Chichester-Constable and his family were enabled to stay on in a wing of the house (without, as he put it, having 'to wake up every morning with an appalling sense of worry as to the future') and Burton Constable was saved.

The significance of the Foundation's link with Leeds City Council lies in that local authority's association with Temple Newsam. This museum's furniture experts have hailed Burton Constable as not only containing a conspicuously fine repertoire of pieces by the great Thomas Chippendale, but also as a key house for the study of works made by such excellent regional firms as Wright & Elwick of Wakefield, Farrer & Reynoldson of York and Joseph Foster of Hull, as well as the Hargraves, Jeremiah and his son Joseph. From a scholarship point of view Burton Constable is uncommonly well

ABOVE Burton Constable: the Elizabethan entrance facade.

PRECEDING PAGES The Great Hall, remodelled by Thomas and Timothy Lightoler in 1713, with a Jacobean-style ceiling by James Henderson of York.

documented, and in its new guise as a museum outpost will indubitably become a mecca for students of craftsmanship and connoisseurship.

As for the layman, he should definitely not be put off by the remoteness of the house. The strange flatlands of the Holderness may not be to all tastes but for those who like the big skies of the eastern counties, they have an eerie beauty of their own. Few, at any rate, could fail to be excited by their first glimpse of Burton Constable, set within the landscape like a great ship at sea.

On slightly closer inspection, the red-brick pile appears typical of the country seats erected by the *nouveaux riches* of the Elizabethan period. In reality, nothing could be further from the truth.

For a start, the Constables, an old recusant dynasty, have been here since the 12th century. The bottom of Stephen's Tower – on the right of the entrance front as you look at it – is said to date from that period.

If one looks carefully at the facade one notices 18th-century remodelling: the main door was moved to the centre, an attic floor added and also two bay windows rising to onion domes. Such is the sympathy and taste shown by the chief remodeller, William Constable, however, that the original Elizabethan exterior seems somehow intact.

RIGHT The Great Hall's oak overmantel was carved by John and Samuel Fisher of York, with armorial achievement in scagliola by Domenico Bartoli.

LEFT The Long Gallery, as altered and lengthened in the 18th century. The bookcases (mahogany with elm veneer) house the remains of William Constable's library. The late 17th-century Dutch-style chairs were gilded in the 1850s.

RIGHT William Constable, the corpulent connoisseur of Burton Constable, as portrayed by Jean-Étienne Liotard.

Nonetheless, in the fashion of the mid-18th century, William Constable considered brick unworthy for the seat of the Lord Paramount of the Seignory of the Holderness, as the squires of Burton Constable are formally styled. Strange as it may seem to modern eyes, the whole building was faced with yellow stucco until 1896 when Walter Chichester-Constable, grandfather of the present squire, sensibly uncovered the vibrant brickwork once more.

Inside comes the big surprise. Nearly all the rooms are 18th-century rather than Elizabethan or Jacobean, though the original Great Hall has a touch of 'Jacobethan' revival about the ceiling, and the Long Gallery still has a 17th-century feel (even if it was altered and lengthened in the 18th), with its series of family portraits by Marcus Gheeraerts, Sir Peter Lely and others.

The 18th-century improvements to the Long Gallery are thought to have been put in motion by William Constable's father, Cuthbert Tunstall, a scholarly bibliophile who assumed the surname of Constable on succeeding his uncle, the 4th (and last) Viscount Dunbar, to the Burton Constable estate in 1718. This Scottish viscountcy had been created in 1620 for Henry Constable (only son of Sir Henry Constable of Burton Constable, High Sheriff of Yorkshire in 1586), who was to die of wounds received at the siege of Scarborough Castle in the Civil War.

Despite the penalties for recusancy, the Constables remained true to the old faith and somehow managed to hang on to their ancestral acres. Deprived of the opportunity to take any part in politics, William Constable, Cuthbert's even more scholarly son, devoted himself to his studies and to modernizing Burton Constable.

William Constable was a man of parts: connoisseur, patron of the arts, scientist, geologist and Fellow of the Royal Society. His portrait by Jean-Étienne Liotard shows him in a fur-trimmed cap and gown, an outfit favoured by his friend Jean-Jacques Rousseau.

Constable went on three Grand Tours to Italy, collecting expeditions which brought in layer after layer of fine objects. The art dealer James Byers steered many treasures in his direction and it was probably he who persuaded

Constable and his sister, Winifred, to have their portraits painted as citizens of Ancient Rome rather than Grand Tourists of the 18th century.

Constable was fascinated by the phenomena of nature – geology, botany and physics – and collected numerous specimens. His 'Cabinet of Curiosities', a bizarre rag-bag of fossils, shells and other phenomena, was discovered in the attics in the late 1960s and installed in the Museum Room in the house.

Another remarkable recent discovery in an attic at Burton Constable is a bell-crater made in Apulia, southern Italy, in the 4th century BC. William Constable may have acquired the vase directly from an archaeological excavation site, as he visited several on his Grand Tour of 1764–5. Decorated in red-figure technique, this antique vase features a maenad seated on a rock, holding a floral staff; behind her is a young satyr and Dionysus.

The vase and other antiquities are on display in the Long Gallery, along with some of William Constable's important collection of 18th-century scientific instruments, made for him by William Cole, instrument-maker to King George III. Constable conducted his experiments in the Long Gallery, which also houses his exercise chair, wheelchair and crutches; he became distinctly portly in his later years and was a martyr to gout.

The Museum Room also illustrates another of Constable's collecting passions: firearms. Sadly, the collection was sold in 1952, but the Foundation is gradually buying some of it back.

Constable's patronage of the arts is documented in an astonishingly well-stocked archive which reads like a directory of 18th-century art, architecture and crafts. In carrying out a major programme of exterior and interior alterations, redecoration and refurnishing, Constable dealt with everybody from the finest architects and craftsmen of the day to local tradesmen.

The architects from whom advice was sought included John Carr and Thomas Atkinson, both of York, Robert Adam, 'Capability' Brown and James Wyatt, although in the end most of the new neo-classical interiors were executed by Thomas and Timothy Lightoler. Timothy was responsible for the spectacular Staircase Hall, originally designed as a picture gallery. It makes an impressive setting for the three vast historical canvases by Andrea Casali, formerly at Fonthill Splendens, the demolished seat of the Beckfords in Wiltshire.

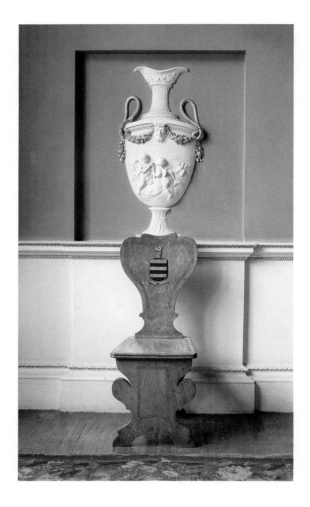

ABOVE A neo-classical bas-relief by William Collins of London in the dining room.

LEFT The dining room, designed by the Lightolers in 1767 to reflect William Constable's classical tastes and to celebrate Bacchus. The fireplace is by Thomas Atkinson, the ceiling by Giuseppe Cortese.

ABOVE The Great Drawing Room, or ballroom, by James Wyatt, 1775–6, with furniture and pier glasses by Chippendale. The room, originally in shades of blue and green, was redecorated in gold in 1840.

The Lightolers were also busy in the Great Hall (where John Cheere chipped in with statues of Hercules and Demosthenes), and the dining room, which is a shrine to Bacchus, god of wine and hospitality. The marble fireplace in the dining room – with a tablet showing the sacrifice to Aesculapius, the god of medicine, and Hygea, the goddess of health – is by Thomas Atkinson, who also had a hand in the chapel and the Blue Drawing Room (now being restored), with its airy bow window on to the garden.

Wyatt weighed in with the Great Drawing Room, or ballroom, an imposing exercise in the Adam manner executed in 1775–6. Two years later Thomas Chippendale was commissioned to equip this stately interior with a suite of furniture, pier glasses and also side tables to accommodate the marble slabs brought back from Italy by William Constable. Chippendale charged £1,000 – a sizeable sum in 1778.

The Constable family's connoisseurship did not cease with William's death in 1791. In the 19th century they acquired a notable collection of French furniture (much of it by Saunier of Paris), thanks to their close links with the exiled King Louis XVIII – who, so tradition claims, stayed in the King's Suite at Burton Constable in the early years of the century. If he really did so, there is a nice irony in the fact that the King's Drawing Room was formerly William Constable's drawing room before he became so fat and infirm that he had to move his quarters to the ground floor, as Louis XVIII himself was so stout that he could hardly move at all.

ABOVE A corner of the Chinese Room, redecorated in 1842 after a family visit to the Brighton Pavilion.

ABOVE RIGHT The east front and old stables as they were *circa* 1700 (later replaced and rebuilt by Thomas Lightoler).

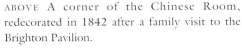

LEFT An atmospheric corner of an upstairs bedroom, awaiting re-arrangement.

William Constable's new downstairs bedroom (with hand-painted Chinese wallpaper by William Reid) was completely redecorated in 1842 as the Chinese Room by Sir Thomas Clifford Constable, 2nd Bt., and his wife, the former Marianne Chichester from Calverleigh Court, Devon. The Clifford Constables seem to have been carried away by visits to the Brighton Pavilion; the result is a marvellously exotic room with flying dragons guarding the window and a fantastic dragon chair designed by Marianne herself and executed by Thomas Wilkinson Wallis of Louth, Lincolnshire.

Thomas and Marianne's other decorative flights of fancy at Burton Constable include the boulle furniture in the Blue Drawing Room; the plush redecoration of Wyatt and Chippendale's ballroom; the cheval glass in the Gold Bedroom; and the gilding of the set of William and Mary walnut chairs in the Long Gallery.

Led by the trustees, who include Christopher Gilbert, director of Leeds City Art Galleries and a leading authority on furniture, the Burton Constable Foundation is constantly making stimulating re-assessments and extending knowledge about the history of the house. Since it took over the running of the place several new rooms have been opened for the first time – such as the former housekeeper's room off the Great Hall, which has been done up as a display room to show some of Burton Constable's large collection of 18th-century architectural drawings and estate plans.

Memorably atmospheric is the Lamp Room, with its artless clutter of lighting paraphernalia – candles, oil, paraffin, gas, electricity – evoking centuries of backstairs life in the country house. It is one of many hitherto hidden treats at Burton Constable, waiting to be discovered.

12

LONGLEAT

WILTSHIRE

*T*HE LATEST of the diverse attractions offered at Longleat in Wiltshire – which range from the Safari Park and the *Dr Who* exhibition to the new Marquess of Bath's *Kamasutra* murals in the west wing – is an exhibition on the life and times of Henry, Lord Bath, who died in 1992.

As the present Marquess, who commissioned the show as a memorial to his father, explains, it is also the story of Longleat, 'the house he loved, and saved'. Henry Bath was the 'founding father of the stately home industry': the first owner of a great house to open it to the public on a full-blown commercial basis after the Second World War. Faced with a bill of £750,000 in death duties, he threw open the doors of Longleat in 1949 and entered enthusiastically into the then novel role of titled showman. By 1957 he was able to welcome, with a characteristic flourish, the millionth visitor.

Lord Bath deployed every tripperish magnet conceivable: a funfair, pedal boats on the mile-long lake, a putting green and tearooms. To the disapproval of his fellow peers he even allowed 'Capability' Brown's dramatically plunging park to be used for staging pop concerts – a practice subsequently copied at other great houses.

It was in the 1960s when the Longleat tourist venture really took off. The circus impresario Jimmy Chipperfield suggested introducing game to roam the estate. Led by the celebrated lions, it grew into a safari park of international fame, with tigers, baboons, chimpanzees, giraffes, hippos and sea lions.

Yet the 6th Marquess of Bath deserves to be remembered for more than 'the Lions of Longleat'. He laid out a new formal garden in keeping with the house; planted extensively in the park; sat for a portrait by Graham Sutherland (wearing his familiar, tramp-inspired polka-dot tie); commissioned new furniture by John Makepeace and other works of art; added many hundreds of books to the libraries (even if he spent little time reading them); and was an inveterate collector of memorabilia: Churchilliana, Hitleriana (Bath found the Führer's watercolours of particular interest) and Thatcheriana (including 'Maggie' toilet-paper rolls and *Spitting Image* puppets and mugs).

Above all, though, he kept Longleat alive as a going concern – even if, as he pointed out, the net takings from the tripper attractions failed to cover the costs of daily maintenance and repair of the great house – the first of what Sir John Summerson has called 'the Elizabethan prodigy houses'.

Longleat was built in at least three stages by Sir John Thynne, an ambitious and archetypal Tudor 'New Man', who bought the old priory here in 1541 for a mere £55. Thynne was a nephew of William Thynne, Clerk-Comptroller of King Henry VIII's household, who probably insinuated him into the entourage of Edward Seymour, the future Duke of Somerset and Protector of the Realm.

PRECEDING PAGES Longleat: a Wiltshire wonderland.

BELOW Renaissance roofscape.

RIGHT Roman busts adorn the stonework.

As 'Protector' Somerset's steward and man of business, Sir John Thynne accumulated a large fortune and also developed a passion for building. He was intimately involved in the building work for his master's houses on the Thames, at Somerset House and Syon.

At his own property in Wiltshire, Thynne began by converting the modest remains of the priory into living quarters for himself and his wife, Christian Gresham [*sic*], sister of Sir Thomas Gresham, builder of the Royal Exchange in the City of London. In the 1550s and 1560s he gradually enlarged, extended and rebuilt his new mansion with stone dragged across the combes from his own quarry at Box near Chippenham, with the help of such masons as John Chapman and William Spicer (subsequently Queen Elizabeth I's Surveyor of Works), and the sculptor Allen Maynard, a naturalized Frenchman.

A perfectionist, Thynne was forever scrapping plans and starting again on his beloved project, the perfect house. His neighbour, William Darrell of Littlecote, devised a satirical complaint from Longleat itself to its owner:

> But now see him that by these thirtie years almost
> with such turmoyle of mynd hath byn thinking of me,
> framing and erecting me, mussing many a tyme with
> great care and now and then pulling downe this or
> that parte of me to enlardge sometyme a foote, or
> some few inches, uppon a conceyt, or this or that
> man's speech, and by and by beat down windows for this
> or that fault here or there.

The setback of a fire in 1567 only spurred Thynne on to renewed efforts. Soon after the fire, the significant name of Robert Smythson, one of the great geniuses of English architecture who was later to work at Hardwick, first turns up in the records of Longleat.

The accounts show that Smythson, who spent a dozen years at Longleat, carved much of the house's exterior detail, but it is difficult to apportion credit for the overall design of the building that began to take its final shape after 1572. Probably the spoils should be shared between Maynard, Smythson and Thynne himself.

RIGHT The Great Hall, with its Mannerist chimneypiece, beamed roof (lowered late in the 17th century to fit in Bishop Ken's Library above), and screen of *circa* 1600. On the right are two of the equestrian paintings by John Wootton that fill the upper walls. Commissioned by the 2nd Viscount Weymouth (seen in the picture above the fireplace, with hand on hip), they tell the story of an orphan taken on as a stable lad at Longleat, who was killed at the age of 14 trying to separate two fighting stallions.

LEFT Detail of the chimneypiece, showing a mermaid with two tails.

In any event, at the time of Thynne's death in 1580 Longleat had become a remarkable Renaissance palace, combining innovative classical outline and detail with the English Gothic tradition. Its vast mullioned windows, allowing the light to flood in, made Longleat the first great 'lantern house'. Here, in the words of Mark Girouard, Smythson's biographer, was 'a sudden efflorescence of splendour that ushered in the great age of Elizabethan architecture'.

In Girouard's view, Longleat was 'the first Elizabethan house to have more than the charm of naivety or freshness. It is a work of art, noble, delicate and intelligent.'

Four hundred years on, the exterior remains little altered. The baroque doorway and the statues on the balustrade (itself inspired by Somerset House, which had a decisive influence on the symmetry and classical flavour of Longleat) were added at the end of the 17th century during the time of the 1st Viscount Weymouth.

Lord Weymouth had inherited Longleat in 1682 from his dissolute cousin Thomas Thynne, known as 'Tom o' Ten Thousand', who lived at the house in extravagant style. Tom had married the heiress Lady Elizabeth Percy of Alnwick, to the fury of another fortune hunter, the Swedish Count Königsmark, who arranged for a hired thug to blast Thynne away with a blunderbuss in his coach in Pall Mall a few months later.

In the 1690s the 1st Viscount Weymouth commissioned George London to lay out extensive formal gardens at Longleat, with parterres stretching in front of the house, clipped hedges, canals and statues. These were run down by the 18th century, when they were removed by 'Capability' Brown.

Inside the house Lord Weymouth, a High Churchman and patron of the Non-Jurors (Anglican clergymen who declined to take the oath of allegiance to William and Mary after the 'Glorious Revolution'), built a chapel and gave shelter to the Non-Juror Bishop Ken of Bath and Wells. Bishop Ken's Library, a charmingly plain and simple room of the 1690s, is still to be found above the Great Hall at Longleat.

The Elizabethan beamed roof of the Great Hall was flattened to accommodate this insertion, and the 1st Viscount Weymouth was probably also responsible for the balcony with open-work scrolls in the same room. There are still some original touches in the Great Hall such as the Mannerist chimneypiece, with two-tailed mermaids, which is probably by Maynard, but the 'Jacobean' panelling is most likely 19th-century work. Indeed most of the interior of Longleat is 19th-century – and none the worse for that, as it displays craftsmanship of the highest quality, first by Sir Jeffry Wyatville (of Windsor Castle fame) and then, later in the century, by John Crace.

ABOVE The Italianate State Drawing Room, with a ceiling adapted from that in the library of St Mark's Cathedral, Venice, and an original frieze, composed of genuine Venetian work and attributed to Pietro Liberi, depicting the story of the goddess Circe. The paintings include Old Masters by Tintoretto and Titian, collected by the 4th Marquess of Bath.

ABOVE RIGHT The Red Library contains some 6,000 volumes, mainly collected by the 4th Marquess of Bath. The drawing displayed on the easel on the extreme left of the photograph is by John Singer Sargent, and shows the wife of the 5th Marquess.

BELOW RIGHT Detail of a marquetry door leading from the breakfast room into the dining room at Longleat.

Wyatville's patron was the 2nd Marquess of Bath, whose father, previously the 3rd Viscount Weymouth – a gambler and drunkard who served briefly as Lord Lieutenant of Ireland without ever setting foot in that kingdom, and later took on the largely honorific post of Groom of the Stool (bowdlerized as 'Stole') – had, hardly deservedly, been given a marquessate in 1789. Between 1801 and 1811 Wyatville rebuilt the north front of Longleat; added the Elizabethan revival stables and clock tower (which now houses the memorial exhibition about the 6th Marquess of Bath); and radically re-arranged and remodelled the interior of the main house. He inserted passages round the inner courtyard and constructed the 'Imperial' Staircase (rising in one flight and returning on itself in two).

In the 1960s a guide at Longleat made the mistake of patronizing a group of schoolgirls going round the house. 'This', she trilled, 'will doubtless be the grandest staircase any of you have ever seen!' 'Not at all', drawled a duke's daughter in the party. 'The one at home is far grander.'

Similarly, Wyatville's surviving marble chimneypieces at Longleat look small beer among the grandiose transformations of the 1870s carried out for the 4th Marquess of Bath by John Crace. The 4th Marquess – who, according to the gossipy *Society in London* (1885), had 'frozen down into the very exemplar of an immaculate, unemotional self-possessed English aristocrat' – had acted as Envoy Extraordinary to Lisbon and Vienna and was an avid collector of both paintings and furniture. Keen on all things Italian, especially Venetian, this Lord Bath had Crace set mythological canvases of the Titian school into a scrolling gilt ceiling in the State Dining Room. The pick of the paintings in the drawing room is Titian's *Rest on the Flight into Egypt*, which hangs near a small gallery containing Meissen birds and animals made by Kändler, *circa* 1730, for the Japanese Palace at Dresden. The drawing room is also stuffed with French furniture, including a Louis XVI *bureau plat* which once belonged to Talleyrand.

The saloon, 90 feet long, is less overpowering and still has an Elizabethan feel thanks to its huge windows. It once was the Long Gallery and is now hung with tapestries, including a Flemish set of the life of King Cyrus of Persia. The cyclopean chimneypiece, supported by figures of Atlas, was copied from the Doge's Palace in Venice.

Besides Crace and his firm, the 4th Marquess of Bath also employed George Fox in the decoration of some of the seven Italianate rooms at Longleat. For example, it was Fox – responsible for similar work at the Brobdingnagian Eastnor Castle in Herefordshire – who inlaid the exotic doorcases in the Ante-Library and he also helped Crace in the saloon and drawing room.

RIGHT Detail of an 18th-century Italian oval library table, part of a suite decorated with a serpent motif.

BELOW Staircase landing at the top of the Brown Stairs.

RIGHT A royal gallery in light and shade.

Of the portraits at Longleat, there are memorable studies of the Duchess of Richmond by Van Dyck at the foot of the Imperial Staircase and of the 5th Marquess of Bath by Sir William Orpen in the Breakfast Room. The 5th Marquess's elder son was killed in the First World War and on his own death in 1946 he was succeeded in the marquessate and in the Longleat estate by his younger son, Henry.

Henry's first wife, Daphne Vivian (later Fielding), wrote an evocative memoir of her life at Longleat entitled *Mercury Presides*. When the 6th Marquess and his second wife, Virginia, a granddaughter of the actor-manager Sir Herbert Beerbohm Tree, were finding it difficult to conceive in the late 1950s, they climbed a Dorset hillside in order to call on the help of the generously endowed chalk giant of Cerne Abbas. Their exertions duly

The delightful 1690s library of Bishop Ken, to whom the 1st Viscount Weymouth gave shelter at Longleat after the 'Glorious Revolution'.

resulted in the birth of a daughter, Lady Silvy Cerne Thynne, an artist who restored the superb carved giltwood looking glass in the Music Room.

The sexual and artistic endeavours of Henry Bath's eldest son, Alexander, the present Marquess, have generated much publicity over the years. *The Times* described his murals and bas reliefs as 'a sub-Freudian phantasmagoria'. He has also written novels, championed the Wessex Regionalist cause and changed the spelling of the family surname from Thynne to Thynn – 'in order', as he says, 'to arrest the drift in its pronunciation', which was increasingly rhyming it with 'Pine' instead of 'Pin'.

13

HARDWICK HALL

*T*HERE was something so vivid and larger-than-life about the Tudor age that its great figures, such as King Henry VIII and Queen Elizabeth I, have projected their personalities with such strength down the centuries that they still seem to be living memories. Another Tudor Elizabeth, 'Bess of Hardwick', no less formidable in her own way, ensured her immortality through building surely the most remarkable Elizabethan house of them all, Hardwick Hall in Derbyshire.

'Hardwick Hall/More glass than wall' goes the old jingle and drivers on the M1 motorway far below in the valley must echo the refrain when the rays of the sun strike the four storeys of huge windows. The result is a glittering wall of flame. On the more frequent dark days of the English Midlands, it stands silhouetted against the sky, massive and mysterious like a great galleon.

John Byng visited Hardwick in 1789 and described it as 'like a great old castle of romance. Such lofty magnificence! And built with stone, upon a hill! One of the proudest piles I ever beheld!'

Bess's extraordinary life was intimately tied up with the building of Hardwick, which remains her memorial and monument. She was born at Hardwick in 1527, one of four daughters of John Hardwick, a local squire whose family had been settled hereabouts for at least six generations. The family seat was a modest manor house now subsumed by the ruins of Hardwick Old Hall.

Her father died when Bess was still an infant and she was brought up in straitened circumstances. Young Bess began her career in the household of the neighbouring grandees Sir John and Lady Zouche of Codnor Castle, but then accumulated a fortune through a progression of shrewd marriages – so shrewd as to make one mildly suspicious of her husbands' causes of death.

First, in 1543, she married an ailing cousin, Robert Barlow, who died a few months later – 'before they were bedded', according to one account – and left

her a reasonable income. Then, after a probable stint as a gentlewoman in the household of the Marchioness of Dorset (mother of Lady Jane Grey, the 'Nine Days' Queen'), she married, in 1547, Sir William Cavendish of Cavendish in Suffolk, an immensely rich widower who had served as one of the commissioners for the Dissolution of the Monasteries. Bess persuaded him to concentrate his landholdings in Derbyshire – among the new acquisitions was the estate of Chatsworth.

ABOVE A gateway to history.

PRECEDING PAGES The main staircase at Hardwick, made of local stone, leading one ever upwards.

ABOVE *ES* for Elizabeth Shrewsbury, *alias* Bess of Hardwick: her name is shouted from the roof-tops.

BELOW Bess in pride of place above her son, the 1st Earl of Devonshire.

By the time Sir William Cavendish died, ten years later, Bess, who had borne him eight children (of whom six survived), was hitting her stride as an acquisitive, ambitious schemer with a passion for building. Next she married Sir William St Loe, a West Country landowner and influential figure in the court of Queen Elizabeth. St Loe's death five years later, in the winter of 1564–5, put her on an even sounder financial footing; and in 1567 she snapped up her fourth and most spectacular catch, the 6th Earl of Shrewsbury.

Lord Shrewsbury, Premier Earl of England (the earldom had been conferred on his ancestor 'Le Grand Talbot', Shakespeare's 'Great Alcides of the Field', who won 40 battles against the French before being defeated by Joan of Arc), was a powerful Tudor tycoon with interests in all manner of commercial concerns besides vast land-holdings. The union – one might almost say merger – did not turn out well. Apart from the clash of two strong personalities, one of the flies in the ointment was the exiled Mary Queen of Scots, of whom Lord Shrewsbury was appointed custodian in 1569.

The intriguing (in both senses of the word) Mary was shuffled around Lord Shrewsbury's numerous seats, much to Bess's annoyance. The Scottish Queen certainly stayed at Chatsworth, Worksop and other houses under the Shrewsburys' sway, but there is no evidence to support the legend that she stayed at Hardwick. After all, Lord Shrewsbury stopped acting as Mary's custodian in 1584 and Bess is not thought to have started new building work there until at least 1585.

Bess was still concentrating her energies on aggrandizing Chatsworth. She was eventually to relieve her frustrations about the Marian complications by spreading a scandalous story that there had been an improper intimacy between the Scottish Queen and her husband. Earlier, in 1574, she had provocatively arranged the marriage of her daughter Elizabeth to Charles Stuart, Earl of Lennox, brother of Lord Darnley, Mary Queen of Scots' murdered husband. The issue of the marriage – in the event, a daughter, Arabella, to whom Bess became guardian – would have a claim to the English throne. Queen Elizabeth was furious, Lord Shrewsbury deeply embarrassed.

Another bone of contention was the amount of time and money Bess was lavishing on Chatsworth – which Lord Shrewsbury insisted belonged to him anyway under the marriage settlement. In the early 1580s the marriage came apart at the seams. Bess decided to decamp to her own stronghold of Hardwick, which she had recently acquired from her bankrupt brother, James.

It was as if she said 'I'll show them!' And she did. First of all, between 1585 and 1590, when Lord Shrewsbury died, she transformed her old family home into a rambling, rather haphazardly designed mansion. Then, flush with almost limitless wealth, she decided to start all over again on a new house only about 100 yards away.

This was to be her conclusive statement: Hardwick Hall, a triumphant, symmetrical, deceptively simple expression of the English Renaissance in glass, stone, tapestry and embroidery. Her initials *ES* (Elizabeth Shrewsbury), carved repeatedly on the parapets of the six towers, shouted her ownership from the roof-tops.

The extravagant use of glass, an expensive commodity in Tudor times, was a status symbol, and Bess was in a strong position to show off in this connection as one of the many assets she had inherited from Lord Shrewsbury was a glass works. Hardwick was also conveniently placed for other materials. Stone came from a quarry halfway up the drive; slate from

ABOVE Detail of the elaborate painted plaster frieze in the High Great Chamber.

The black Derbyshire marble and Derbyshire alabaster brought from Bess's own quarries and carved by her own craftsmen are a constant delight at Hardwick. Also ubiquitous as a design motif is the stag, reflecting the heraldic emblem of both the Hardwick and Cavendish families.

An inventory drawn up in 1601 shows that Bess filled Hardwick with treasures. Many of the items are still *in situ*, notably the tapestries, furniture and, above all, the embroideries. Hardwick's collection of late 16th- and early 17th-century embroidery is without equal. Bess herself was an expert and prolific needlewoman and presided over a hive of embroiderers – even if, legend notwithstanding, Mary Queen of Scots was not one of the team.

RIGHT Another of Hardwick's superb decorated doorways.

Bess lived on at Hardwick into the new century, finally dying in 1608. She was buried in great state at Derby. The epitaph on her tomb describes her, aptly enough, as *'aedificatrix'*.

Hardwick passed to her Cavendish descendants, who became Dukes of Devonshire and based themselves largely at Chatsworth. Yet they far from neglected the great Elizabethan house, at least in the summer months. With all the glass, it must have been bitterly cold. The 6th ('Bachelor') Duke of Devonshire recorded in his *Handbook to Chatsworth and Hardwick* (1844) how he made a vain attempt to pass some evenings in the Long Gallery: 'although surrounded by red baize curtains, the cold frosty East wind got the better of us'.

It was the Bachelor Duke who assembled the present range of portraits in the Long Gallery, including a flamboyantly attired Queen Elizabeth I, a more austere likeness of the widowed Bess and a study of the toothless old philosopher Thomas Hobbes, tutor to the 2nd and 3rd Earls of Devonshire, who died at Hardwick in 1679. Hobbes sought to prolong his life by walking up and down the hill until, as a chronicler recorded, 'he was in a great sweat, and then give the servants some money to rub him'.

The Bachelor Duke enhanced the antiquarian atmosphere at Hardwick, importing appropriate tapestries, furniture and pictures from Chatsworth and elsewhere. In this century an enormous amount of skilled repair work on the tapestries and embroideries was carried out by Evelyn Duchess of Devonshire, who settled at Hardwick after the death of her husband, the 9th Duke, in 1938. The programme of sensitive conservation has continued under Hardwick's new owner, the National Trust, which took the place over in 1956.

Symmetry in the snow.

14

BLICKLING HALL

THAT IT was possible for the National Trust to take on Hardwick Hall, and several other great houses featured in this book, such as Powis Castle, Knole, Petworth, Kedleston and Waddesdon, was due to the vision of the 11th Marquess of Lothian, the Liberal statesman who inherited the title and the estate of Blickling in Norfolk in 1930.

As Philip Kerr, he had first made his mark in public life as private secretary to David Lloyd George, the Liberal Prime Minister who did more than anyone else to erode the supremacy of the British aristocracy. When Lloyd George wrote to congratulate him on his inheritance Lord Lothian replied: 'Largely as a result of your all too admirable work, a well diluted peerage is now possessed of almost no power, and I discover that I shall have to pay to our exhausted Exchequer almost 40% of the capital value of a mainly agricultural estate. In my capacity as an ordinary citizen I think highly of these arrangements but as an inheritor of a title and estates thereto they will prove somewhat embarrassing.'

Concerned about the seepage of family seats and their contents on to the market, Lord Lothian made an historic speech in 1934 to the annual general meeting of the National Trust, which had previously only concerned itself with the protection of the landscape. He warned of the perils facing England's great houses and urged the Trust to devise a 'Country Houses Scheme' whereby, instead of being dispersed as a result of death duties, whole houses and their contents could be left to the nation intact with their estate income as an endowment.

The upshot was a Bill in Parliament, created in 1937, which allowed the National Trust to save country houses. Lord Lothian himself initiated the process by bequeathing Blickling to the National Trust on his death *en poste* as British Ambassador to the United States of America in 1940.

LEFT Double vision in the Stone Court.

RIGHT The Great Staircase, with its curious newel figures, as redecorated in the 19th century by the 8th Marquess of Lothian.

BELOW A bird's-eye view of Blickling.

Nearly 100 other country houses have followed Blickling into the Trust's care but none can displace it as a perfect representative of the English country house. Writing in *Country Life* in 1930, the year that Lord Lothian succeeded to the property, Christopher Hussey remarked on how

> The suddenness and completeness with which the scene
> bursts upon the eye strikes a simultaneous chord
> rather than a scale of impressions: a backwater in time...
> a vanished line of Norfolk grandees, the generous vitality
> of Shakespeare's England, the childhood of Anne Boleyn,
> and, muted by the imprisoned mist of time, faint memories
> of famous knights, the pomp of bishops' courts, and the
> last of the Saxon kings passing through the water-meadows
> that gave his manor its name.

Heady stuff, but then the first sight of Blickling's south front, with its gables, chimney stacks, towers and central cupola, is breathtaking in a gloriously English way.

Hussey may have piled it on rather, but the Shakespearean allusion is justified by the fact that the Bard borrowed the surname of a 15th-century squire of Blickling, Sir John Fastolfe, a soldier, for his character Sir John Falstaff. It was Fastolfe who sold Blickling – originally a moated manor house of *circa* 1400, built by Sir Nicholas Dagworth – to the Boleyn family. According to tradition, Blickling was the birthplace of Anne Boleyn, King Henry VIII's bewitching second queen. True or not, this legend contributes significantly to Blickling's air of romance.

In 1616 the estate was bought by Sir Henry Hobart, Lord Chief Justice of the Common Pleas and one of the first baronets created by King James I. Sir Henry set about rebuilding the old manor house in such a grandiose and expensive fashion (the expenditure for 1619 to 1621 alone was £5,451, 18s 1d) that Blickling became one of the stateliest Jacobean seats.

PRECEDING PAGES Blickling: the north front, seen in the morning from across the lake.

LEFT Detail of the fire irons in the grate of the Long Gallery fireplace.

RIGHT Blickling's most remarkable interior, the Long Gallery, with its original, heavily symbolic, ceiling by Edward Stanyon and bizarre Victorian frieze by John Hungerford Pollen. The Long Gallery became a library in the 18th century.

As his architect, or 'Surveyor' (as they still tended to be called), Hobart went to the top: Robert Lyminge, who had previously built Hatfield House in Hertfordshire for King James's Lord Treasurer, Robert Cecil, Earl of Salisbury, son of William Cecil, Lord Burghley (see pages 132-43). In architectural terms the two houses have obvious stylistic similarities, such as the angle turrets that define the bulk of the building, the shaped gables that punctuate the skyline and the entablatures that mark the floor levels and bind the complexities of mass together. At Blickling, Lyminge showed particular imagination in devising the thrusting service ranges at the two sides of the main house to form an imposing forecourt.

Blickling's trump card over Hatfield is the variety of its elaborate plaster ceilings, carved by the stuccoist Edward Stanyon. The ceiling in the Long Gallery is the house's chief wonder – a dense and intricate pattern of bands enclosing heraldic and emblematic panels. There are symbols of the five senses and some 20 emblems derived from Henry Peacham's *Minerva Britannia* (1612). Peacham claimed that the true use of emblems was 'to feede at once both the minde, and eie, by expressing mistically and doubtfully, our disposition, either to Love, Hatred, Clemencie, Justice, Pietie, our Victories, Misfortunes, Grefes, and the like: which perhaps could not have been openly but to our praeiudice revealed'. One could certainly spend the best part of a day on one's back in the Long Gallery feeding 'the minde, and eie' by peering up at the ceiling with its charmingly chunky and naive plasterwork.

The extravagance of the building operation became rather out of hand and Sir Henry Hobart, who died in 1625, did not live to see its completion. The cruel truth is that, like Sir Nathaniel Curzon at Kedleston (see pages 362-71), he had built above his station. He lumbered a far from great family with a great house. Blickling proved a burdensome inheritance for the fairly dim line of Norfolk baronets that followed him.

There were few incidents of note in the subsequent family history, save for the 3rd Baronet's entertainment of King Charles II at Blickling in 1671 and the death in 1698 of the 4th Baronet in a notorious duel with Olivier Le Neve of Great Witchingham, who fought left-handed and against his will, and had to flee abroad for some years. Nonetheless, in the 18th century the

Hobarts advanced to the earldom of Buckinghamshire, not so much through any merit as by the charms of the 1st Earl's sister, Henrietta, the Countess of Suffolk, who was King George II's mistress.

There is a striking portrait of Henrietta, attributed to Thomas Gibson, in the South Drawing Room at Blickling. It shows her dressed for a masquerade and exhibiting the good looks that lasted into old age when Horace Walpole knew her: 'Of a just height, well made, extremely fair, with the finest light brown hair.'

Henrietta was a woman of style and taste who lived at the exquisite Palladian villa of Marble Hill on the Thames at Twickenham, but she appears to have exercised little influence on her brother other than gaining him an earldom. The 1st Earl's only contribution to Blickling appears to have been the installation of a library in the Long Gallery, subsequently removed.

The 2nd Earl of Buckinghamshire, however, spent much of his childhood with his Aunt Henrietta at Marble Hill, and was to be a key figure in Blickling's late 18th-century revival. It was fortunate indeed that thanks to his aunt, the new Lord Buckinghamshire was in the forefront of advanced architectural taste, with its new-found enthusiasm for what Lady Suffolk's friend and neighbour Horace Walpole of Strawberry Hill called 'King James's Gothic'.

ABOVE & ABOVE TOP Initials on the walls and drainpipes: *HD* for the marriage in 1761 of John Hobart (2nd Earl of Buckinghamshire) to Mary Anne Drury, whose jewels paid for the completion of the west front; and *B* for 'Buckinghamshire'.

LEFT The Peter the Great Room, dominated by the tapestry of the Russian monarch defeating the Swedes at the Battle of Poltawa in 1709. The tapestry was presented to the 2nd Earl of Buckinghamshire by Catherine the Great, who appears to have been susceptible to his manly charms when he was *en poste* in St Petersburg. The carpet was woven specially for the room.

Not long before, Blickling had been the object of derision, looked down upon by admirers of Norfolk's other great houses – for example the Palladian palaces of Holkham and Houghton (see pages 330-41 and 316-29). Charles Lyttelton called Blickling 'a bad old house' and in the valuation taken at the death of the 1st Earl of Buckinghamshire in 1756, its price was estimated chiefly in terms of the salvage of its building materials.

Happily, though, the 2nd Earl had no intention of pulling Blickling down. As Hannah More, the poet, wrote to Horace Walpole: 'You admire Houghton, but you yearn for Blickling; you look at Houghton with astonishment, at Blickling with desire.' In one of the earliest instances of 'Jacobean Revival', the 2nd Earl of Buckinghamshire bucked the classical style and made a series of sympathetic alterations to Blickling between the mid-1760s and the mid-1780s. 'Gothick it was', he told his Aunt Henrietta, 'and Gothick it will be in spite of all the remonstrances of modern improvers and lovers of Grecian architecture.'

The Ivory dynasty of architects and craftsmen was brought in from Norwich to rebuild the west front and part of the north front, and to refashion Lyminge's dramatic staircase with its delightfully dotty series of newel figures, most of which had to be replaced. The new west front, paid for by the sale of Lady Buckinghamshire's jewels, was not very successful – Silas Neville observed in 1782 that it looked 'more like a hospital than a nobleman's seat' – but the north front is much more in keeping. Even the texture and bond of the brickwork is hard to distinguish from the genuine Jacobean article.

Not all Lord Buckinghamshire's tickling of Blickling, however, is in the Jacobean manner – and the great house is none the worse for that. The old Jacobean withdrawing chamber was partitioned and exotically decorated in

RIGHT The State Bedroom, finished *circa* 1782. The tester and backboard of the bed are made up from a canopy of state issued to the 2nd Earl of Buckingham-shire for his Russian embassy. The royal arms on the coverlet, though, are those of Queen Anne, and must have come from an earlier canopy. The Axminster carpet was made for the room.

the Chinese taste in the early 1760s as the Chinese Bedroom and the Chinese Dressing Room. Later, in the 1770s, Lord Buckinghamshire created Blickling's two major 18th-century rooms – the Peter the Great Room and its adjoining state bedroom – in order to commemorate the high point of his career, when he was sent by King George III to be Ambassador in St Petersburg.

Portraits of the King and his Queen, Charlotte, together with the rich canopy of state adorn the state bedroom, which may have been completed by Samuel Wyatt after Thomas Ivory had his leg crushed by a piece of timber. The neo-classical Peter the Great Room takes its name from the vast tapestry hanging there of Peter defeating the Swedes at the Battle of Poltawa in 1709. This tapestry was presented to the 2nd Earl of Buckinghamshire by the

The east front from the parterre.

Empress Catherine, a lusty monarch who seems to have taken a fancy to the handsome British envoy.

Although endowed with looks and charm, the 2nd Earl does not seem to have deceived his contemporaries as to more sterling qualities. Horace Walpole likened him to a confection known as 'the Clearcake' which was 'fat, fair, sweet, and seen through in a moment'. Lord Buckinghamshire had a wretched time as Viceroy of Ireland, describing himself as 'a man whose mind has been lacerated with a variety of embarrassments for thirty weary months'. He was also a martyr to gout and, according to Walpole, his death in 1793 was brought about by thrusting his inflamed foot into a bucket of icy water.

The title then passed to his brother George, 'a conductor of the opera entertainments' according to *The Gentleman's Magazine*. He was ancestor of a line that became increasingly impoverished – the 9th Earl of Buckinghamshire was to be found working as a corporation gardener in Southend-on-Sea.

Blickling, though, was inherited by the 2nd Earl's younger daughter, Lady Suffield. During her long tenure of Blickling she commissioned Joseph Bonomi to build a pyramidal mausoleum in the park and John Adey Repton to carry out various improvements, all in sympathy with the Jacobean flavour of the house. It was Repton who was largely responsible for the reconstruction of the central clock tower in the 1820s – a three-storey wooden affair which seems alarmingly flimsy from within when the east wind is blowing – and for the linking arcades between the main house and the wings.

On Lady Suffield's death, childless, in 1850, Blickling passed to her great-nephew, the 8th Marquess of Lothian, who renovated the house with the help of the architect Benjamin Woodward (designer of the Oxford Union Debating Hall) and the decorative painter John Hungerford Pollen. With the increased appreciation of Victorian taste it can now only be a matter for regret that the 11th Marquess of Lothian and his sister, Lady Minna Butler-Thwing, should have swept away so much of Pollen's fascinating decoration – which was certainly of more interest than the conventional 'safe' taste that replaced it. However, although Pollen's extraordinary neo-Byzantine chimneypiece has gone from the Long Gallery, his ornate bookcases and bizarre painted frieze can still be seen.

By the time that James Lees-Milne, first secretary of the National Trust's Country House Scheme, saw Blickling during the Second World War it was 'a sad, lonely, unloved house with a reproachful air'. He soon grew to love it, however, for the more he gazed 'the more I was impressed by the dowagerial majesty of this ancient pile; and then bewitched by its rosy brick complexion'.

Lees-Milne's diaries and his book *People and Places* paint an evocative picture of the National Trust's sensitive restoration of Blickling. Although, like so many other Trust properties, it is no longer actually a family home (one might say that only an idealistic bachelor such as the 11th Marquess of Lothian could have imagined such a conflicting state of affairs ever being a working reality), Blickling is an outstanding example of a great house beautifully preserved for posterity by expert and sympathetic hands, thanks to the foresight of its former owner.

15

WOBURN ABBEY

BEDFORDSHIRE

*I*T IS a curious irony that though Woburn has been a household name since its phenomenal success in the stately home industry of the 1950s, the name itself is invariably mispronounced. Although the old Cistercian abbey in Bedfordshire, granted to the Russell family after the Dissolution of the Monasteries, had always been pronounced '*Wooburn*', the 13th (and present) Duke of Bedford, who opened the place to the public in 1955, democratically took to calling it '*Woeburn*', so as not to confuse his paying customers.

'Ian' Bedford had inherited the traditional Russell shyness and endured an extremely strange upbringing – he was kept in ignorance of his ducal destiny and was reduced to eating the chocolates put out for his eccentric father 'Spinach' Tavistock's beloved parrots – but he gallantly forced himself to face the glare of publicity as a pioneer of 'stately' showmanship. He did so in order to save Woburn Abbey, which would otherwise have had to be sold, owing to the exceptionally heavy death duties incurred by the demise of both his reclusive grandfather and his quixotic pacifist father within a few years.

By the time he inherited the dukedom in 1953 Woburn and its 16,000-acre estate had fallen into an almost derelict state. In the ensuing years the 13th Duke stopped at virtually nothing – even allowing a nudist film to be shot in the grounds – so that the great treasure house could be preserved for posterity. Some of his fellow aristocrats shuddered at the relentless vulgarity of the 'Maverick' Duke of Bedford's publicity stunts – the funfair, souvenir shop, safari park, the embarrassing film and television appearances, 'dinner with the Duke' at so much a head – but Ian Bedford was unrepentant. 'I do not relish the scorn of the peerage', he said, 'but it is better to be looked down on than overlooked.'

The visitors flocked to Woburn and the more discerning found plenty to admire beside the tripperish attractions. Indeed the contents of the house are overwhelming in their variety and splendour: an outstanding collection of

16th- and early 17th-century portraits, including the celebrated 'Armada' portrait of Queen Elizabeth I; later portraits by Van Dyck, Reynolds and John Hoppner; pictures by Frans Hals, Rembrandt, Tintoretto, Murillo, Claude, Poussin and Teniers; and a series of Canaletto views of Venice. The furniture includes marquetry commodes by Pierre Langlois, 'Chinese Chippendale', French marquetry and Boulle; there is fine English and Sèvres porcelain and fabulous services of silver, silver-gilt and gold plate. The catalogue of treasures is unending.

The Duke himself always claimed, though, that the most important factor in the stately home business was less the presence of great works of art than a sufficiency of lavatories. Far from feeling degraded at having to share Woburn with the public, he felt 'flattered that they seem eager to share it with me'.

'I have learned the most important lesson of my life from opening Woburn', he said. 'It is that the pleasure you give to other people is the most rewarding thing in the world. I regard it as the main purpose of my life to keep Woburn Abbey for my family.'

Ian Bedford once described the Russells as thinking themselves 'slightly grander than God'. Certainly they rank with the Cecils of Burghley as one of the great British families who rose to prominence in the Tudor age. Originally medieval wine merchants, the Russells had risen to the status of county gentry in Dorset by the end of the 14th century. The durable Tudor diplomatist Sir John Russell was given a barony by King Henry VIII and created Earl of Bedford by King Edward VI.

ABOVE The ground-floor hall.

RIGHT Looking down the cantilevered Great Staircase, probably built by Henry Flitcroft for the 4th Duke of Bedford.

PRECEDING PAGES The Palladian west front of Woburn Abbey glows in a stormy autumn dusk.

ABOVE The Blue Drawing Room, where the wife of the 7th Duke of Bedford took afternoon tea – and indeed is credited with the 'invention' of this light repast.

The 1st Earl of Bedford was described by Edmund Burke as 'a prompt and greedy instrument of a levelling tyrant' on account of the vast acreages he acquired – though in fairness, it should be recorded that ten peers actually received larger grants of former monastery land than he. Among the abbeys that came into Bedford's possession were Tavistock, Dunkeswell, Thorney, a site in London that is now called Covent (after 'Convent') Garden, and the Cistercian house at Woburn, founded in 1145 by Hugh de Bolebec.

The last Abbot of Woburn, Robert Hobbes, had been turned out in 1538, and supposedly hung from an oak tree in the park, having been found guilty of treasonable utterances against King Henry VIII. Nine years later, King Edward VI granted Woburn Abbey to the 1st Earl of Bedford, as he soon became.

The original monastic buildings at Woburn followed the usual Cistercian pattern, with a church (where the north wing now stands) and a cloister and garret (the site of the present courtyard). Initially the Russells did not make Woburn their principal seat, preferring to base themselves in London and at

BELOW Detail of the Blue Drawing Room, showing the set of watercolour miniatures of the Russell family by George Perfect Harding.

the manor house of Chenies in Buckinghamshire. It therefore came as an unwelcome surprise when Queen Elizabeth I decided to put up at Woburn on her Progress of 1572, as the old abbey was far from being in a fit state of habitation.

It was not until the early 17th century and the tenure of the 4th Earl of Bedford, who increased the family fortunes by draining the Fens (the scheme that came to be known as 'the Bedford Level') and developing Covent Garden, that Woburn came into its own. This Lord Bedford pulled down most of the old monastic buildings and erected a handsome new Carolean house on the same site, perpetuating the courtyard plan.

The interior features included a saloon known as the 'Star Chamber', from the golden astral decorations on its walls, a state bedroom which the 4th Earl's close friend King Charles I is known to have occupied on three occasions, a Long Gallery and, most notably, a Fountain Room or Grotto in the north wing. This deliciously cool cavern of shells and stucco is very much in the Italian mannerist style and, inevitably, there is a tradition that it must have been designed by Inigo Jones, who was certainly associated with the 4th Earl of Bedford's Covent Garden improvements. The likelihood, though, is that it was designed by Jones's assistant, Isaac de Caus, who also worked at Wilton.

BELOW The delightful 17th-century Grotto, originally designed as an open loggia where the Russell family could sit and breathe in the good clean air of Bedfordshire. The stonework is carved to resemble seaweed and adorned with shells.

ABOVE Queen Victoria's Bedroom: though Charles I stayed here, this room was completely redesigned during the 4th Duke's rebuilding and it now takes its name from Queen Victoria's stay. The wall hangings, a copy of the previous silk of 1820, were renewed in 1973.

The 4th Earl's younger son, John, a legendary dancer, may have been the model for Addison's 'Sir Roger de Coverly', but the elder boy, William, was made of sterner stuff, and became an active Parliamentarian in the Civil War. 'The Puritan Earl' (as he was known), according to the memoirs of the Earl of Ailesbury, 'kept a good house for eating amongst themselves, but no hospitality...'. He seems to have begun the Woburn tradition of entertaining paying guests; even his children had to account for their board and lodging.

The Puritan Earl lived to a great age, and was predeceased by his heir, Lord Russell, who came to be regarded as a martyr to the Whig cause, having been executed after the Rye House Plot of 1683. Eleven years later the Puritan Earl was raised to the dukedom of Bedford, partly in honour of the memory of his son, who was described in the preamble to the patent of creation as 'the ornament of his age, whose great merit it was not enough to transmit by history to posterity'. (Non-Whig historians have taken a less roseate view of 'this since canonized ruffian', as Vicary Gibbs put it.)

Something Lord Russell was able to transmit to posterity was a vast fortune, enhanced by his marriage to the former Lady Rachel Wriothesley, heiress of the Bloomsbury estate in London. Buttressed by this further influx of wealth, the Russells were at the forefront of the Whig oligarchy, and in the mid-18th century the 4th Duke of Bedford – unfazed by the interfering tendencies of his grandmother-in-law, Sarah Duchess of Marlborough – commissioned the architect Henry Flitcroft to give Woburn a Palladian face-lift.

ABOVE A detail of the gilt decoration in the State Dining Room.

LEFT Whig identity parade.

RIGHT View through the *enfilade* of state apartments at Woburn – a distance of some 220 feet.

Flitcroft built the long west front, facing the park, with its very proper Ionic centrepiece linked to the wings by two lower ranges. Inside, he created a grand series of state rooms, beginning with the exotic Chinese Room (where the wallpaper dates from 1753) and proceeding through the State Apartment, the State Bedroom, the central saloon, the State Dining Room and the Breakfast Room to the Carolean Long Gallery, which Flitcroft remodelled.

The 4th Duke was ahead of his time in installing such domestic comforts as hot and cold baths, a water closet (for his exclusive use, in the garden) and earthenware stoves to warm the corridors and staircases, but Woburn still lacked a set of family rooms. These were installed by his bachelor grandson, the 5th Duke of Bedford, an agriculturalist with revolutionary leanings (he was said to have been a friend of Danton), who brought in the fashionable Whig architect Henry Holland, designer of the Prince of Wales's Carlton House and Brooks's Club in St James's.

From 1787 onwards Holland rebuilt the southern range of Woburn Abbey, transforming some old offices into an *enfilade* of handsome living rooms, including a superb Long Library with two pairs of Corinthian columns, and a corner 'eating room', which was hung with Canalettos brought down from Bedford House when the family's London residence was demolished in 1800. Holland was also responsible for creating the enchanting Chinese Dairy, a conservatory, tennis court and riding school.

ABOVE The Long Library, the most attractive of the rooms designed by Henry Holland at Woburn, with screens of fluted Corinthian columns. The Marquess and Marchioness of Tavistock use this as a family room and it is not generally open to the public.

On the death of the 5th Duke of Bedford in 1802 – as a result of a tennis ball aggravating an earlier rupture caused by a cricket ball – the dukedom and Woburn passed to his brother, the 6th Duke, who carried on improvements with the help of Sir Jeffry Wyatville. A keen botanist, the 6th Duke erected flower houses for his plant collections, though he converted Hollands' conservatory into a sculpture gallery, at one end of which Wyatville devised a circular temple to house Antonio Canova's *The Three Graces*. (This sculpture was removed and put on the market in the 1980s.) The 6th Duke also brought in Humphry Repton to landscape the park.

Later in the 19th century Woburn enjoyed a halcyon period when the 7th Duke of Bedford, described by the diarist Charles Greville as 'affable, bland, and of easy intercourse', entertained on a princely scale. Queen Victoria recorded in her journal for July 1841 how, after inspecting all the tenants 'drawn up on either side of the house', she 'left Woburn with great regret having spent a very pleasant time there'.

The 7th Duke, though, died the same year as the Prince Consort (1861), and thereafter 'pleasant' was no longer a word that could be applied to Woburn. A series of withdrawn, misanthropic Dukes presided in lonely grandeur over feudal formality. The 9th Duke entered left-wing demonology for his apparent indifference to the lot of his slum tenants in London ('If one

ABOVE Marble busts of the 6th Duke and Duchess by Nollekens.

RIGHT Classical stance. The 5th Duke of Bedford suffered a rupture playing cricket; it was later aggravated by a tennis ball, with fatal consequences.

hadn't a few acres in London at these times of agricultural depression', he remarked, 'I don't know what one would do'), though he was in fact a 'progressive' himself. Having built his own crematorium he then proceeded to inaugurate it after he shot himself.

The wife of the 11th Duke (who saved from extinction the Père David deer from China in the park) took refuge in aviation, becoming famous as 'the Flying Duchess' before being lost on a solo flight over the North Sea (a room at Woburn now celebrates her exploits). In the late 1940s her son, 'Spinach', the 12th Duke, demolished the dry rot-ridden east range by Holland, as well as the same architect's riding school and tennis court. The neo-Georgian architect Sir Albert Richardson was employed to undertake a tidying-up operation, which involved flank walls to seal off the truncated wings, and steps leading up the hill towards Flitcroft's twin mid-18th-century stable blocks.

After 20 bustling years of rescusitating the estate, Spinach's son, the 13th Duke of Bedford, made over Woburn to his eldest son and heir, the Marquess of Tavistock, who together with his energetic wife, the former Henrietta Tiarks, has valiantly carried on the constant struggle to make Woburn a paying proposition. Besides opening more rooms – the tour of the house covers three floors, including the crypt – the Tavistocks' enterprises have included pop concerts (Neil Diamond performed before 60,000 people at Woburn in 1977), an antiques centre, two championship golf courses, a flourishing stud, a pottery, corporate hospitality and catering. In 1985 they gave some Père David deer to the People's Republic of China, in the hope that the species might become re-established in its natural habitat.

In short, Woburn is a hive of activity and, as Lady Tavistock says, the best way to describe the chatelaine's day is 'like running up a down escalator'. The Tavistocks are determined to follow the example of the 13th Duke who, in the words of his son, 'realized the importance of providing a full and enjoyable day out for every member of the family, while preserving the beauty of the house and its setting'.

ABOVE The results of Sir Albert Richardson's tidying-up operation, which set off Flitcroft's twin mid-18th-century stable blocks.

LEFT The Canaletto Room, containing the celebrated collection of Venetian views commissioned by the 4th Duke of Bedford.

16

TREDEGAR HOUSE

GWENT

ALTHOUGH this book is entitled 'Great Houses of England *and* Wales', the Principality is modestly represented for the simple reason that Wales has very few 'great houses'. What it lacks in quantity, however, is amply compensated for in terms of quality by the magnificence of Powis Castle, and the curiously little-known Tredegar House in what used to be Monmouthshire and is now called Gwent.

Tredegar is an exceptionally splendid example in brick and stone of that glorious late 17th-century period in architecture when symmetry and the classical Renaissance still had a slightly rustic, home-bred feel. This was the late Stuart age when the gentleman architect Sir Roger Pratt flourished, with his 'double-pile' designs for Coleshill in Wiltshire (later burnt and demolished), Kingston Lacy in Dorset (given a heavy Italianate going-over by Sir Charles Barry in the 19th century) and the vanished Clarendon House in Piccadilly. Tredegar, however, is not by Pratt, nor – as tradition once had it – by Inigo Jones and John Webb, though there are certain similarities between Tredegar and the river front at Wilton. Indeed no architect is known for sure to have worked at this family seat of the Morgans and there are no obvious parallels with other houses – the quadrangular plan and use of corner pavilions distinguish it from 'double-pile' houses, while its lavish external decorations appear to be *sui generis*.

The only possible comparisons that come to mind are with Ragley Hall in Warwickshire (see pages 232-43) and Maiden Bradley in Wiltshire, seat of the Dukes of Somerset. It happens that the master-carpenters Roger and William Hurlbutt, or Hulbert, from Warwick, worked at both these places and this has led the architectural historian Howard Colvin to suggest that the design of Tredegar might be attributed to either of them. Moreover, Giles Worsley of *Country Life* has also put forward the Hurlbutts as possible designers of the handsome flanking stables, which bear a resemblance to the (now demolished) stables of 1667 at Warwick Castle.

Overall, the style of Tredegar's principal facade has a 'Dutch' feel, with the brick adorned by carved stone swags round the windows. The spiral columns of the entrance doorway are also reproduced within two of the interiors.

Inside, one is quite bowled over by the exuberant wood carvings of the Brown Room and the Great Staircase, with its balustrades of scrolling acanthus. The *pièce de résistance* is the gorgeously ornate Gilt Room, with its richly twisted columns and elaborate painted ceiling, illustrating how Pope Urban VII nobly overcame lust – portrayed by an ample, naked, female figure. There are more barley-sugar columns in the robust and muscular Cedar Closet upstairs.

No precise dates can be put on Tredegar's lavish rebuilding but *circa* 1664 to *circa* 1672, with the fitting-up of the interiors going on well into the 1680s, seems a reasonable presumption. In the course of this 17th-century re-modelling the north-east wing of the original medieval house was completely

ABOVE The decorative climax of the state rooms at Tredegar, the Gilt Room, with its pine panelling painted to resemble walnut, and gorgeous gilding.

PRECEDING PAGES Tredegar House, from across the lake.

ABOVE & BELOW Details of the glittering chimneypiece in the Gilt Room, reminiscent of an Italian baroque altarpiece.

rebuilt, and the old screen wall replaced by an additional wing which was designed as the principal facade. The 17th-century roof was higher than it is today and surmounted by a cupola and balustrade – removed around the end of the 18th and the beginning of the 19th century.

The Morgan family's connection with Tredegar goes back to at least the early 15th century. Llywelyn ap Morgan is recorded as living there in 1402, but he subsequently had to forfeit his estates for supporting the rebellion of Owain Glyndwr against the English. Later, Sir John ap Morgan was a faithful ally of the ambitious Welshman Henry Tudor, who became King Henry VII, and was rewarded with the post of Constable of Newport Castle. Sir John appears to have rebuilt the house at Tredegar; the surviving south-west wing, which now houses the servants' hall, probably dates from his time.

In 1540 the traveller and topographer John Leland found Tredegar 'a very faire place of stone... neither castle nor pile, but a manor place'. A century later, during the Civil War, it was considered commodious enough to accommodate King Charles I and his retinue, plus two troops of horse, for a night in July 1645.

The then squire, Sir William Morgan, lived to the age of 93, but the most likely person to have carried out the major remodelling is his grandson and namesake, who married the heiress of another William Morgan, a rich lawyer who was King's Attorney for South Wales. Flushed with fortune and a fine family seat, the Morgans went up in the grand Whig world across the Severn.

The elaborately carved doorway of the Brown
Room. A bust of the Emperor Augustus is
supported by intricately carved trophies of arms.

Early in the 18th century yet another Sir William Morgan of Tredegar married Lady Rachel Cavendish, whose father was the 2nd Duke of Devonshire of Chatsworth and whose mother was a sister of the 2nd Duke of Bedford of Woburn. Judging by the copious Tredegar accounts for coaches, cockpits, racehorses, blackamoors, musicians and fancy clothing, this grand match seems to have gone literally to Sir William's head – among other extravagances he found it necessary to hire the services of a French peruke- (or wig-) maker. Having filled only briefly the post of Lord Lieutenant for Monmouthshire and Brecon he died, at the age of 30, in 1731.

Lady Rachel lived on for another 50 years, but hard as she tried she could not protect the interests of her daughters after her only son died a bachelor in 1763. Tredegar then passed to her brother-in-law, Thomas Morgan of Ruperra Castle, whose own male line also expired when finally, in 1792, the property was inherited by his daughter Jane Gould.

Jane's husband, Sir Charles Gould, Bt., Judge Advocate-General and president of the world's first life assurance society, the Equitable Life, duly took the name of Morgan. A remarkable tycoon, he exploited the coal and iron on the Tredegar estate and built a chain of canals and tramroads in the neighbourhood. A mile of the tramroad passed through the park at Tredegar and was known locally as 'the Golden Mile', owing to the tolls levied on the vehicles availing themselves of it.

Sir Charles's son and namesake was probably responsible for the early 19th-century remodelling of the house, to accommodate his eight children and ever expanding household. The surviving warren of servants' rooms at Tredegar bear eloquent witness to the elaborate rituals of 'downstairs' life.

In 1859 the next Sir Charles Morgan, the 3rd Bt., was raised to the peerage by Benjamin Disraeli as Lord Tredegar. His son Godfrey took part in the Charge of the Light Brigade and survived into the 20th century to become a generous public benefactor in South Wales. He was advanced in the peerage from a barony to a viscountcy. There is a charming Edwardian portrait at Tredegar of this benevolent bachelor. It shows him nursing his Skye terrier, Peeps, with whose whiskers Godfrey's soup-strainer moustache seems to droop in sympathy.

The 2nd Viscount Tredegar, like many early 20th-century aristocrats, devoted himself largely to hunting, shooting and fishing, but his son, the 3rd Viscount, had more exotic tastes. Indeed this Lord Tredegar, otherwise the artist, poet and novelist Evan Morgan, can claim a special niche in the gallery of aristocratic eccentrics. An aesthete with a passion for animals, he maintained a bizarre menagerie at Tredegar which included such creatures as bears, gorillas and kangaroos, with whom His Lordship liked to box.

Lord Tredegar had a peculiar affinity with birds – possibly derived from the fact that his mother, Lady Katharine Carnegie, seemed to be under the impression that she herself belonged to the avian species. There is a celebrated 1930s photograph of Evan swanning around at one of his numerous garden parties at Tredegar with his parrot, Blue Boy, perched on his shoulder, while the worthy local gentry look on aghast. One of his party tricks, apparently, was to let Blue Boy crawl up his trouser legs and then peep his beak out from the fly buttons.

A Roman Catholic convert, Evan somehow managed to combine a string of impressive-sounding papal appointments – he was Privy Chamberlain of Cape and Sword to Popes Benedict XV and Pius XI – with a passion for black magic (the occult, not the chocolate). In association with the notorious 'Beast', Aleister Crowley, Evan would engage in strange voodoo rituals

LEFT The Great Staircase: a 17th-century carved curiosity, with balustrades of scrolling acanthus which may have been remodelled in the 19th century.

RIGHT The Master's Bedchamber, decorated in the style of the early 18th century. The bed is on loan from the Victoria & Albert Museum in London.

BELOW The New Hall, once the entrance hall, with a cast-iron fireplace set in marble and historical portraits on loan from the Dulwich Picture Gallery.

involving pythons. There are hair-raising stories of seances at Tredegar, with owls fluttering around the ceiling. The American-born diarist and socialite Sir Henry 'Chips' Channon, MP, has left a disturbing picture of Tredegar House in the 1930s: 'The feel and even smell of decay, of aristocracy in extremis, the sinister and the trivial, crucifixes and crocodiles...'.

Yet Lord Tredegar did not entirely neglect public life. In 1929, before succeeding to the peerage, he stood as Conservative candidate for the Limehouse division of Stepney, in the East End of London. This must surely rank as one of the Tory Party's more inspired electoral choices; the imagination boggles at what the dockers and stevedores must have made of this *rara avis*. He was not elected.

Evan's luxurious 'Cow Bathroom' (so called because it housed his collection of Staffordshire pottery cows), complete with bidet, evokes Tredegar's 'Indian Summer' as a country house in the 1930s. As it turned out, Evan, who died in 1949, was the last Morgan to live in the house. In the 1950s, Tredegar was sold, and the place became a boarding school run by the Sisters of St Joseph.

By the 1960s Tredegar House had virtually disappeared off the map. In the *Country Life* series of books on country houses, the Carolean volume (published in 1966) by Oliver Hill and John Cornforth devoted only a paragraph to Tredegar. Soon afterwards the school was absorbed into the 'comprehensive' system: blackboards, desks and hideous strip lighting dominated the interiors, now painted in institutional colours. It looked as if this great house had gone forever.

However, in 1974 Newport Borough Council stepped in and acquired the house, stables, home farm, gardens and 90 acres of parkland. Notwithstanding Tredegar's unpromising position, engulfed by the M4 motorway and the urban sprawl of Newport – and its poor state of repair, aggravated by dry rot and the attention of woodworms – the council determined to restore the building and to present it as a furnished country house.

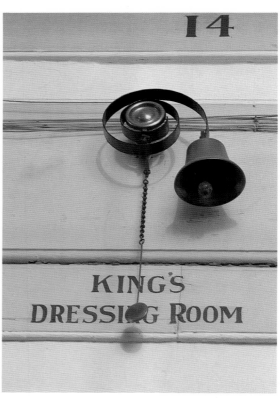

TOP, ABOVE & RIGHT Three generations of service bells 'below stairs'.

ABOVE The entrance front of Tredegar.

LEFT One of the atmospheric, evocative corridors at Tredegar.

Thanks to the sympathetic skills of its imaginative curator, David Freeman, Tredegar House somehow manages to avoid the deadly atmosphere of a museum. Gradually, some of the original contents are returning – through loan or acquisition – and the Dulwich Picture Gallery has lent some 50 16th- and 17th-century paintings, including 'primitive' portraits of Tudor kings and queens. A family armorial dinner service has returned to the dining room; a fine 17th-century Flemish cabinet has gone back to the King's Room; the last Lord Tredegar's widow (the title finally became extinct in 1962) has generously returned many of the family portraits. The '10 red curtains', recorded as hanging in the Gilt Room in 1688, have been ingeniously reproduced and the fascinating old kitchens – featured in the BBC's *Victorian Kitchen* series – have been restocked with antique items, gathered together by the thriving 'Friends of Tredegar'.

This hitherto neglected great house, so surprisingly exhumed, deserves many more friends to discover its unusually atmospheric charms.

17

BADMINTON HOUSE

GLOUCESTERSHIRE

THE NAME Badminton has sporting connotations that are world famous. It was in the magnificent baroque entrance hall, with its Corinthian columns and vast hunting canvases by John Wootton, that the children of the 8th Duke of Beaufort invented the game of 'Badminton' during the bleak winter of 1863. And the north front of the exterior, designed, in all probability, by James Gibbs and William Kent in the 1740s, has become one of the most familiar country house views through the annual television coverage of the Badminton Horse Trials, an international three-day event started by the 10th Duke of Beaufort in 1949.

The 10th Duke – always known as 'Master', a sobriquet going back to his childhood, when he was given his own pack of harriers, the Brecon, at the age of eight – was a legendary fox-hunter and Master of the Horse to three sovereigns. His ground-floor sitting room was a shrine to the chase, complete with signed photograph of the television-puppet fox, Basil Brush. As his neighbour, the writer James Lees-Milne put it, 'More learned in fox lore than lettered he was possibly the only man who neither wrote nor even read his own autobiography.'

The present writer, when interviewing 'Master' in connection with these *Memoirs* (1981), made the appalling *faux pas* of bringing up the subject of his uncles, Lord Henry and Lord Arthur Somerset, both of whom found themselves obliged to live abroad after allegations of homosexuality (probably quite unfairly in the case of Lord Henry). Neither gentleman was permitted to be mentioned in Master's hearing.

He also did not care to be reminded, as a loyal servant of the Crown, of the story that his ancestor Lord Herbert (later the 1st Duke of Beaufort) had courted Oliver Cromwell – and possibly even sat in the Rump Parliament as 'Mr Herbert' – in order to recover the family estates, confiscated by the Roundheads from his father, the 2nd Marquess of Worcester. This Lord

Worcester was a many-sided genius with a claim to have invented the steam engine and to have narrowly missed the feat of making an artificial bird fly, chirp and even hover.

During the Civil War the family seat of Raglan Castle in the Welsh Marches – acquired through the 1st Earl of Worcester's marriage to an heiress of the Herberts – had been 'slighted' by the Parliamentarians, and Badminton, across the Severn in Gloucestershire, subsequently became their principal residence. The manor of Badminton, originally owned by the Boteler family, had been acquired in 1608 by the 4th Earl of Worcester for his second son, Thomas Somerset, who transformed it into a Jacobean mansion. In 1655 Thomas's spinster daughter left it to her cousin 'Mr', or Lord, Herbert.

Master's touchiness on the question of any Roundhead sympathies was understandable in view of the fact that his family, the Somersets, are really Plantagenets, descended in the direct male line (albeit illegitimately) from King Edward III's son, John of Gaunt. In all fairness, too, it must be recorded that 'Mr Herbert', having recovered his estates, made his peace with the restored King Charles II, who eventually created him Duke of Beaufort in 1682.

Previously, while still the 3rd Marquess of Worcester, he had begun aggrandizing the rambling pile of Badminton. An attempt was made at a classical facade on the north, or entrance, front by an unknown architectural hand – possibly John Webb, Inigo Jones's protégé. Grinling Gibbons contributed some luscious carvings in limewood of lobsters, fruit and game in the dining room (which was given a rococo treatment in the form of pilasters, cornice and doorcases in the 18th century, probably by Edward Poynton), and he was also responsible for the spectacular marble monument to the 1st

PRECEDING PAGES A landing on the oak staircase, which rises to the height of the house.

RIGHT Worcester Lodge by William Kent, *circa* 1746.

BELOW RIGHT The rusticated front door on the north front.

BELOW Badminton: east front.

Duke of Beaufort in the church attached to the south-east corner of the house.

The 1st Duke, by all accounts, lived at Badminton in princely style with a household of more than 200. In the park he devised an impressive array of intersecting avenues. 'You may stand on Ye Leads', recorded the traveller Celia Fiennes from the vantage point of the roof at Badminton, 'and look 12 wayes.' Roger North noted that 'divers gentlemen cut their trees and hedges to humour his [the 1st Duke's] vistas, and done planted their hills in line, for compliment at their own charge'.

Such obliging behaviour chimes with Badminton's extraordinarily feudal tradition. To this day the Beauforts are like local royalty, and people in the vicinity tend to think of themselves as living in 'Beaufortshire', the hunting country of the Beaufort Hunt, rather than Gloucestershire (let alone 'Avon', the odious new county foisted – surely only temporarily – on the map in the mid-1970s, much to Master's fury).

The next significant changes to Badminton's architecture came in the time of the 3rd Duke of Beaufort, who succeeded to the property as a boy in 1714. First, he engaged Francis Smith of Warwick who tinkered with the west, east and even the north fronts – although, as the Duke wrote in a letter to his Duchess, a Scudamore heiress, in 1737, 'Smith was here yesterday and shakes his head sadly about a pediment.' It appeared to the architect that the existing walls of the north front would not take the weight of additional stone.

After the head-shaking Smith's death the next year the Duke turned to James Gibbs, whose precise role in Badminton's architectural history remains rather hazy. He may have been responsible for the pair of wooden cupolas on the north front and he probably started the pair of pavilions; he could also have designed the splendid entrance hall, which is usually attributed to William Kent.

Kent was introduced to Badminton by the 4th Duke of Beaufort, who succeeded his brother, the 3rd Duke, in 1745. The 4th Duke was a notable patron of the arts who was instrumental in bringing Canaletto to England; the two views of Badminton painted by this great topographical artist are among the house's most important treasures.

They show Kent's newly completed remodelling in its pristine state. The Palladian all-rounder constructed a wooden pediment and a third storey to the flanking wings, as well as beefing up Gibbs's pair of pavilions with pediments and a pyramidal roof. Three miles down the principal axis of the landscape from the house, Kent designed, with the assistance of his Clerk of Works, Stephen Wright, the nobly domed Worcester Lodge in the great flat park – which was once of nine miles circumference.

BELOW The entrance hall: by William Kent or James Gibbs? The hunting and equestrian scenes are certainly by John Wootton; the Landseer painting on the easel is of the 8th Duke of Beaufort as a boy, standing with his pony in the hall.

LEFT A chair in the entrance hall.

BELOW Trophies of the chase.

The delightful library, designed by Sir Jeffry Wyatville for the 6th Duke of Beaufort.

'Capability' Brown was consulted about landscaping the parkland, but there is no evidence that his proposed plantations were carried out. Thomas Wright of Durham (no apparent connection of Stephen's) adorned the surroundings with various follies and fancy touches.

Later in the 18th century the 5th Duke of Beaufort, who entertained Queen Charlotte at Badminton (thus bringing to an end the family's Jacobite leanings towards the Stuarts), commissioned Charles Evans to rebuild the parish church adjoining the house as a sort of St Martin's-in-the-Fields in miniature. The interior boasts a majestic series of sculpted memorials by John Michael Rysbrack, as well as Gibbons's tribute to the 1st Duke.

Early in the 19th century the 6th Duke of Beaufort employed Sir Jeffry Wyatville to tackle the *enfilade* of rooms on the east side of the house. His most successful effort was the library, a delightful interior begun by the 3rd Duke of Beaufort, where the chimneypiece is surmounted by a carved panel of botanical specimens.

In more imposing mode, the heavily gilded Great Drawing Room (or ballroom), at the other end of the east range, has a chimneypiece of Carrara marble, porphyry and ormolu. This room also used to house the so-called

'Badminton Cabinet', a massive affair of *pietre dure,* made in the Grand Ducal Workshop of Florence in 1726 for the 3rd Duke of Beaufort during his Grand Tour. It was sold in 1990 to Mrs Johnson, the baby lotion heiress from New Jersey.

During the Victorian era, sporting rather than artistic matters tended to hold sway at Badminton, though the 7th Duke of Beaufort was a patron of the popular animal artist Sir Edwin Landseer, who often came to stay. He painted a charming picture of the future 8th Duke, standing in the entrance hall beside his pony.

The 8th Duke, who did two stints as Master of the Horse, was a legendary sportsman and joint editor of *The Badminton Library,* a series of authoritative studies of hunting, shooting, fishing and other country pursuits. One of the most popular grandees of his time, he would purposely drive in his carriage through the poorest quarter of Bristol, believing that it gave pleasure to the people to see him go by. Indeed it seemed to, for the sight of the ducal conveyance brought the Bristolians hurrying out on to the street, crying 'The Dook, the Dook!'

'Master's' sitting room, complete with equestrian portraits and fox puppet in Beaufort Hunt coat.

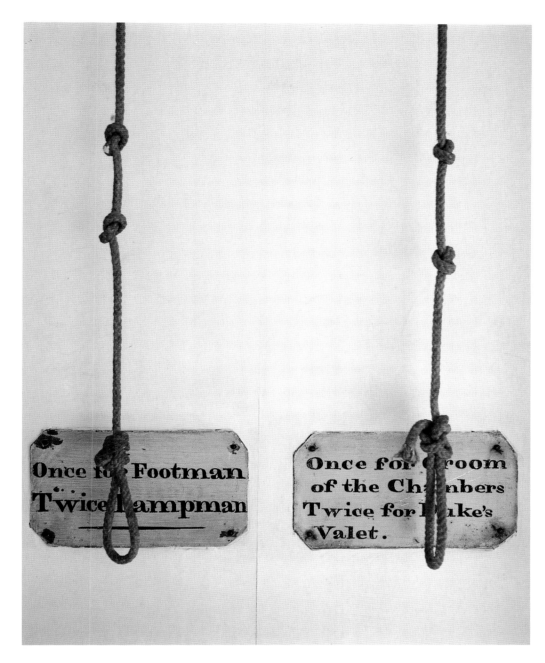

ABOVE Pull for service.

LEFT A view of the octagonal inner hall,
with its fine plasterwork decoration.

It was near the end of the 8th Duke's long tenure, in the 1890s, that the Oak Room at Badminton acquired its name and its panelling (brought in from another family house, Troy, near Monmouth). By this time two of the 8th Duke's younger sons, Lords Henry and Arthur Somerset, had both decamped abroad – Lord Arthur in the wake of a scandal concerning a male brothel popular with the aristocracy in Cleveland Street, near Euston Station, and Lord Henry after being accused, probably erroneously, of homosexuality by his wife.

Lord Henry, a promising politician and a protégé of Disraeli's, wrote a touching book of poems entitled *Songs of Adieu,* and was immortalized in the autobiography of his cousin, Sir Osbert Sitwell, who described him in old age as living in 'an elaborate, and taken in all, rather hideous little palace in Florence; a very tall Don Quixote in broad-brimmed hat and gold mono-grammed carpet slippers taking the air in the side-car of a motor-cycle through streets lined with an appreciative, indeed rocking, crowd'.

His ramrod-straight nephew, Master, favoured more robust attire and began his career in the Blues before marrying Queen Mary's niece, the former Princess Mary of Teck. During the Second World War, the redoubtable old Queen decided to base herself at Badminton, though she had never previously showed much liking for rural life. Her Majesty did 'her bit' by exhorting teams of loyal workers to cut down trees and tear away the dreaded ivy.

Sometimes her enthusiasm for collecting scrap metal for the war effort would go too far. There are stories of her ordering perfectly good field harrows and other farming implements to be carted away to the salvage dump.

When, after the war, someone inquired of Master's wife, Duchess Mary, what part of the great house the old Queen had lived in, the Duchess replied: 'She lived in all of it.' Although attended by numerous servants and decked in diamonds, Her Majesty would religiously stick to wartime rations.

BELOW The dining room: the most complete
17th-century survival at Badminton, with
carvings by Grinling Gibbons of lobster, fruit
and game.

Master continued to preside in feudal manner at Badminton until his death in 1984, in the 60th year of his dukedom. The title and estate then passed to his cousin, David Somerset, a great-grandson of the exiled Lord Henry.

The new Duke, a dashing and stylish figure, combines the Somerset strands of sport and art. As well as being a dedicated fox-hunter and former president of the British Horse Society, he is chairman of the Marlborough Fine Art Gallery in London, and an internationally recognized expert on paintings. His Duchess was formerly Lady Caroline Thynne, daughter of the late Marquess of Bath, the Stately Showman of Longleat.

The Beauforts, however, do not open Badminton to the public on a regular basis. They have carried out a sympathetic renovation of the house and gardens, village (recolour-washing the houses and cottages) and park (planting many thousands of trees), perfectly preserving Badminton's potent mixture of intimate informality and regal splendour.

The 'Horse Trials' view, across the lake to the north front.

18

RAGLEY HALL

WARWICKSHIRE

THE SECOND World War marked a watershed in the fortunes of the English country house. Many families moved out in 1939, never to return, as their family homes were taken over by the military (as in Evelyn Waugh's novel *Brideshead Revisited*) or by hospitals, schools or other institutions. The consequent damage done to the fabric was often irreparable, or so it seemed at a time when egalitarian zeal was influencing opinion against the very morality of living in a great house.

Ragley Hall in Warwickshire, the vast Carolean and Georgian seat of the Seymours, Marquesses of Hertford, set in one of 'Capability' Brown's most delightful parks in the heart of England, did 'its bit' as a hospital throughout the war. Afterwards it seemed likely that it would never be lived in by the Seymours again.

That, at least, was the official view – but as another country house owner, Charles Clive-Ponsonby-Fane of Brympton d'Evercy in Somerset, once observed, 'the worst damage done to the heritage was not so much by the taxman and dry rot but by the fuddy-duddy family adviser'. The present Marquess of Hertford, looking back to the austere days of the 1940s, recalls: 'It was obvious to everyone (except me) that the days of living in great houses had gone for good.'

Hugh Hertford had succeeded his uncle, the stage-struck 7th Marquess, as a boy of ten in 1940; his father, Brigadier-General Lord Henry Seymour, who won a DSO and Bar in the First World War, having died in the last summer of peace. Young Hugh and his mother, the youngest daughter of the 1st Duke of Westminster, moved into a farmhouse on the estate, which had been placed in the hands of trustees by the 6th Marquess of Hertford, but nonetheless reduced by a quarter due to death duties.

The trustees made plans to sell the big house to a firm of demolition contractors, but the young Marquess fought hard to prevent this. Then, in

PRECEDING PAGES Ragley: the Great Hall, James Gibbs's splendid baroque interior, 70 feet long, 40 feet wide and 40 feet high.

LEFT The doorway from the Great Hall into the Red Saloon.

RIGHT, TOP, MIDDLE & BELOW Details of the chimneypiece in the Great Hall.

the 1950s, he amazed everyone by bucking the contemporary trend that such stately homes were white elephants and moved back into Ragley Hall. He found it almost derelict – 'the house was in some danger of becoming a ruin' – and set about an extensive programme of restoration, with the expert help of his wife, Louise de Caraman Chimay. 'A smaller house might have given us an easier life', he recalls, 'but we both felt that Ragley is too precious to be allowed to fall down.'

In 1958 they began opening Ragley regularly to the public and were 'greatly encouraged, not only by the financial support, which does indeed help, but also by the appreciation expressed by so many people'. As well as renovating and redecorating many of the house's 115 rooms, the Hertfords also added a remarkable new feature which illustrates that the age of country house patronage is far from extinct.

In the 1960s Lord Hertford had the happy notion of cheering up the bare walls and ceilings of Ragley's South Staircase Hall. He spotted the young artist Graham Rust at work on a mural in Virginia, and decided that he was the ideal person for the job.

Rust was accordingly commissioned to interpret, as he wished, the theme of *The Temptation*, chosen by Lord Hertford because he had once climbed to the top of the Mount of Temptation, or Sinai, back in 1952. On the flat ceiling of the South Staircase Hall Rust painted an open-topped dome through which is seen the Mount of Temptation at the moment when the

Devil is offering Christ the world with all its riches, as chronicled in the Gospel of St Matthew. On the balcony are depicted the Hertfords' four children – the Earl of Yarmouth and Ladies Carolyn, Diana and Anne Seymour – with their godparents.

Rust began painting the mural in 1969 and finished in 1983. *The Temptation* is entirely his own design and his own work: he had no assistants. The mural is painted in indelible gouache on a heavy rag pure paper on the walls, and directly on to the plaster on the ceiling.

By any standards, it is an extraordinary achievement. When first seen, in the early 1980s, it struck some as rather garish and overpowering. Doubtless, though, the work of Verrio and Laguerre in the 18th century must have seemed a bit over the top when new. Viewed today, Rust's *Temptation* certainly has an abundant exuberance. The attire of the modern figures

LEFT Wyatt's Red Saloon, which was restored in 1970.

BELOW A detail of the Red Saloon, with a display of Sèvres porcelain on the table. The painting is of *Antiochus and Stratonice* by Celesti.

already has an amusing 'period' flavour – that of the 1970s, with its polo necks, thick ties, velvet jackets, flamboyant open-neck shirts and – thankfully largely obscured by the balustrading – flared trouserings.

Some of the best touches are the animals, varying from family pets such as William the spaniel and Roland the Pyrenean Mountain dog to leopards, monkeys and exotic parrots. All in all, it is a triumphant reflowering of a grand tradition, which reflects credit on both patron and artist.

Ragley's traditional history goes back to the 6th century, the date of a large brooch made of gilded bronze and supposedly worn by a Saxon Lady of the Manor, which is now on display in the Red Saloon. Later the lands were owned by Evesham Abbey and then the Rous family, who built a small castle on the site, bought at the end of the 16th century by Sir John Conway of Conway Castle in North Wales, who married the heiress of the neighbouring Arrow estate.

The present house at Ragley dates from the late 1670s, when Sir John's great-grandson, Edward, the 3rd Viscount Conway (later the 1st Earl of Conway) became involved, as he put it, 'in playing the fool in laying out money upon building'. A scholarly man who wrote a philosophical work in Latin, Lord Conway was a Fellow of the Royal Society, where Robert Hooke – a close associate of Sir Christopher Wren, another Fellow – was secretary. Hooke worked with Wren on the reconstruction of the City of London after the Great Fire of 1666, and was one of the three 'Surveyors' for the building of churches in London, along with Wren and Edward Woodroffe.

Although he does not sound an attractive personality – 'cantankerous, secretive and always in ill health', as one chronicler put it – Hooke is under-rated as an architect, probably because so few of his buildings survive. At Ragley he produced a French-influenced plan for the interior that survived the Georgian improvements. A cross formed by the state features, the 'ceremonies' – the hall, saloon and two swagger staircases – separates each corner into an apartment of four rooms and a back stair. For the exterior, erected in a not particularly attractive local white lias, or limestone rock, he designed flanking pavilions which were never built.

RIGHT *The Temptation* mural by Graham Rust in the South Staircase Hall.

LEFT The Music Room, with its pretty plasterwork and an 1840 Broadwood piano.

The dining room in full fig, with Georgian silver.

Building operations took place from 1679 until Lord Conway's death in 1683, when his titles became extinct. The Ragley estate passed to his cousin, Popham Seymour (later Seymour-Conway), son of Sir Edward Seymour of Berry Pomeroy, Devon. Sir Edward had been Speaker of the House of Commons in the reign of King Charles II and was one of the chief authors of the Habeas Corpus Act. His line of the Seymour family descended from 'Protector' Somerset, who was the brother of King Henry VIII's third Queen, Jane Seymour.

Popham, however, soon popped off, being fatally wounded in a duel at the age of 23, and Ragley was inherited by his brother, Francis, who was newly created Lord Conway. Building work at Ragley after the death of the previous Lord Conway seems to have proceeded at a sluggish pace. Indeed it was not until 1751 that the roof was finally completed.

By this time the veteran Catholic Tory architect James Gibbs had been brought in by Francis's son, the 1st Earl of Hertford, to finish off the interior. There are few surviving elements of the interior decoration of Hooke's time save for some carving in the style of Grinling Gibbons in the library.

James Gibbs's great contribution to Ragley was the magnificent Great Hall. This alone justifies Ragley's reputation as a great house; many consider the hall to be the finest late baroque interior in England and Wales. A glorious pink and white edifice, it is 70 feet long by 40 feet by 40 feet, and is adorned with rococo plasterwork by Giuseppe Artari. In style, the room harks back to the Italy of Gibbs's youth, half a century before, when he studied under Carlo Fontana, surveyor to Pope Clement XI.

There is more rococo plasterwork in the Music Room, with its vines and Bacchic overmantel. Bacchus, however, does not appear to have been much of an inspiration to the 1st Earl of Hertford. As Ambassador to Paris in the 1760s he was criticized in a publication called *The Royal Register* for practising 'all the narrow principles of his beggarly economy to the increase of his own fortune, but at the expense of his country's honour'. Nonetheless, he went on to become Viceroy of Ireland, Master of the Horse and Lord Chamberlain, and was given a marquessate in 1793, the year before he died 'of mortification from a slight hurt received when riding'.

The 1st Marquess had hoped to entertain his royal master, King George III, at Ragley, and in the 1780s commissioned James Wyatt to give the house a fashionable face-lift. Outside, Wyatt added the giant portico, with its paired staircases, and the crowning balustrade. Inside, he redesigned a number of the state rooms in the 'Adam' manner, notably the dining room, with its panels for state portraits, the Mauve Drawing Room and the Red Saloon.

If George III never turned up, his son, the pleasure-loving Prince of Wales certainly did – though the attraction was not so much the beauty of Ragley as that of its chatelaine, Isabella, the second wife of the 2nd Marquess of Hertford. Known as 'the Sultana', Lady Hertford ousted Frances Lady Jersey in the profligate 'Prinny's' affections, though Sir Nathaniel Wraxall, Bt., claimed in his memoirs that the influence she exerted over the Prince Regent (as he became) depended 'from the first moment of its origin, more on intellectual than on corporeal qualities, and reposing principally on admiration and esteem'.

Since 'the Sultana' was, according to a ditty of the day, 'All gentle and juvenile, curly and gay/In the manner of Ackerman's Dresses for May', Sir Nathaniel's claim seems hard to believe, even if the Seymour family faithfully maintain that the Prince and Isabella were, in the present Lord Hertford's words, 'just good friends'. In any event, the Prince Regent's bedroom at

19

CHATSWORTH

DERBYSHIRE

C HATSWORTH, a treasure-trove in the most beautiful of English settings, exemplifies the *beau ideal* of a benevolent, paternalistic ducal estate. In describing many great houses one is tempted to use the past tense for their days of glory are so often long gone; at Chatsworth, though, there is a strong feeling that 'the House' is enjoying its golden age today, under the consummate leadership of the present Duke and Duchess of Devonshire.

In the past the Dukes of Devonshire possessed so many great houses, including the mighty Hardwick Hall nearby (see pages 166-79), that they could only spend part of the year in each, but the present Duke has concentrated his attention on 'the Palace of the Peak'. The result is that Chatsworth has really come into its own for the first time in its long history.

After the Second World War, when Chatsworth became a girls' school (and bust-bodices jokily adorned the statues), it seemed that the Cavendishes would never live in the house again. Confiscatory capital taxation of '80 per cent of everything' on the death of the 10th Duke of Devonshire threatened to destroy this part of the 'heritage' as it had so many other great houses. One of the Cavendishes' other seats, the Elizabethan Hardwick Hall, went to the National Trust.

During the 1950s numerous landed proprietors retreated to lesser houses on their estates. 'Debo and I lived in the village', the present Duke recalls, 'and we would go for a drive in the park and she would say "That's a nice house. I wonder who lives there...".' They decided to give it a go and finally moved back in 1959; today the house is owned by a charitable trust.

The sympathetic and thoroughly practical changes wrought by the present Duchess have redefined life in the country house. A Mitford who writes as well, if not better, than her celebrated sisters, Deborah Devonshire has produced several books celebrating the house, the estate, the treasures and her beloved farm animals in an irresistibly breezy way. They capture the *joie de vivre* which permeates the atmosphere of Chatsworth and can be savoured by even the most casual visitor.

Important as the history of the architecture, art and landscape are at Chatsworth, it is the human qualities of a living community that seem to matter more in the scheme of things. The Devonshires and their estate seem psychologically sure of their identity and purpose. Chatsworth succeeds in being at once a working, well-run estate, a tourist attraction, a great house and a family home.

The Duke and Duchess do not live in a poky wing: they maintain an unostentatious but fitting ducal style in the most attractive part of the main house and their frank enjoyment of their good fortune is refreshingly infectious. The redecoration and re-ordering of their own apartments – from re-gilding the glazing bars of the windows to adding modern works of art by Lucian Freud and Angela Conner – has shown that the 'heritage' need not be an ossified, museumified affair but a constantly evolving organism. Outside, too, the gardens have been rejuvenated with sculptures by Elisabeth Frink and imaginative new horticultural designs – such as the Duchess's jolly 'cottage garden'.

ABOVE The Duke of Devonshire, a devoted bibliophile, takes a nap in the Duke's Sitting Room, or Lower Library. Asked why he referred to this room as his sitting room rather than his study, the Duke replied: 'Because I sit in it more than I study.' As the 'Bachelor Duke' of Devonshire recorded in his *Handbook to Chatsworth and Hardwick* (1844), it was John Crace who transformed the old breakfast room into 'something between an illuminated MS and a café in the Rue de Richelieu... two bearded artists in blouses were imported from Paris and completed the ceilings and pilasters'.

PRECEDING PAGES The south front, designed by William Talman in 1685, with almost sculptural detail and in a *palazzo* style. Talman, a quarrelsome character, was subsequently dismissed by the 1st Duke of Devonshire, who became keen on directing the building operations himself with the help of Thomas Archer.

RIGHT Colossal foot, 1st century BC, in the West Sub-Corridor. It was sold to the Bachelor Duke in Rome by the sculptor Carlo Finelli and was formerly in the Quirigi family's palace at Lucca. This pedal extremity was long thought to be spurious but is now known to be one of a pair from a giant female figure.

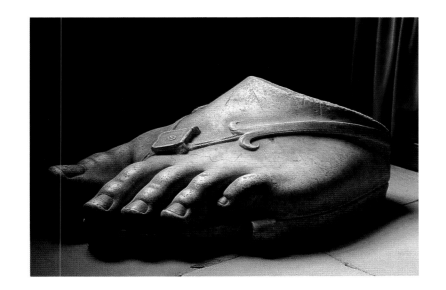

BELOW The Blue Drawing Room which, according to the Bachelor Duke's *Handbook* (when it was called the Music Room), 'used to be the most joyous and frequented of all the rooms at Chatsworth'. It now very much is again for this is the room, overlooking the south, that the present Duke and Duchess use as a family sitting room. Much of the decoration dates from the 5th Duke's time, when Carr of York was employed here. The silvery trio by Sargent are the Acheson sisters (granddaughters of the 'Double Duchess' who married both the 7th Duke of Manchester and the 8th Duke of Devonshire). The modern family portraits around the jib door are by Lucian Freud; the one actually on the door is of the present Duchess aged 34, though she once heard a visitor observe 'That's the Dowager Duchess. It was taken the year she died.'

ABOVE RIGHT View down the stairs to the Painted Hall. The staircase has been altered twice since the 1st Duke of Devonshire's twin curved stairs were built: first in 1833 by Sir Jeffry Wyatville, who designed a single flight and matching galleries along the east and west; and then in 1912 by W.H. Romaine Walker for the 9th Duke of Devonshire. The flower paintings are by Jean-Baptiste Monnoyer. Some people, including the present Duchess, regret that the 9th Duke – or rather his Duchess – did not put back the 'much prettier curved flight, as not only would they have looked better but they would have allowed more space than the ponderous stony mass which protrudes so far over the floor'.

LEFT '*Et tu, Brute...*'. Shadows fall across the death of Julius Caesar, one of the scenes of his life depicted in the Painted Hall by Louis Laguerre from 1652 to 1694. The gilt ironwork on the left of the photograph was copied in 1912 by the Bromsgrove Guild from the balustrade wrought (in 1648) by the French smith Jean Tijou.

A churl would complain that all this takes money and that the Cavendish family have always been too rich and powerful for their own good. Yet there is no finer example in the British Isles of *noblesse oblige*, of privilege amply compensating for its advantages by providing such a glorious and user-friendly show.

The Duke of Devonshire is quite evidently not being affected when he says that the visitors are 'very welcome'. 'They really are', he adds. 'I would feel uneasy not sharing all this with the public.'

'All this' certainly encompasses a great deal: there are, for instance, 175 rooms, 3,426 feet of passages, 17 staircases, 359 doors and 7,873 panes of glass. Although the original Tudor house cannot be seen, it is there embedded in the skeleton of the central block of the new classical house of the late 17th and early 18th centuries.

Building operations began at Chatsworth in 1552, five years after the formidable 'Bess of Hardwick' (whom we encountered in her element in the chapter on Hardwick Hall) married, as her second husband, Sir William Cavendish, a Suffolk squire who had done well out of the Dissolution of the Monasteries. Bess persuaded – ordered, more likely – Cavendish to settle in her native Derbyshire. Having sired six surviving children by her (including the 1st Earl of Devonshire), he died in 1557 and Bess, who continued building, married twice more, lastly to the 6th Earl of Shrewsbury, who acted as custodian to Mary Queen of Scots at various times.

RIGHT The Violin Door in the State Music Room – a brilliant piece of *trompe-l'oeil* which really does deceive the eye. Even close up, it is almost irresistible not to touch it to see if it is real. It was painted by Jan van der Vaart (1653–1727) on a door brought to Chatsworth in the 1830s from the family's London residence, Devonshire House in Piccadilly (demolished in 1924).

LEFT The Tapestry Gallery, a private corridor which leads to the drinks tray and (turning right at the portrait on the easel) to the Blue Drawing Room. The tapestries are Lille *circa* 1730, after designs by Teniers, and were brought here from Hardwick when it passed to the National Trust. The mirror comes from Chiswick House. The blue-green velveteen came from Peter Jones (and cost, as the Duchess tells us '£1 a yard').

A century on, in the 1680s, the Tudor Chatsworth was found to be 'decaying and weake', so the 4th Earl of Devonshire (created Duke of Devonshire in 1694 for his part in bringing William of Orange to the English throne) set about some improvements. Initially, he only intended to remodel the south front (which he did in 1688), but he found building so enjoyable that he carried on right the way round, adding a new east front in 1691 and then the west, finally completing the north front before he died in 1707.

William Talman was the architect for the south and east fronts and Thomas Archer may have been responsible for the west and north, though the Duke himself probably took a hand. Outside, the Duke laid out spectacular water gardens including the Cascade and a 314-yard-long canal. The travel writer Celia Fiennes, who came here in 1697, was much impressed by 'a fine grottoe all stone pavement roofe and sides, that is designed to supply all the house with water besides severall fancyes to make diversion'. Inside was a 'batheing room' with a marble bath:

> You went down steps into the bath big enough for two people; at
> the upper end are two Cocks to let in one hott the other cold water
> to attemper it as persons please; the windows are all private glass.

The 1st Duke's formal gardens were largely swept away by the 4th Duke in the 1760s at the hands of the ubiquitous Lancelot 'Capability' Brown, controversial champion of the 'natural' landscape and peerless planter of trees. The 4th Duke, who married the great heiress of the architect 3rd Earl of Burlington, also brought in James Paine to build the monumental stables (now a restaurant) and the bridge over the river which affords such a fine view of the west front.

The 5th Duke of Devonshire, an idle fellow (who observed of his cousin Henry Cavendish, the scientist, 'He's not a gentleman. He works'), married the legendary beauty Lady Georgiana Spencer, immortalized as 'The

ABOVE The sumptuous library, originally the 1st Duke's Long Gallery, took on its present appearance *circa* 1830. The recently restored ceiling of gilded stucco by Edward Goudge, with paintings by Verrio, dates back to the 1st Duke's time. The bookcases are by Wyatville, the sofas and chairs came from Devonshire House in London, and the portrait of Henry VIII is after the original by Holbein.

Chatsworth, the *beau ideal* of an English
estate, on an ideal English day

LEFT The bronze figure of Mercury, cast for the Bachelor Duke after the original in Florence by Giambologna, on the Great Staircase. The 1st Duke had the *grisaille* panels on the wall painted to resemble sculpture. The real sculpture above is by Caius Gabriel Cibber (1630–1700).

RIGHT The Sabine Bedroom, with its diverting frescoes of *The Rape of the Sabines*, attributed to Sir James Thornhill. The bed is by Lesage of Paris. Purists have objected to the hanging of a chandelier in the room but the Duchess (who describes this as 'a useful bedroom except for nervous guests') feels that 'the glass and candles cheer up the rapists and the raped'.

ABOVE Looking down the *enfilade* of state rooms from the State Dining Room. The gilt side tables are by William Kent.

Face Without a Frown' by Gainsborough and Reynolds. Their son, the 'Bachelor Duke', devoted himself to improving his multifarious properties, particularly Chatsworth. 'I enjoy being here before all earthly things', he wrote. 'I adore it'; and 'I am drunk with Chatsworth.'

The Bachelor Duke's invaluable *Handbook to Chatsworth and Hardwick* (1844) shines through with his love of the place and his enthusiasm for all he did there. As the present Duchess of Devonshire (who formed a passionate attachment to the Bachelor Duke through reading his *Handbook*) has written: 'It reveals the mixture of grandeur and humility in his character, of pride of ownership and the extreme liberalism in his wish to share the enjoyment of his possessions with anyone who might be passing. His generosity and keen appreciation of work done for him by his employees... his passionate interest in building and gardening'.

The Bachelor Duke engaged the architect Sir Jeffry Wyatville to build the long and rather ponderous north wing, which houses many of Chatsworth's state apartments. In the gardens the Bachelor Duke forged a wonderful relationship with his tubby head gardener Joseph (eventually Sir Joseph) Paxton, a relationship described by the Bachelor Duke's biographer James Lees-Milne as 'one of the most satisfactory in the history of master and man'. They went on expeditions to collect plants and are largely responsible for the present layout of the Chatsworth gardens.

It was Paxton who designed and constructed the Emperor Fountain (a jet in the Canal Pond which can reach 280 feet on a calm day) and the now-vanished Great Conservatory, forerunner of the Crystal Palace which he built for the Great Exhibition in London's Hyde Park in 1851. The Bachelor Duke was not only on the best of terms with Paxton but with all who worked for him. In the *Handbook* he delights in recording the personalities at Chatsworth such as Miss Bunting, 'the most prim and punctual of ladies' maids, walking as if she went upon wheels, generally in a riding habit, passionately fond of horsemanship... It was supposed by some that she was not averse to manship either; but that I am persuaded was a mistake arising from her zeal in teaching the groom his Catechism.'

In her own book on *The House* (1982), which brings the 6th Duke's *Handbook* up to date, the present Duchess says that the Bachelor's influence on Chatsworth was immense: 'his benign and generous nature pervades the place to this day. You cannot go far, inside or out of doors, without being aware of him.' She stresses that it is the Bachelor Duke's 'sense of humour which makes one love him more than all the rest put together'.

Those qualities apply equally to the present Duchess, whose love of jokes and fun illuminates Chatsworth. 'It is a terrible place to house-train a puppy', she observes in *The House*. The new door in the library covered with false book-backs contains such titles as *Sideways Through Derbyshire* by Crabbe, *Consenting Adults* by Abel N. Willing, *The Battle of the Bulge* by Lord Slim and *The Day After Gomorrah* by the Bishop of Sodor and Man. It is typical of the Duchess to nominate *Ronalds on the Apple* as her favourite book in the library and Beatrix Potter as her favourite artist in preference to, say, Veronese, Murillo, Rembrandt and Poussin – all well represented on the walls of Chatsworth.

Perhaps the enchanted world created so meticulously by Miss Potter is the key to appreciating the *genius loci* of Chatsworth at the end of the 20th century. The doors of the farm shop, for example, open straight into the pages of *Ginger and Pickles* ('although it was such a small shop it sold nearly everything') and the award-winning farmyard for children is also pure Potter.

For all its grandeur, its frescoed and treasure-filled state apartments, its Old Masters, boulle furniture and 17th-century Delft pottery, the peculiar charm of Chatsworth is the way the Duchess, in the words of her friend Elizabeth Winn, 'has managed to turn the whole place into a smallholding'.

LEFT View along the east front to Flora's Temple, which has recently been restored. The temple was built in 1695 by the 1st Duke of Devonshire as a bowling-green pavilion and was originally sited elsewhere in the grounds. It was moved to its present position in 1760. Wyatville's Italianate tower soars up on the left.

RIGHT A corner of the west entrance hall, complete with the present Duke's walking-sticks and a bust of Byron. This is in the private part of the house, on the west front.

The Sculpture Gallery, housing the Bachelor Duke's collection of mythologies, including works by Canova (for example the *Sleeping Endymion with his Dog* in the right foreground). The *Wounded Achilles* (left foreground) is by Filippo Albacini.

20

PETWORTH HOUSE

SUSSEX

LTHOUGH Petworth House, the Sussex seat of the Wyndham family, can boast masterpieces by Van Dyck and Titian, as well as a notable series of 17th- and 18th-century Dutch, Italian and French paintings, for once in a great house, the 'home side' comes out on top. Besides fielding such artists and sculptors as Grinling Gibbons, Gainsborough, Reynolds, George Romney, Richard Wilson, John Flaxman and Sir Richard Westmacott, Petworth has two outstanding home-grown stars: 'Capability' Brown and J.M.W. Turner.

The incomparable 18th-century parkland created by Brown – surely one of the greatest man-made landscapes in the world – inspired Turner in the early 19th century to such an extent that the artist took up residence at Petworth, under the hospitable roof of his friend and patron, the 3rd Earl of Egremont. Turner was given a room to work in, and one of his delightful series of watercolours shows him painting there.

A curmudgeonly cockney, the son of a barber, Turner kept the door locked. No-one was allowed in except Lord Egremont, and he always knocked first.

The results of Turner's labours now adorn the walls of Petworth, and the Tate Gallery in London. A set of watercolour and gouache sketches of the interiors *circa* 1827 has recently inspired the National Trust (which was given the house in 1947 by the 3rd Lord Leconfield) to carry out an ambitious redecoration scheme to revive the spirit of the place during the time of the 3rd Earl of Egremont. As for the exterior, Turner's great oils show a scene which is happily – despite the ravages of the hurricane of October 1987, which destroyed 600 trees in the park – little changed today.

In his hauntingly evocative painting of *A Stag Drinking*, Turner depicts Petworth Park at sunset. Clumps of trees throw long shadows across the lake, and in the foreground, in a golden haze, a stag slakes his thirst.

Turner used to say that if he could have begun life again he would rather have been an architect. It is intriguing to speculate what he might have done to Petworth. The present pile, a magnificent baroque palace, was built between 1688 and 1696 by the 'Proud Duke' of Somerset to replace an old manor house, of which little now remains except for the 13th-century chapel.

The Proud Duke had acquired Petworth through his marriage to Elizabeth Percy, heiress to Alnwick, Syon and the other Percy estates, and widow of the murdered 'Tom o' Ten Thousand' Thynne of Longleat (for whose dramatic history, see page 158). The Percy family, who became Earls of Northumberland, had come into the manor in the 12th century and a licence to crenellate was granted in 1309. The 9th 'Wizard Earl' of Northumberland began assembling the fine library at Petworth in the late 16th century, and the 10th Earl started collecting the house's great treasury of pictures.

PRECEDING PAGES Petworth: the back view of the house across the trees.

BELOW Detail of the hall: a portrait of Sir William Wyndham by Sir Godfrey Kneller and John Wootton.

ABOVE Looking down the *enfilade* from the North Gallery.

LEFT Door furniture.

The Proud Duke adopted a curious attitude to the pictures at Petworth. According to Jeremiah Miles, who visited the place in 1743 towards the end of what can only be described as the 6th Duke of Somerset's 'reign', he 'studiously concealed' the artists' names 'out of an unusual and ridiculous whimmy'. Miles noted that the Proud Duke lived -

> in a grand retirement peculiar and agreable only to
> himself. He comes down to breakfast at 8 of ye clock
> in ye morning in his full dress with his blue ribbon;
> after breakfast, he goes into his offices, scolds and
> bullys his servants and steward till dinner time; then
> very formally hands his Duchess downstairs. His table,
> tho' spread in a grand manner as if company was expected
> consists of his own family ye Duchess and his 2
> daughters; and when he has a mind to be gracious the
> chaplain is admitted. He treats all his country
> neighbours, and indeed everybody else, with such
> uncommon pride, and distance, yet none of them visit Him.

Among the many anecdotes told of the Proud Duke's absurd arrogance is that he insisted on his children standing in his presence and is said to have disinherited one of his daughters because he found her seated when he woke up after having a nap. He seems to have been under the impression that he was *le Roi Soleil* rather than a Sussex squire, and indeed there is a strong whiff of Versailles about the vast west front – some 320 feet long – at Petworth.

The French influence relates it stylistically to Montagu House in Bloomsbury (later demolished to make way for the British Museum) and to the north front of Boughton House in Northamptonshire (see pages 276-91), both built by the Proud Duke's stepfather-in-law, Ralph Montagu. The architect of the remodelled Petworth is not known. Candidates from the home side who have been floated by architectural historians over the years include John Scarborough, a surveyor, and William Talman, but the French runners, Pierre Puget (a sculptor), Daniel Marot and the mysterious 'Monsieur Boujet' appear more convincing authors – particularly Marot, who is known to have worked for Ralph Montagu and who features, tantalizingly briefly, in the Proud Duke's personal account book at Petworth.

As a composition, the west front suffers from the lack of its original squared dome in the centre which, as a picture of *circa* 1700 shows, relieved the length of the facade. This dome survived a disastrous fire of 1714, which wrecked much of the interior of the centre of the house, save for the Marble Hall (a room reminiscent of King William III's exquisite palace of Het Loo at Apeldoorn in Holland, where Marot also worked), but was removed at a later, unknown, date.

Although the identity of the architect is unrecorded, the various craftsmen are well documented, notably the carvers John Selden and Grinling Gibbons. Selden's and Gibbons's best work for the Proud Duke was later installed in the Carved Room by his great-grandson, the 3rd Earl of Egremont. Horace Walpole considered Gibbons's luscious pendants and pair of double picture frames as 'the most superb monument of his skill', and Selden's efforts are by no means overshadowed. The late 18th-century installation, and restoration, of the carvings in the Carved Room were entrusted to another talented craftsman, Jonathan Ritson, a protégé of the 3rd Earl of Egremont.

Upon the death in 1750 of the Proud Duke's son, the 7th Duke of Somerset, the great Percy inheritance was divided. Alnwick passed to the 7th Duke's daughter, Elizabeth, who married Sir Hugh Smithson, later the 1st

ABOVE, TOP & MIDDLE Details of carving in the Carved Room.

RIGHT The Carved Room: Grinling Gibbons's superlative pair of picture frames.

Duke of Northumberland, whereas Petworth, and the Cumberland estates, went to the 7th Duke's nephew, Sir Charles Wyndham, who also inherited the earldom of Egremont.

Sir Charles – or the 2nd Earl of Egremont, as he became – succeeded William Pitt the Elder as a Secretary of State, and was a notable connoisseur. He collected a cornucopia of classical sculpture from Greece and Rome, including a beautiful head fashioned in the 4th century BC, which has been attributed to Praxiteles and was known as 'the Leconfield Aphrodite'. To house his statuary the 2nd Earl commissioned Matthew Brettingham (the Elder) to build him a sculpture gallery, known as the 'North Gallery', at Petworth; in style it is similar to the same architect's sculpture gallery for Lord Egremont's friend the 1st Earl of Leicester at Holkham.

The 2nd Earl of Egremont, who had to eat his way through innumerable official banquets, joked that 'Well, I have but three turtle dinners to come and if I survive them I shall be immortal.' Alas, he did not survive them and died of apoplexy at his house in Piccadilly (now the Naval and Military Club, or

ABOVE The White Library.

LEFT A view through the doorway into the White Library, Lord and Lady Egremont's private drawing room.

ABOVE The Red Library, Lord Egremont's private study.

ABOVE RIGHT The White and Gold Room in the family's private apartments.

RIGHT The Beauty Room, with a series of portraits by Sir Godfrey Kneller of the ladies of the court of Queen Anne. Her Majesty, not usually regarded as a beauty, is hung above the fireplace.

Among the masterpieces the 3rd Earl collected was John Flaxman's sculpture of *St Michael and Satan*, a bloodthirsty composition all carved from one piece of marble, save for the spear that St Michael is about to stick into Old Nick. The 3rd Earl's own devilish tendencies were limited to his passion for the Turf and his dilatoriness in leading his mistress, who bore him six children, to the altar.

As a consequence, the earldom passed to a nephew (and soon expired) on his death in 1837, but his eldest bastard son was eventually created Lord Leconfield. In 1869 the 2nd Lord Leconfield, concerned about the porous nature of the walls rebuilt after the 1714 fire, asked the architect Anthony Salvin down to Petworth for his advice.

'My Lord', observed this Victorian practitioner after surveying the spectacle, 'there is only one thing to be done. Pull the whole house down and rebuild it.' Lord Leconfield replied: 'You'd better see the inside first.'

Smoking by Servants in Petworth House strictly prohibited
LECONFIELD.

ABOVE Laying down the law on tobacco.

LEFT The Grand Staircase, decorated with murals by Louis Laguerre for the Duke of Somerset after the fire of 1714 had destroyed the old staircase. The balustrade is by Sir Charles Barry, *circa* 1827.

RIGHT Lumber in an attic room.

In the event, Salvin only rebuilt the south-east part of the house, adding the new entrance and *porte-cochère*. Another of the 2nd Lord Leconfield's building enterprises was the construction of a special greenhouse to grow his own bananas. Once he had discovered, however, that the Petworth fruit tasted 'just like any other damn banana!', as he exclaimed, the greenhouse was promptly destroyed.

This and many other amusing anecdotes about the family are related by his grandson, John Wyndham, who revived the title of Lord Egremont when he was created a peer on the recommendation of Harold Macmillan, to whom he

LEFT The upper reaches at Petworth.

ABOVE The long west front from the park.

was private secretary. In his hilarious book, *Wyndham and Children First*, he describes an occasion during the Second World War when his Uncle Charles, the 3rd Lord Leconfield, out fox-hunting, came across a village soccer match; standing up in his stirrups, he shouted: 'Haven't you people got anything better to do in wartime than play *FOOTBALL*?!'

The 3rd Lord Leconfield appears to have lacked the hospitable instincts of his ancestor, the 3rd Earl of Egremont. James Lees-Milne, who visited him on behalf of the National Trust in the 1940s, recalls Lord Leconfield showing him to the back door of the house which leads straight on to the streets of Petworth town and saying: 'I am told they give you very good snacks there. Put yours down to me.' The tea shop to which he pointed, 'Priscilla's Pantry', had an enormous notice in the window saying '*CLOSED.*'

The Trust duly opened the house to the public, but made the mistake of consulting the art historian Anthony Blunt (not yet unmasked as a traitor) about the display of the collections. With all the cold ruthlessness that made him such a successful spy for Stalin, Blunt re-arranged Petworth's treasures in a deadly museumified manner. It is good to record that the Trust is now stylishly turning the clock back to the warmth and characterful clutter of the 3rd Earl of Egremont and Turner's time.

In doing so, the Trust's experts have the full support and consideration of the present Lord Egremont, who has lent more than 100 paintings for the 're-hang' from his private collection. Max Egremont, who still lives with his wife and family in a wing of the main house, is a distinguished biographer and an original and witty novelist. He writes in the morning, attends to estate matters in the afternoon and works out the plots of his books during long walks in the park, accompanied by a Cavalier spaniel. As most visitors to princely Petworth would agree, one could hardly conceive a more ideal existence.

21

BOUGHTON HOUSE

*I*F THE French influence is easily discernible at Petworth, it is positively overwhelming at Boughton House in Northamptonshire, where Ralph Montagu, later 1st Duke of Montagu, gave the north front the appearance of a French château. Montagu had developed a taste for French architecture and decoration while serving as British Ambassador to King Louis XIV in Paris from 1669 to 1678, and on his return to England set about giving both his London house in Bloomsbury and his country seat near Kettering a touch of Versailles.

As at Petworth, it is not known for sure who was responsible for the designs adopted, but Daniel Marot seems the most likely candidate to have been the mastermind both at Montagu House (the site of the future British Museum) and Boughton – as well as at Petworth. A Huguenot, Marot fled from France to Holland after the Revocation of the Edict of Nantes in 1685, and soon afterwards became architect to William of Orange, who was shortly to become King William III of England. Ralph Montagu, who had a chequered political career, was a close friend of the Dutch monarch and is known to have employed Marot to design a series of painted panels for a room at Montagu House.

Certainly the arcaded north front of Boughton bears a remarkable similarity to an engraving in Marot's published *Oeuvres*. Yet, again as at Petworth, there are some curiously English features in the masonry and joinery of the building, which contrast with the more sophisticated French style of the architecture.

Indeed, a significant element of Boughton's potent charm is how, paradoxically, the place combines French and English features. Beneath the elegant French mask of the north facade lies a characteristically English structure of almost village-like proportions. For instance, an aerial view shows 7 courtyards, 12 entrances and 52 chimney stacks; there are also the traditional 365 windows.

PRECEDING PAGES Boughton: the English 'village' behind the French facade.

LEFT The simple panelling, even in the back corridors, is one of Boughton's special charms.

RIGHT Panelling and portraits.

This agglomeration is explained by the fact that, like so many great English houses, Boughton began life as a monastery. In 1528 Edward Montagu, a Tudor lawyer, acquired the property from St Edmundsbury Abbey and tacked on a manor house to the old Great Hall of the monks.

As Sir Edward rose in power so Boughton became progressively more rambling. Courtyards and wings were added during his nigh-on 40-year tenure. He was knighted in 1537 and two years later appointed Lord Chief Justice of the Court of King's Bench. Then, in 1545, he switched to be Lord Chief Justice of the Common Pleas – 'a descent in honour', as the historian Thomas Fuller noted, 'but an ascent in profit'. King Henry VIII held Montagu in such high esteem that he appointed him one of the executors of his will – a burdensome responsibility as it involved him in the power

struggle over the succession to the throne, and landed him in the Tower of London under 'Bloody Mary'.

However, he survived to retire to Boughton and died in 1567. His memorial inscription in the local church bids him –

> Farewell, O Edward Montagu father of Justice and master
> of the Law, you whom sober skill has nourished and
> wicked knaves of men have feared have lived in the
> ancient manner, a lover of peace and unyielding guardian
> of virtue and scourge of vice...

If subsequent generations of Montagus did not always live in 'the ancient manner', they continued to add courts and wings to the hotchpotch of the ancient manor of Boughton. Substantial additions were made to the south-west corner of the house by Sir Edward Montagu's grandson and namesake, another lawyer.

This Sir Edward was, by all accounts, another honourable figure. 'A man of a plain, downright English spirit', observed Sir Philip Warwick, 'viz of a steady courage, of a devout heart, and a true son of the Church of England.' He was created a peer as Lord Montagu of Boughton in 1621, having shown

LEFT The Great Hall: the central feature of the house. Louis Chéron's painted barrel ceiling of the marriage of Hercules and Hebe was added *circa* 1680, obscuring the ancient hammer-beam roof structure. The panelling of Boughton oak was installed in 1912, when Jan Wyck's portrait of the Duke of Monmouth was brought down from Scotland and installed above the fireplace.

RIGHT The Little Hall, in the oldest section of the house. The children depicted in the painting above the door are those of Charles I, by Weessop, *circa* 1645.

RIGHT Cartoon of the meeting of the two Holy Families, attributed to Giovanni Francesco Penni.

LEFT The staircase, with *trompe-l'oeil* ceiling and walls by Chéron. The wrought-iron balustrade is especially noteworthy.

BELOW A set of Van Dyck miniatures.

himself a staunch supporter of the Stuart doctrine of the 'Divine Right of Kings' – and, incidentally, proposed that the date of the abortive 'Gunpowder Plot', the 5th of November, be kept as a cautionary festival. On the outbreak of the Civil War in 1642 he rallied to the Royalist cause despite his great age, and was promptly seized at Boughton by the Parliamentarians. He died in captivity in London two years later.

The 2nd Lord Montagu wisely kept a low profile at Boughton, but his son Ralph, who succeeded to the title and estate in 1684, decided to make a bigger splash. *The Complete Peerage* is very sniffy about his machinations in Paris, 'when he carried on the disgraceful negotiations which resulted in Charles II being heavily bribed by the French King to secure England's neutrality. It is impossible even now to read his letters... without shame and anger.'

However, the gossipy 17th-century chronicler Spring Macky, while noting that Ralph was 'inclining to fat, of a coarse, dark complexion', conceded that he was 'a good Judge of Architecture and Painting as his fine Pictures at his Houses in Northamptonshire do show. He hath one of the best Estates in England, which he knows very well how to improve.' Macky also recorded that Ralph Montagu was 'a great Supporter of the French, and other Protestants who are drove into England by the Tyranny of their Princes'.

Indeed Boughton is a treasure house of French arts and crafts. The use of mansard roofing was quite new to England, as was the '*parquet de Versailles*' flooring in many of the rooms. The *trompe-l'oeil* walls and ceilings in the staircase hall are by Louis Chéron, and some of the most outstanding pieces of French furniture were given to Montagu by *le Roi Soleil* himself. For instance, in the low pavilion anteroom there is an exquisite writing table by Pierre Gole, decorated with pewter and brass inlay with a border of mother-of-pearl in ebony which was made for Versailles *circa* 1675.

In the Little Hall there are flower studies by Jean-Baptiste Monnoyer, one of many Huguenot craftsmen brought to England by Ralph Montagu. Ralph also bought up and ran the Mortlake tapestry factory between 1674 and 1691; there are several fine examples of its work on display at Boughton.

BELOW The late Duchess of Buccleuch's barrel-ceilinged boudoir.

RIGHT A staircase landing, with *trompe-l'oeil* marbling and bust above the door.

The stables were also given the Versailles treatment and in the park Ralph commissioned a formal layout, involving lakes and canals, from a Dutchman, Van der Meulen. In 1695, some eight years after Ralph began the transformation, Boughton was in a fit state for King William III to be entertained there in splendid style.

To help him pay for all this lavish extravagance Ralph had shrewdly married Elizabeth Wriothesley, widow of the 11th Earl of Northumberland and co-heiress of the immensely rich 4th Earl of Southampton, who owned the Bloomsbury estate in London. After her death in 1690, he then married 'the Mad Duchess' of Albemarle, a widow who was under the impression that she was the Empress of China.

Ralph was made Earl of Montagu by King William III in 1695, and advanced to a dukedom by Queen Anne ten years later – 'a distinction', *The Complete Peerage* insists, 'beyond his merits'. His son John, the 2nd Duke of Montagu, Master General of the Ordnance, was more interested in planting trees than building. He failed to finish his father's great scheme at Boughton – hence 'the Unfinished Wing' – but planted avenues of trees which at one time totalled 70 miles in length. The limes are still in remarkable condition after 250 years, even if the elms suffered heavy losses due to the epidemic of the 1970s.

LEFT & RIGHT Entrance and colonnade.

BELOW Doorbell to the private family quarters.

castle of Drumlanrig in Dumfriesshire from his Douglas cousin, the 4th Duke of Queensberry, in addition to his wife's property of Boughton. It was therefore inevitable that Boughton drifted away from the centre of the stage in the lives of the Montagu Douglas Scotts, as they became called, one of the greatest territorial dynasties in Europe, who owned some 460,000 acres in the 19th century.

Boughton House, largely untouched since 1700, fell into a state of slumber. Fortunately, as so often happens, its apparent neglect proved a blessing in disguise. The late-Georgian, Victorian and Edwardian 'improvers' passed it by, serving only to enhance its almost tangible air of timelessness.

A century and more passed. Then, in the 1920s, the bride of the heir to the dukedom of Buccleuch, Mollie Lascelles, a spirited young lady with consummate taste, fell in love with the sleeping beauty of Boughton. She determined to bring it back to life.

She succeeded triumphantly, harmoniously blending the superb collections of paintings, furniture, tapestries, needlework, carpets, porcelain, arms and silver in a series of simple yet grand panelled rooms. She made Boughton much more than a showcase, however, and ranks with Sybil Cholmondeley at

Houghton as one of the great chatelaines of the 20th century. Mollie Buccleuch's *cavaliere servante,* the writer Alan Pryce-Jones, described her as 'visibly descended from the Lady Bessborough who cut a swathe through London Society two centuries ago; she would have been perfectly at home in the Devonshire House of 1820'.

At Boughton, as Pryce-Jones relates in his memoirs, the Duchess entertained 'not only Ambassadors and Royal Duchesses, but off-beat writers... museum experts; dogged American millionaires, who required a

BELOW The north front, reminiscent of a French château.

RIGHT The face at the window.

nap after luncheon, [and] soon tired of Raphael cartoons, Carlin writing tables and Isfahan carpets'. One of the 'off-beat writers', the aesthete Brian Howard (part model for the character of 'Anthony Blanche' in Evelyn Waugh's *Brideshead Revisited*) drooled: 'I have never been in such a magical place, so full of beautiful things.'

Howard was particularly impressed to find that the linen on his bed bore a strawberry leaf coronet, with 'B.1888' embroidered on the sheets, and to learn that the servants employed the dried leaves of the bitter apple plant, imported from Persia, against moths. There was talk of ghosts at some of the house parties and Winston Churchill complained in 1938 that some presence had been in his room 'taking *exshepshion* to my being there'.

Mollie Buccleuch, widowed in 1973, stayed on at Boughton until her death in 1993. Today, while remaining the home of the present Duke and his family, the house is a focal point for Sotheby's study courses – appropriately enough, in view of its visually unrivalled collections of armour, tapestries, Old Masters, portraits, English and French furniture, Sèvres porcelain, to name but a few – and the estate, in the form of the Living Landscape Trust, is an award-winning pioneer in improving schoolchildren's understanding of the countryside.

What strikes the visitor to Boughton most is the gracious understatement of the architecture and the panelled interiors. Here is a beguiling lesson in the difference between late 17th-century taste and the more flamboyant ostentation that came soon afterwards.

22

CASTLE HOWARD

YORKSHIRE

THE APPROACH to Castle Howard, in Yorkshire, through the Howardian Hills, is probably the most dramatic of all the great houses of England and Wales. The five miles of avenue stretch up and then down before you, punctuated by a series of architectural fanfares – the huge monument to the 7th Earl of Carlisle; the exotic Carrmirr Gate by Nicholas Hawksmoor with its pyramids; the mock-fortified curtain walls and gatehouse by John Vanbrugh; and then the 100-foot Obelisk, marking the intersection of avenue and drive.

The Obelisk has an inscription recording how 'Charles the III Earl of Carlisle of the Family of the Howards Erected a Castle where the Old Castle of Henderskelfe Stood and Call'd It Castle-Howard. He Likewise Made the Plantations in this Park and All the Other Out-works, Monuments and Other Plantations Belonging to the Same Seat.'

The 'Old Castle of Henderskelfe' had only been rebuilt in 1683 but ten years later was gutted by fire. The ambitious young Lord Carlisle, who rose to be First Lord of the Treasury, was determined to build a palatial new pile befitting his grand status. In 1698 he commissioned William Talman, the architect who had worked at Chatsworth (see pages 244-59), to draw up some classical designs but the two promptly fell out. The next year Lord Carlisle took the surprising step of entrusting the design of Castle Howard to someone who had never designed a building before, the playwright John Vanbrugh, an acquaintance at the Kit-Cat Club, a haunt of Whig grandees where 'Van's' wit and style were much appreciated.

Vanbrugh, then 35, had led a somewhat picaresque life. The grandson of a Protestant *émigré* from Ghent, one van Brugg, he was brought up in Chester and commissioned into the infantry; in 1691 he was imprisoned in the Bastille on suspicion of being a spy. After abandoning the military life, 'Captain Van' next enjoyed considerable success as a playwright with his Restoration-style comedies, such as *The Relapse* and *The Provok'd Wife*. Towards the end of the 17th century, Dean Swift noted:

Van's genius, without thought or lecture,

Is hugely turned to architecture.

Although brimful of imagination and confidence Vanbrugh had little idea of how to put his grandiose ideas on to paper, but in the spring of 1699, the same year as he was approached by Lord Carlisle, he met the perfect collaborator in Nicholas Hawksmoor, the best-trained professional architect of his day, who had studied under Wren. Hawksmoor became Vanbrugh's right-hand man and they worked in tandem at Castle Howard and later at Blenheim (see pages 304-315).

Together with Lord Carlisle they set about transforming an unpromising chunk of the North Riding of Yorkshire – 'bushes, bogs and briars' as Vanbrugh put it – into a classical arcadia. The most notable of the many original touches in the design of the main house was a central dome; no private house had had a dome before, though those at St Paul's Cathedral and the Royal Hospital at Greenwich (in which Hawksmoor had a hand) were currently much in the news. Another novel idea was to switch the orientation of the house from the traditional east/west axis, which Talman had favoured, to north/south in order to take advantage of the 'prospects'. On a windy hilltop in the North Riding such a scheme was much derided but , once the house was built, Vanbrugh had the satisfaction of reporting that Lord Carlisle did not need to put one candle, even in the hall, in a 'lanthorn' and that 'all his Rooms, with moderate fires Are Ovens'.

Architectural purists, particularly the Earl of Burlington's Palladian circle in the early 18th century, found fault with Vanbrugh and Hawksmoor's cavalier disregard for the classical niceties. For example, the north front has the Doric Order, the south front, the Corinthian; and the south front has a plain surface above a rusticated basement, whereas on the north front there is a rusticated surface above a plain basement. Vanbrugh, more concerned with the magical dramatic effects and the architectural flow of what Robert Adam later called 'movement', was not bothered about such trifles. Hawksmoor, ever practical, pointed out that the two fronts could not actually be seen together.

ABOVE Portrait by Gainsborough of Isabella Byron, the 'bolter' mother of the 5th Earl of Carlisle, in the Tapestry Room. A great-aunt of the poet, she eloped in 1771 to Paris with the *soi-disant* Baron de Weinhein (*alias* Monsieur Latcher). The union did not turn out well. The side table is George III.

LEFT View from beyond the New River, created by Vanbrugh, to the waterfall and bridge, probably designed by Daniel Garrett in the 1740s. The house is visible on the horizon.

PRECEDING PAGES A wintry view of the garden front from the south-east. Vanbrugh broke all the rules – setting the house on a north/south axis and inserting a dome in the middle of his composition – but carried it off with theatrical style.

ABOVE Flower arranging in the Great Hall, in
front of Bacchus's Niche – one of the earliest
examples in England of the use of scagliola, a
mixture of hard plaster and marble chips.

ABOVE Ancient and Modern: a classical figure contemplates the passing of time.

RIGHT The Long Gallery, one of the interiors designed by C. H. Tatham in 1805. The book-cases, of Norwegian oak, were installed in 1827. The table on the right is 1725, with a Peterhead granite top.

ABOVE Looking up from the Great Hall to the dome, 70 feet above. The dome was destroyed in the fire of 1940 but restored 20 years later by George Howard, who commissioned the Canadian artist Scott Medd to restore Pellegrini's fresco of Phaeton falling from his father's chariot: 'The breathless Phaeton, with flaming hair/ Shot from the chariot like a falling star'.

LEFT The Antique Passage: one of Vanbrugh's ingenious and innovative corridors that were a feature rather than merely a utilitarian part of Castle Howard. The gilded plinths for the antique statuary collected by the Howard family were designed by William Kent.

For all his grandeur Lord Carlisle did not have unlimited funds and building work on Castle Howard, which began in earnest in 1700, proceeded at a sedate pace. By 1714, when the Obelisk was erected, the centre block with its dome, the south front, the east wing and the Kitchen Court were more or less complete, but nothing had been done about the west wing. Ten years later Vanbrugh, becoming understandably impatient, was pleading that the loose stones near the site of the west wing should be used for its foundations.

By this stage, though, Lord Carlisle was more concerned about his 'Out-works'. Vanbrugh's last design at Castle Howard, before his death in 1726, was the Temple of the Four Winds at the end of the grass terrace – another domed affair but on a miniature scale with four Ionic porticoes and carved finials. This exquisite building and Hawksmoor's noble mausoleum, beyond the bridge over the New River, are the highlights of any visit to Castle Howard. Sir Sacheverell Sitwell, in his *British Architects and Craftsmen*, considered them to be 'greater works of art than many of our Cathedrals. They belong to the class of Landscape buildings, and probably, of their kind, they are as beautiful as anything in Europe'.

Horace Walpole, in the 18th century, was no less enthusiastic: 'Nobody had informed me at one view I should see a palace, a town, a fortified city, temples on high places, woods worthy of being each a metropolis of the Druids, the noblest lawn in the world fenced by half the horizon, and a mausoleum that would tempt one to be buried alive; in short, I have seen gigantic palaces before, but never a sublime one.'

Small wonder that in his will the 3rd Earl of Carlisle, who died in 1738 having spent £78,000 on his new seat, made reference to 'Sir John Vanbrugh and Nicholas Hawksmoor with whose performance I am very well satisfied'. Unfortunately Lord Carlisle's son-in-law, Sir Thomas Robinson, who belonged to the Burlingtonian school of Palladian purity, did not share these sentiments. 'Long Sir Tom' (as he was nicknamed) fancied himself as an architect and even during his father-in-law's lifetime did not hesitate to give Lord Carlisle the benefit of his architectural wisdom. The ailing Hawksmoor,

LEFT The Orleans Room is named after the pictures bought from the collection of the Duke of Orleans in 1798 by the 5th Earl of Carlisle (together with the Duke of Bridgewater and Lord Stafford). Over the Adam chimneypiece hangs Feti's *The Music Master* (possibly a portrait of Monteverdi). The *Salome with the Head of John the Baptist*, to the left of the fireplace, came from the collection of Sir Joshua Reynolds.

who died in 1736, had to fend off Robinson's tiresome and pedantic criticisms of the mausoleum design.

With his father-in-law out of the way, 'Long Sir Tom' badgered his brother-in-law, the 4th Earl of Carlisle, to let him complete Castle Howard. It was Robinson who was responsible for the long – in fact, far too long – west wing, finally built between 1753 and 1759. While perfectly handsome, this Palladian exercise does not chime sympathetically with the *sprezzatura* style of Vanbrugh. 'Long Sir Tom' also had the satisfaction of destroying Vanbrugh's two rooms at the end of the south front, including a bow-windowed Cabinet with two painted domes.

Fortunately, before he could do further damage to Vanbrugh's legacy, Robinson's enterprises were curtailed by the death of his brother-in-law and the succession to the earldom of Carlisle of ten-year-old Frederick, whose trustees were not inclined to continue building operations. Frederick, the 5th Earl, was summed up by the elderly Horace Walpole as 'A young man of fashion, fond of dress and gaming, by which he has greatly hurt his fortune, totally unacquainted with business, and though not void of ambition, has but moderate parts and less application.' His gambling debts were not helped by his also standing surety to the bibulous Charles James Fox. Nonetheless he picked up some fine Italian paintings from the Orleans Collection and wrote poetry and plays that were not quite so bad as Lord Byron made out in *English Bards and Scotch Reviewers* ('So dull in youth, so drivelling in his age,/ His scenes alone, had damn'd our sinking stage').

RIGHT An interior view of the burnt-out east wing which was gutted by fire in 1940, when Castle Howard was occupied by a girls' school.

Frederick's main contribution to Castle Howard, apart from the pictures in the Orleans Room, was commissioning C.H. Tatham, in 1805, to finish the interior of the west wing, notably the Long Gallery, the Museum Room and the chapel.

The chapel was originally planned as a columned dining hall. The ceiling was based on the Chapel Royal in St James's Palace. Later in the 19th century the chapel was extensively altered by Lord Lanerton (formerly Admiral Edward Howard), who lived at Castle Howard during the tenure of his brother the 8th Earl of Carlisle, a bachelor clergyman badly affected by sunstroke.

Their nephew George, the 9th Earl, was a talented painter in the Pre-Raphaelite manner and a friend of Sir Edward Burne-Jones, whose designs for the stained-glass windows in the chapel were executed by William Morris. George tidied up some of Robinson's less happy efforts on the west wing but largely left the running of the place to his formidable wife, 'Radical Rosalind', who was a member of the high-minded dynasty of Stanley of Alderley, a staunch teetotaller and an alarmingly illiberal Liberal.

After one unfortunate incident when a drunken guest slipped under the table and the footmen were not sober enough to rescue him, Rosalind banished alcohol from Castle Howard (the wine was actually given away to a hospital, not poured into the lake, as popular history has it) and sacked all the menservants. They were replaced by a redoubtable phalanx of parlour-maids – 'a row of Grenadier Guardsmen in skirts', as one nervous guest described them.

Rosalind rode roughshod – to be more precise, she advocated barefootedness – over the principles of primogeniture and on her death in 1921 bequeathed Castle Howard, according to her feminist principles, to her eldest daughter, Lady Mary Murray. Lady Mary, however, preferred to stay on in Oxford with her husband Professor Gilbert Murray, the Greek scholar, and it passed to a younger brother, Geoffrey Howard.

During the Second World War Castle Howard, like several other great houses (including Chatsworth), was occupied by a girls' school. One night in November 1940 a fire broke out which gutted the entire east and central sections of the south front and destroyed the dome. Molten lead cascaded from the burning dome to the floor 70 feet below. Several sumptuous interiors, including the High Saloon and Garden Hall, with their Pellegrini murals and mirrored walls, were lost.

Vanbrugh's masterpiece was a forlorn shell, seemingly destined for dereliction. The trustees, assuming that Castle Howard would never be lived in again, had begun to sell the contents when Geoffrey Howard's son, George, returned from the war. An expansive, vigorous figure, he confounded all the Jeremiahs and proceeded to move in.

He and his wife, Lady Cecilia (daughter of the 8th Duke of Grafton), opened the house and park regularly to the public from 1952. 'I am used to the public', he would say. 'Indeed I would feel unhappy if I wasn't sharing Castle Howard with people. Anyway it was open from the day it was built; one of my ancestors built an inn nearby so tourists could make an early start on the house in the morning.' A flamboyant personality who took to wearing kaftans in the 1960s and later became chairman of the governors of the BBC and a life peer as Lord Howard of Henderskelfe, he maintained that 'park walls were put up to keep the deer in, not the people out. Privacy is a 19th-century taste: I would be quite happy for people to see me sitting on the loo – provided they were prepared to pay for the privilege!'

The 'Brideshead' view of the south front, with the Atlas Fountain by W. A. Nesfield in the foreground. The fountain dates from the 1850s. Rosalind Countess of Carlisle swept away Nesfield's parterres and replaced them with lawns and hedges.

Nothing daunted, this robust Whig grandee succeeded in restoring the dome 20 years after the fire. He commissioned the Canadian artist Scott Medd to re-create Pellegrini's fresco of Phaeton's fall so that once more the climax of the interior, the Great Hall, is an inspirational *tour de force*, resembling, as Mark Girouard has written, 'a dramatic slice of a Baroque Cathedral inserted into an English house'. The eye feasts on antique sculpture, a rococo chimneypiece (by Bagutti, 1710), frescoes by Pellegrini and iron balustrading by Jean Tijou.

Another of George Howard's outstanding re-creations was the new Garden Hall in the spirit of Vanbrugh with the help of the architect Julien Bicknell and the artist Felix Kelly. Kelly's panels depict imaginary, indeed fantastic, follies that might have been designed by old 'Van' himself. It is a charming conceit, a fitting tribute to Vanbrugh's genius and a permanent reminder of Castle Howard's most recent claim to international fame, as the setting – even star – of Granada Television's lavish film of Evelyn Waugh's romantic novel *Brideshead Revisited*. For the Garden Hall is the room in which we saw Jeremy Irons (as Charles Ryder) dabbing away with his paintbrush at the panels on the wall. Like the narrator of the novel, any visitor to Castle Howard can conclude '*Et in Arcadia Ego...*'

23

BLENHEIM PALACE

OXFORDSHIRE

S URVEYING the ornately baroque palace in Oxfordshire built in honour of the 1st Duke of Marlborough's smashing victory at Blindheim, or Blenheim, in Bavaria in 1704, King George III ('Farmer George', as he was known) muttered that he had 'nothing to equal this'. Indeed there can be little doubt that Blenheim is the greatest palace in Britain, far outstripping those in possession of the Royal Family. Some of its interiors, notably Sir John Vanbrugh's Great Hall and saloon and Nicholas Hawksmoor's library, can vie with the most splendid palace rooms in Europe.

Yet for all that, ever since building operations began on the old royal estate of Woodstock, granted by 'a munificent Sovereign', Queen Anne, to the triumphant Marlborough in January 1705, Blenheim has tended to receive somewhat mixed notices from its visitors. 'That celebrated palace', noted Arthur Young in *A Southern Tour* (1767), 'which has been by some so excessively abused, and so praised by others. The front is a clutter of parts, so distinct that a Gothic Church has as much unity; and withal, a heaviness in each part, which is infinitely disgusting.' That inveterate sightseer considered the palace to consist 'of such innumerable and trifling parts, that one would think them the fragments of a rock jumbled together by an earthquake'.

It is possible that Young's intemperate views and those of another celebrated 18th-century onlooker, Horace Walpole, may have been influenced by the disobliging behaviour of the palace staff. Young recorded the 'excessive insolence of the porters' and earlier, in the 1730s, Walpole – who summed up Blenheim as 'execrable within, without & almost all round' – found the place inhabited only by 'a cross housekeeper and an impertinent porter'.

Again, in the 19th century, Prince Puckler-Muskau was not impressed by 'some very dirty shabby servants' who produced an imperious housekeeper, wrapped in Scotch plaid, to show him 'many chill and faded rooms'. Sir Winston Churchill – Blenheim's most famous son, who was born in the palace in 1874 and was actually heir to the dukedom of Marlborough

ABOVE The front door key of Blenheim with ducal coronet.

LEFT Niche in the Great Hall.

RIGHT The elaborate 'door furniture', or lock, on the front door of the palace, copied from the gates of Warsaw.

until the birth of his cousin 'Bert' in 1897 – maintained loyally that 'the cumulative labours of Vanbrugh and "Capability " Brown have succeeded in setting an Italian palace in an English park without apparent incongruity '. Bert's widow, on the other hand, Laura Duchess of Marlborough, described Blenheim in her memoirs as 'so terribly gloomy... built as a monument not a house to live in'. To her it was always known as 'The Dump'.

To complain of Blenheim's lack of homeliness, however, is rather beside the point. The object, after all, was not only to house a national hero but to celebrate England's newly won supremacy over the French in a blaze of architectural glory that would rival Versailles.

The triumphal mood of Vanbrugh's dramatic composition is everywhere apparent – from the Grinling Gibbons carvings of English lions lacerating French cocks on the towers, to the trophies on the entrance steps underneath the giant portico presided over by Pallas Minerva, goddess of

PRECEDING PAGES The Great Hall: cool, marbled, majestic and 67 feet high. The Duke of Marlborough's banner hangs above the front door.

victory. On the ceiling of the cool marbled Great Hall within, the 1st Duke of Marlborough, kitted out by the artist Sir James Thornhill as a Roman general, shows the Blenheim battle-plan to Britannia. The ceiling of the saloon, painted by Louis Laguerre, shows the victorious Duke driving a chariot through the sky. The Duke's armorial bearings, complete with the black double-headed eagle – the crest of the Holy Roman Empire, of which he was a prince – are displayed over the doors. In the Green Writing Room hangs the tapestry of Marlborough accepting Marshal Tallard's surrender at the Battle of Blenheim; more tapestries of his other great victories adorn the three state rooms.

Naturally, the state apartments at Blenheim were not intended to be 'lived in'; they were for pomp and parade. Vanbrugh, in an innovative and imaginative gesture, designed the east wing for the family to base themselves and they are there to this day. The central block and the west wing were to comprise courtly chambers in which to entertain the Sovereign. Queen Anne, an unlikely (and frankly dumpy) figure to preside over an age of national glory, is commemorated in the library by a Rysbrack statue – commissioned after the Duke's death by Her Majesty's erstwhile friend, the fiery Duchess Sarah. In the chapel, Marlborough, attired in Roman armour, stands atop a monument so noble as to make you wonder whether one is supposed to be worshipping God or the Great Duke. In the park, the Duke, again dressed as a Roman general, surmounts the Column of Victory.

Born plain John Churchill in Devon in 1650, he became one of the very few men in British history to rise from obscure beginnings – well, minor West Country gentry – to a dukedom. He owed his early advancement to the

LEFT Sir Joshua Reynolds's grandiose group of the 4th Duke of Marlborough and his family, which hangs in the Red Drawing Room. The 1st Duke is represented by the statue on the right of the picture. The 4th Duke, a scholarly connoisseur who reigned at Blenheim for nearly 60 years is shown in his Garter robes, holding one of his sardonyx collection. His heir, the 5th Duke, grasps a box containing some of the Marlborough Gems, while the older girls are teasing, with a mask, their little sister Lady Anne, who had declared to Sir Joshua: 'I won't be painted!'

ABOVE Looking across the grand entrance to the family's private apartments in the east wing.

fact that his sister Arabella was a doxy of the Duke of York (later King James II) and, quite possibly, his own romps with King Charles II's tempestuous mistress, Barbara Villiers – who is said to have remarked that young Jack had cost her a good deal of money 'for very little service'.

His subsequent triumphs on the battlefield gave more widespread satisfaction, none more so than at Blenheim on 13 August 1704. The battle scene is faithfully and vividly reproduced on the Blenheim Tapestry which hangs in the Green Writing Room at the palace. Also on show, in the First State Room, are the historic dispatch the Duke scribbled to his wife on the back of a tavern bill and the Blenheim Standard, one of which is sent every year to Windsor Castle on the anniversary of the battle as 'quit-rent' for the Royal Manor of Woodstock, the site of the future 'Blenheim Palace'.

ABOVE RIGHT Detail of one of the gilt tables in the saloon.

LEFT The saloon, which was decorated with murals by Louis Laguerre after Sir James Thornhill was sacked by Sarah Duchess of Marlborough (she thought his painting 'not worth half a crown a yard' let alone the 25 shillings he charged). Laguerre (who inserted himself among the figures depicted) charged £500 for the job. The result is one of the most splendid palace rooms in Europe.

The building of Blenheim Palace remained a source of delight and diversion to the 1st Duke of Marlborough to the end of his life in 1722, even if its long drawn-out labours became the despair of his Duchess. To Sarah, the Duke's love of Blenheim was his 'greatest weakness', but to Jack Churchill, the boy who had never really had a family home, the monumental new palace represented the fulfilment of his dreams. 'Pray press on with my house and garden', he urged Sarah from his campaigning on the Continent, 'for I think I shall never stir from my own home.' In the event, he had little enough time there: he suffered a stroke in 1716, having finally retired from military manoeuvres, and peregrinated from spa to spa. Towards the end of his days, wandering around the palace, he stopped beside a portrait of himself in his prime, painted by Sir Godfrey Kneller (and now hanging in the Green Writing Room). He stood in front of the picture, lost in thought. 'That', he is said to have observed, 'once was a man.'

'About his achievements', wrote Sir Winston Churchill in his biography of his illustrious ancestor, 'he preserved a complete silence... His answer was to be this house'. Sarah Marlborough wanted Sir Christopher Wren as architect (he later designed Marlborough House near St James's in London), but Queen Anne, and the Duke himself, opted for John Vanbrugh.

Following his triumph at Castle Howard (see pages 292-303) for the 3rd Earl of Carlisle, 'Van' had become Comptroller of Her Majesty's Works, and effectively Wren's No.2 at the Board of Works – a remarkable

LEFT Two of the six ocular panels by Colin Gill on the ceiling of the great portico on the entrance front. The blue eyes belonged to the 9th Duke of Marlborough's second wife, the former Gladys Deacon, who in order to help the artist with his task, climbed the scaffolding to show Gill a scarf of the same icy blue as her eyes. The owner of the brown eyes remains a puzzle: they might have been the Duke's first wife, the former Consuelo Vanderbilt.

RIGHT View down the Long Library towards the Willis organ. The 9th Duke of Marlborough converted it into a library from a picture gallery. Vanbrugh originally planned the vast chamber (180 feet long and 32 feet high) as 'a noble room of parade', which Hawksmoor then cleverly broke up into five separate compartments. The plasterwork on the ceiling is by Isaac Mansfield, while the pilasters and doorcases are by William Townsend and Bartholomew Peisley.

ABOVE Detail of a finial on the Willis organ, installed in the Long Library in 1891.

achievement for an amateur. Marlborough knew 'Van' through their joint membership of the Kit-Cat Club, the convivial Whig meeting place off Temple Bar, and they shared an assured, if cultivated, aristocratic outlook. As Robert Adam pointed out later in the 18th century, Vanbrugh understood better than either Inigo Jones or Christopher Wren 'the art of living among the great'.

As the site of the new palace Vanbrugh chose a broad plateau at the southern end of Woodstock Park which appealed to his sense of theatre. In front, to the north, was a dramatically steep valley down to the River Glyme. On the other side of the valley – to be approached by a bridge which, in Lytton Strachey's phrase, 'positively gives one an erection' – were the picturesque ruins of Old Woodstock Manor.

Vanbrugh's design for the palace, which had a superficial similarity to his plan of Castle Howard, provided the main building with wings projecting at right angles, thus forming a forecourt. To achieve a symmetrical effect, Vanbrugh employed his favourite trick of placing four massive towers at the corners of the main block. These give the building the look of a fortress rather than a palace; there is a blending of classical grace and rugged strength, evoking, as Laurence Whistler has observed, 'the Rome and Middle Ages of the soldier, of hard campaigning and triumphant returns'.

In his biography of Vanbrugh's right-hand man, Nicholas Hawksmoor, Whistler points out that 'though Blenheim as a whole is Vanbrugh's, yet there is not one detail of which one could say with certainty that Hawksmoor had not designed it'. Certainly Hawksmoor helped Vanbrugh lay the foundation stone in June 1705 and his hand can be clearly detected in various commissions carried out for Duchess Sarah after the Duke's death – notably in the Triumphal Arch or Woodstock Gate; in the gallery (now the Long Library) and the ceilings of the Green Drawing Room, the Red Drawing Room and the Green Writing Room.

Duchess Sarah had fallen out spectacularly with Vanbrugh, who described her as 'that BBBB old B the Duchess of Marlborough'. The Duchess, for her part, had a withering contempt for the architect's

24

HOUGHTON HALL

NORFOLK

T HE SURVIVAL of historic houses, opined Commander Michael Saunders Watson, the ebullient president of the Historic Houses Association in the 1980s, 'depends on two Ws – the Will and the Wife.' Certainly the role of the chatelaine in the modern age has been of vital importance to the rejuvenation of several great houses, as exemplified by the late Countess of Ancaster at Grimsthorpe (see pages 106-115), Lady Victoria Leatham at Burghley, the present Duchess of Devonshire at Chatsworth, the late Duchess of Buccleuch at Boughton and, by no means least, the late Marchioness of Cholmondeley at Houghton Hall in Norfolk.

When the Earl of Rocksavage, heir to the 4th Marquess of Cholmondeley, married Sybil Sassoon, descendant of banking sheikhs from Baghdad, in 1913, the Palladian palace of Houghton, which had passed to the Cholmondeleys from the Walpole family, was in a bad state. The 3rd Earl of Orford – grandson of the first 'Prime Minister', Sir Robert Walpole, who built the house in the early 18th century – had removed the two sets of grand exterior steps to save the cost of repairs, and sold the fabulous picture collection to the Empress Catherine of Russia to meet his gambling debts in 1779. In the 19th century Houghton was offered for sale to both the Duke of Wellington and the Royal Family, who, strange to relate, respectively preferred Stratfield Saye and 'dear old Sandringham' to this most princely of seats.

Fortunately Sybil Cholmondeley (as she became in 1923 when her husband inherited the marquessate), like her brother the politician and socialite Sir Philip Sassoon, Bt., owner of Trent Park in Middlesex and Port Lympne in Kent, had an eye and a taste for beautiful things and she could afford to collect and conserve. An exotic beauty of the Edwardian era – her striking dark features were captured by John Singer Sargent – she retained an aura of old world luxury into the last dozen years of the 20th century.

At Houghton she carried out a superb restoration of the house, made good the gaps in the collections with paintings, French furniture and porcelain of the highest quality and, above all, replaced the double staircase which rises in front of the basement to the *piano nobile* on the west front. The steps bear a Latin inscription which, freely translated, reads: 'These stairs which were built by Robert Walpole and removed by his grandson were rebuilt for Houghton Hall in 1973 to their original design in memory of George 5th Marquess of Cholmondeley.' There is no mention of 'Sybil fecit', but it was surely this redoubtable and stylish figure who put Houghton back where it belongs as one of the very noblest houses in England and Wales.

The 'original design' to which the inscription refers was drawn up by the Palladian architect Colen Campbell, celebrated as the author of the three-volume *Vitruvius Britannicus*, the first volume of which, published in 1715, probably provided the stimulus for that Palladian champion the Earl of Burlington's interest in architecture. Campbell prepared the plans for

PRECEDING PAGES Houghton: the east front (reminiscent of the palaces of Vicenzo) and the white deer.

RIGHT Classical repose: a corner of the great Stone Hall.

BELOW LEFT The Stone Hall, a 40-foot cube, with balustraded balcony and chimneypiece by Rysbrack.

LEFT The climax of the Houghton interior: the saloon, a case of *Kentissimo* – William Kent at his best. The portrait above the splendid chimneypiece is of Catherine the Great, to whom the 3rd Earl of Orford sold Sir Robert Walpole's great collection of pictures. The Empress gave Lord Orford this portrait in return.

RIGHT Detail of the hunting frieze in the saloon.

BELOW Detail of a chair by William Kent in the saloon. The covering is of Utrecht wool velvet.

RIGHT The Marble Parlour, or dining room, with Bacchic overmantel relief by Rysbrack, and another Kent ceiling.

Houghton in 1721 and subsequently published them in the third volume of *Vitruvius Britannicus* (1725). His client, Sir Robert Walpole, had not only recently become Prime Minister and Chancellor of the Exchequer, but also inherited the family estate of Houghton near King's Lynn on the death of his father.

The Walpoles had held the manor of Houghton since the late 12th century, and were then seated in a Jacobean house. Because of this solid background, the popular image of Robert Walpole tends to be that of a bluff, down-to-earth Norfolk squire growling 'Let sleeping dogs lie.' In reality, apart from his canny political and economic skills, he was a highly cultivated man with a passion for art and architecture. He had begun collecting Old Master paintings before he inherited Houghton, and when his father died in 1720 he determined to create a splendid setting for his pictures.

Having studied Campbell's plans in 1721 he then engaged his protégé, Thomas Ripley, a carpenter who had married one of Walpole's servants, to take charge of the building operations. Ripley, who succeeded Grinling Gibbons as Master Carpenter to the Crown, was not highly regarded by his

peers – Sir John Vanbrugh, seeing his name in a newspaper with 'esquire' attached to it, recorded that 'such a Laugh came upon me, I did like to have Beshit my Self' – but Walpole had great faith in his capabilities. It was Ripley who took the sensational step of using Aislaby sandstone, brought by sea from Yorkshire. While this was regarded as a considerable extravagance and luxury in Norfolk at the time – where Carr stone from Snettisham, used for the stables at Houghton, was easily available – it has proved a master-stroke. For Aislaby stone is extremely durable, and its cool, creamy gold colour has weathered the east wind wonderfully over the centuries.

Campbell's designs for Houghton show four square pedimented towers, but the plans were altered on the advice of James Gibbs to substitute domes with cupolas – a delightfully continental touch. Gibbs was also responsible for the rusticated surrounds to the windows of the *piano nobile* on the east front, which is more opulent and less purely Palladian than the west front.

As the chatty Lord Hervey observed, the 'base or rustic storey' at Houghton was for 'hunters, hospitality, noise, dirt and business', while from the entrance hall (which runs the width of the house), rises the staircase to the *piano nobile,* designed 'for taste, expense, State and parade'. The 'taste and expense' was entrusted to a brilliant team of artists and craftsmen. The sculptor John Michael Rysbrack executed statues of Britannia and Neptune on the east front, and a heroic chimneypiece in the Stone Hall, a 40-foot cube with a stucco ceiling and frieze of *amorini* by the Venetian Giuseppe Artari. Rysbrack also carved the bust of Sir Robert Walpole that can be seen here, as well as the chimneypiece in the Marble Parlour, depicting *The Sacrifice to Bacchus.*

BELOW LEFT Sir Robert Walpole, the first 'Prime Minister' and builder of Houghton, by John Wootton. The portrait hangs in the Stone Hall.

RIGHT A corner of the library.

LEFT Every prospect pleases: looking from the Stone Hall to the Great Staircase.

RIGHT The Great Staircase, which made extravagant use of the newly introduced mahogany. On the walls Kent tells the story of Meleager and Atalanta in grisaille.

The star of the show, however, is William Kent, who Walpole brought to Houghton in 1727. Originally an apprentice to a coach and house-painter in Hull, Kent had been sponsored by Burrell Massingberd and other local squires to study as a 'history painter' in Italy. Here he became known as 'the *Signior*', and eventually acquired a grander patron in the Earl of Burlington and became a passionate Palladian. At Houghton, Kent was responsible for the decoration, including furniture and painted ceilings, and he achieved the most lip-smackingly gorgeous Palladian interior in England and Wales.

Houghton is Kent *in excelsis*. His hand is everywhere. He painted the staircase walls in grisaille and designed the Tuscan pedestal for the bronze gladiator by Le Sueur (given to Sir Robert Walpole by the the 'Architect Earl' of Pembroke, who may also have designed the waterhouse in the park). In the spectacular saloon, he not only painted the deeply coved ceiling in gold mosaic, but designed everything from the gilt sofas and stools to the pier tables and glasses. The ceiling paintings here, in the Marble Parlour, the White Drawing Room, the Cabinet Room and the Green Velvet Bedchamber are all his work.

The Green Velvet Bedchamber also contains one of Kent's most sublime creations, a culmination of all that is exquisite at Houghton – a state bed in sumptuous green velvet with architectural needlework and a giant cockleshell

themselves at Cholmondeley Castle throughout the 19th century, but on the marriage of the 4th Marquess's heir, the Earl of Rocksavage, to Sybil Sassoon in 1913, Houghton was handed over as a wedding present, and a new golden age began.

Sybil's son, Hugh, the 6th Marquess of Cholmondeley, had a special affection for the place and married a Norfolk girl, Lavinia Leslie. In the event, he only survived his mother by a few months and today Houghton is the home of his son, David, the 7th Marquess, who continues to open it to the public.

The attractions range from the pretty white deer in the majestic park, laid out in the 18th century by Charles Bridgeman, to Shetland ponies and heavy horses on show in the stables, and there is a special exhibition devoted to the 6th Marquess's remarkable collection of 20,000 model soldiers. Above all, though, there is the Palladian grandeur of William Kent, Colen Campbell and James Gibbs – not forgetting poor old Thomas Ripley – and a feast of statuary, tapestries, portraits, silk hangings and gilt and mahogany furniture. The sheer quality of Houghton makes superlatives redundant: this is a house which can rival anything in Europe.

25

HOLKHAM HALL

NORFOLK

ONLY A few miles down the road from Houghton in north Norfolk is another even grander Palladian palace at Holkham, the seat of the Coke family, Earls of Leicester, on a scale worthy of a continental sovereign prince. Going from one to the other in the same day, as many visitors do, offers as noble a prospect as can be experienced anywhere in the world.

Holkham is a staggeringly vast monument to the Augustan Whig confidence of the 18th century; even its four pavilions (double the usual number) would, on their own, constitute a sizeable country house anywhere else. Comparisons with Houghton are inevitable, but the mood and atmosphere of the two places are surprisingly different, despite the fact that they are both Palladian in concept, and that they both draw on the genius of William Kent.

Whereas Houghton (see previous chapter) was built of Aislaby stone brought in from outside the county, Holkham was constructed of locally baked yellow-grey brick, which from a distance looks like stone. And whereas Sir Robert Walpole, though an enthusiastic follower of the arts, was essentially an amateur patron who left the details to experts, his friend and neighbour Thomas Coke of Holkham (later the 1st Lord Lovell and 1st Earl of Leicester) was very much a hands-on connoisseur. Indeed, unlike Walpole, he was actually a member of the Earl of Burlington's Palladian group; and had learnt, and collected, much on his six-year-long Grand Tour, during which, in Italy, he met 'the *Signior*', William Kent (then still studying to be a 'history painter' under the patronage of Burrell Massingberd).

The three of them – Burlington, Kent and Coke – formed a committee of taste to plan Coke's new seat at Holkham in the 1720s. The old family home, an Elizabethan manor house, which had been good enough for his ancestor Sir Edward Coke, Attorney-General to Queen Elizabeth I and Lord Chief

Justice to King James I and best known for his dictum 'An Englishman's home is his castle', was demolished as unworthy of this disciple of Andrea Palladio.

Undaunted by a site that was little more than a bare windswept heath overlooking the North Sea – 'a most unpleasant place', in the view of the acidulous Lord Hervey – Coke was set on recreating the glory that was Rome. He began planting trees to improve the landscape but his ambitious building plans hung fire after he lost much of his fortune in the 'South Sea Bubble' speculation of 1720.

Thereafter the creation of Holkham proceeded at a fairly cautious pace; indeed it was only completed in 1762, three years after the death of Coke, or the Earl of Leicester as he then was. By that time the architect Matthew Brettingham (the Elder), who published *The Plans and Elevations of the Late Earl of Leicester's House at Holkham* in 1761, was bragging that it was more or less all his own work. He managed to avoid mentioning William Kent.

Brettingham certainly drew up a plan in 1726 – though emphatically under Coke's direction – which shows the house already thought out in most essentials, but with no attic storey, flanking outside staircases to the portico, and no wings. A later drawing by Kent proposed a south front with a rusticated *piano nobile* not dissimilar to the east front at Houghton, without an attic but with wings.

There is no doubt that the final result – when the foundations were at last laid in 1735 – was the responsibility of Coke himself (by now Lord Lovell), who had definite ideas of how he wished the house to look. The original designs were pared down to achieve a greater purity, even austerity.

The enormous centre block was planned not, of course, for everyday use but for 'state and parade'. The four wings contained, respectively: the kitchen; visitors' rooms; the family apartments (including Kent's delightful library with its Ionic chimneypiece and ingenious ceiling of lozenges and hexagons); and the Corinthian chapel, decorated by James Miller.

It was the family wing, to the south-west, that was the first to be completed, in 1741. Only after that was a start made on the main block.

The most stupendous interior at Holkham – one might almost add 'or anywhere else' – is the Marble Hall, which rises from basement level up through the *piano nobile*, surrounded by no less than 18 fluted Ionic columns, to

ABOVE The curving colonnade of the Marble Hall gallery.

RIGHT The Marble Hall: Derbyshire alabaster, fluted pink Ionic columns, coved and coffered ceiling.

BELOW LEFT The Statue Gallery: antique sculpture and Kent furniture.

PRECEDING PAGES Holkham: the monumental south front.

LEFT View down the *enfilade*.

RIGHT Kent's Long Library, with pedimented bookcases, modillion cornice and lozenged ceiling.

BELOW Looking from the small library down the south *enfilade* to the chapel.

a richly coffered and ornamental ceiling. Originally planned as a 46-foot cube with Corinthian pillars, the hall changed shape in 1757, as it was being built, when Coke altered it to the more oblong design we see today (reminiscent of Lord Burlington's Assembly Rooms at York and Palladio's Egyptian Hall in Rome). The Ionic columns are a crib from the Temple of Fortuna Virili, also in Rome, and the whole space is bristling with classical allusions.

What matters, however, is the overall impression: a vibrant combination of pink, ivory, purple and green, emanating from the Derbyshire alabaster used lavishly for the columns and lower walls. The agriculturalist Arthur Young memorably observed that it all resembled a great bath waiting to be filled.

Up the stairs one comes to a magnificently proportioned progression of state rooms, beginning with the North Dining Room, a restrainedly classical 27-foot cube, which leads, via the octagonal North Tribune, to the Statue Gallery, an enlarged version of Lord Burlington's gallery at Chiswick House. The walls are lined with niches for the antique busts Coke picked up on his Grand Tour, and the gilded furniture, covered in velvet, is by Kent.

Along the garden front we find an *enfilade* of splendid rooms, the saloon in the centre, all hung with crimson Genoese velvet and major pictures, and with gilded ceilings and doorcases. The fine works of art at Holkham include paintings by Claude and Poussin, Rubens's *Holy Family*, portraits by Van Dyck, and tapestries from Brussels and Mortlake.

That the visitor to Holkham can enjoy such a dazzling Coke's tour owes as much to the builder's wife, Lady Clifford in her own right, as to her husband. We learn from the 1st Earl of Egmont's diary that he (Lord Egmont)

was not pleased with the account of my Lord Lovell... as
that my Lady Clifford his wife (who is a very agreeable and
good lady) brought him £80,000 and when he was near undone
in the South Sea year by that vile scheme, recovered his affairs,
has never so much as received of him her pin money; moreover,
half a year after her marriage he resumed his debaucheries,
and continues them with several ladies of quality and fashion.

Indeed, just as Sir Robert Walpole was more cultivated than the traditional picture of a Norfolk squire, so Thomas Coke, 1st Lord Lovell and 1st Earl of Leicester, was more bucolic than his reputation as a scholar might suggest. In one of Sir Charles Hanbury Williams's ballads he is described as 'the oddest character in town/A lover, statesman, connoisseur, buffoon' and in addition to his patronage of the arts he found time to be the leading supporter of cockfighting in his day. It has even been suggested that his death in 1759 might have occurred in a duel with his neighbour, George Townshend.

In any event, his long-suffering widow, who had always kept the building accounts, pressed on with the building of Holkham, where, according to a contemporary account, she lived 'a cankered, solitary life'. Her dissolute only son, who inherited his father's less intellectual qualities, had died in 1753 and she was unwelcoming to the future heir to Holkham, her nephew by marriage, Thomas Coke (*né* Roberts). 'Young man', she told him, 'it is possible that one day you will be master of this house but understand that I will live as long as I can.'

Old Lady Leicester plugged on until 1775 when young 'Coke of Norfolk' (as he was to be known) came into the property. He was to reign at Holkham for some 65 years and made the estate famous through his agricultural improvements.

RIGHT The saloon: crimson Genoese velvet, Old Masters, Kent furniture and the grandest ceiling in the house, by Desgodetz.

BELOW The North Dining Room: classical restraint in a 27-foot cube. The chimneypiece is by Thomas Carter.

A pioneer of the Agricultural Revolution, Coke of Norfolk introduced the four-course rotation – wheat, grass, barley and turnips – and shocked his fellow landowners by farming some of his ever-expanding acreage directly himself. Every summer he would invite hundreds of people to sheep-shearing displays – known as 'Coke's Clippings' – at Holkham, which grew into a national event, the precursor of modern agricultural shows. He also planted about a million trees on the estate.

Coke of Norfolk was MP for the county on and off for nearly 50 years, and revelled in his status as 'the first Commoner of England'. He had no wish to be made a peer or even a knight – 'I had rather remain the first of the ducks than be the last of the geese', he used to say. When the Prince Regent threatened to knight him, Coke of Norfolk is supposed to have exclaimed: 'By God, I'll break his sword.'

After he finally retired from public life in the early 1830s, Coke of Norfolk consented to receive a peerage but promptly dished his chances by referring to His Late Majesty King George III as 'the worst man that ever sat on a throne, that bloody King!' Finally, in 1837, the young Queen Victoria gave him a new creation of the earldom of Leicester.

Like the sensible fellow he was, Coke of Norfolk made few changes to the big house at Holkham, which obviously did not need any. He did, however, commission the sculptor Sir Francis Chantrey to execute a series of busts and reliefs on Whig themes in the Marble Hall – 'the Political Sculpture of Holkham' – including *The Passing of the Reform Bill*. To put matters into the proper Norfolk perspective, the sculptor also carved a plaque depicting the two woodcocks he himself killed with one shot while staying at Holkham in November 1829.

As well as being sculpted by Chantrey, Coke of Norfolk was portrayed in earlier days by Thomas Gainsborough (perhaps the artist's last portrait). We see him in appropriately rustic mode, loading his gun, with a dead bird and frisky dogs at his feet. Another study of the even younger Coke, however, by Pompeo Batoni, reveals an unsuspected side to the great agricultural reformer. In this picture, painted in Rome during young Thomas's Grand Tour, there poses a surprisingly effete young gentleman, togged up in fancy dress and carrying a feathered hat.

BELOW 'Coke of Norfolk' in distinctly non-agricultural mode: a reminder of his dashing youth in Rome by Pompeo Batoni. The picture was commissioned by Coke's lover, Princess Louise of Stolberg (wife of Bonnie Prince Charlie), and her features can be detected on the statue of the Vatican Ariadne in the background.

LEFT & RIGHT The Green State Bedroom, the principal bedroom at Holkham Hall, where Princess Victoria (later Queen) slept in 1835. The picture above the fireplace is Hamilton's *Jupiter Caressing Juno*; the tapestries are from Brussels and Mortlake; the furniture by Kent.

The plot thickens when one examines the face of the stone Ariadne behind 'the handsome Englishman', as Coke was known in Rome in 1773. For the features are those of the lovelorn Princess Louise of Stolberg (wife of the then not-so-Bonnie Prince Charlie), with whom Coke had a fling. It was she who commissioned Batoni to paint her lover. The Princess's broken dreams are symbolized by the fragments at Coke's daintily clad feet. The moral is that it is by no means all sheep and turnips in Norfolk.

Coke of Norfolk died in 1842 and the Holkham tenantry erected a column crowned by a wheatsheaf in his memory, to the designs of W.J. Donthorne. This structure to the north of the house 'answers' the obelisk by William Kent to the south. Coke of Norfolk's son and successor, the 2nd Earl of Leicester, another eminent agriculturalist, added the rather unsightly Victorian *porte cochère* to the entrance front and, even more unhappily, replaced the glazing bars in the windows with plate glass. It is good to record that Viscount Coke, heir of the present Earl of Leicester, has recently replaced the glazing bars, restoring the exterior of Holkham to its true glory.

There is an endearing photograph showing four generations of the family together at Holkham in 1908: the octogenarian 2nd Earl of Leicester, an endearing old buffer with a woolly beard lying recumbent in a carriage, with the future 3rd, 4th and (a babe in arms) 5th Earls standing respectfully beside the conveyance. Between them, Coke of Norfolk, his son (the 2nd Earl of Leicester) and grandson (the 3rd Earl) reigned at Holkham for an amazing total of 165 years.

The present Earl of Leicester lives in South Africa and the 25,000-acre estate is managed by his enterprising son, Eddie Coke, deputy president of the Historic Houses Association and a model landlord who has recently commissioned portraits of his estate staff to hang at Holkham. The house is open regularly to the public and the attractions include a bygones museum, traction engines, a farm centre, a pottery, a deer park and a private beach for visitors. The estate is so vast that Holkham feels like a world apart, and in the centre is the *beau ideal* of the English Palladian movement.

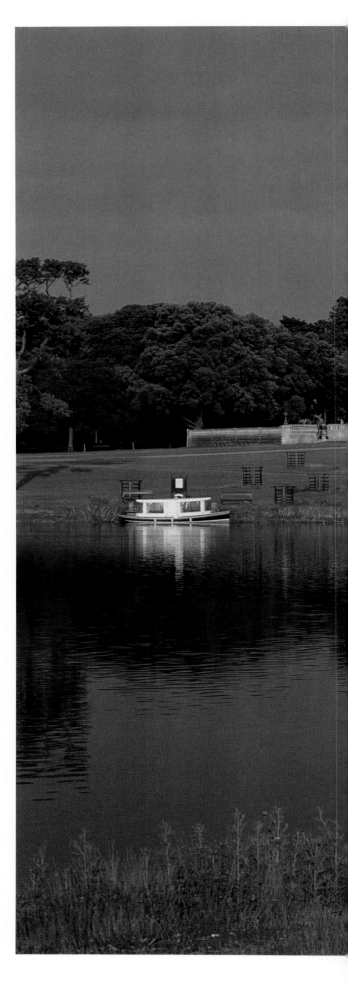

The north front from across the lake on
a high summer evening.

26

SLEDMERE HOUSE

A CONTEMPORARY of 'Coke of Norfolk', and an equally remarkable late 18th-century agriculturalist was Sir Christopher Sykes, 2nd Bt., of Sledmere in the East Riding of Yorkshire. He reclaimed a vast area of the Yorkshire Wolds and transformed a bleak landscape of furze-break and rabbit-warren – where wolves roamed in the 17th century – into a magnificent agricultural estate.

The Sykeses of Sledmere are one of the few dynasties outside the peerage to have risen to territorial magnate status in the 18th century. Moreover they are the only family featured in this book who happen not to have entered the peerage, and some might argue that Sledmere, as the seat of mere baronets, hardly qualifies as a 'great house'. Yet it indubitably contains one of the great Georgian interiors: a magnificent library, with a semicircular vault evoking the baths of ancient Rome, which runs the whole length of the 120-foot-long park front on the first floor.

This spectacular interior has recently been stylishly restored to a glorious vision of blue, white and gold by Sir Tatton Sykes, the 8th and present Bt., with the expert advice of the architect Francis Johnson, a considerable authority on the Georgian period, and the practical assistance of Dobson & Sons of Driffield, nearby. An enthusiastic and knowledgable connoisseur, Sir Tatton has also brought in Alec Cobbe to transform the boudoir into a veritable picture cabinet, Roderick Gradidge to design a new library upstairs and the ingenious team of Royston Jones and Fiona Gray from Norwich to create an intricate doll's-house replica in miniature of the drawing room, with its exquisite Grecian ceiling.

Another of Sir Tatton's sympathetic touches has been the creation of a new formal garden. For the future, he is hoping to build a new orangery and a sculpture gallery. Indeed, a visit to Sledmere affords striking evidence of a new golden age for the country house, in which aesthetic landowners are once again pursuing the practice of beautifying and embellishing their estates.

PRECEDING PAGES Sledmere: the west elevation from across the park. The pediment was added in the 1912 rebuilding.

LEFT Detail of a chimneypiece in the library.

With its model village, and landscape immaculately laid out with belts of beech, 'Capability' Brown parkland, Georgian architecture, paddocks and monuments, Sledmere seems the epitome of a landed estate.

To come across such a well-ordered paradise is all the more surprising in the rugged Yorkshire Wolds, and one has to remind oneself that the whole ensemble was man-made. The Sykeses – rich Hull merchants descended from a long line of merchants in Leeds – came into the Sledmere property through marriage into the Kirkby family, who had acquired the original Tudor manor house in the mid-17th century.

In 1748 Sledmere was inherited by Richard Sykes, Captain of the Hull Volunteers, who decided to aggrandize the place. He demolished the old house and noted in his diary for 17th June 1751: 'Laid the first stone of the new house at Sledmere.' The new house was a two-storey (plus attic), seven-bay affair with a pediment; built of brick with rather heavy stone facings, and approached by two formal avenues from the uncomfortably close village.

During Richard's building schemes, his friend Lord Robert Manners, MP for Hull, wrote to him: 'Till Sledmere is quite completed, the delight you take in that pretty place, I dare say, will not let you stop your hand, but afford you daily employment and the most delightful amusement till all is completed; I hope all your improvements there answer your most sanguine expectations.'

BELOW The spectacular library, recently restored by Sir Tatton Sykes, Bt., and Francis Johnson. Its semicircular vault is based on the baths of ancient Rome.

On Richard's death, without children, in 1761, Sledmere passed to his younger brother Mark, 'Parson Sykes', who was eventually created a Baronet in recognition of his pioneering agricultural work in the Wolds – though, in fact, this was largely the responsibility of his son, Christopher, who took over the Sledmere estate in 1776. Christopher commissioned 'Capability' Brown to lay out a 2,000-acre park, which entailed the demolition of the old village and its rebuilding on the eastern boundary – safely out of sight from the idyllic new landscape.

Sir Christopher (as he became on his father's death in 1783) then set about remodelling his uncle's house. From the mass of surviving drawings it seems clear that he was his own architect and draughtsman, though he consulted both John Carr ('of York') and Samuel Wyatt. The design owed something to the former and rather more to the latter. Two cross-wings were added to the 1750s block, to the north and south, thereby forming an *H*. The house was

Sir Mark Sykes, Bt.'s exotic Turkish Room, designed by David Ohanessian. It is a copy of one of the Sultan's apartments in the Valideh Mosque, Istanbul.

also 'turned round,' so that its main front now faced south. The whole building was encased in Nottinghamshire stone, and a service court was constructed to the north.

The new building work began in 1786 and the whole shell was completed by about 1790. Whereas the core of the house, Richard Sykes's 1750s block, had been slightly old-fashioned – harking back to a Queen Anne style – the remodelling was in the van of fashion: neo-classical, impressively austere and anticipating the later work of the Wyatts with its recessed triple-windows.

The interior was far from austere and even more impressive, thanks to the efforts of the plasterer Joseph Rose, who had previously worked for Robert Adam at Kedleston, Harewood (see next chapter) and Syon. Sir Christopher met Rose, a fellow Yorkshireman, in 1789 and the next year the great craftsman began an association with Sledmere which lasted until Rose's death in 1799. Besides designing and executing all the plasterwork, he took a hand in all the interior details – from designing rooms to ordering furniture, upholstery and wallpapers. Patron and plasterer enjoyed a warm relationship, as is evident from their letters, and his self-portrait in the library at Sledmere is shown to visitors with a special pride.

The library was originally planned by Sir Christopher as a gallery. Then he decided to combine it with a book room so as to accommodate his growing collection of rare volumes. It was planned and executed on a monumental scale. 'It is', John Cornforth, the architectural historian, has written, 'as if recollections of the Baths of Caracella [*sic*] and Diocletian have been combined with those of Renaissance galleries of the Palazzo Farnese and Villa Madama looking out over formal gardens, but here terraces and fountains are replaced by the amphitheatre of Brown's landscape.'

Sir Christopher's son, Sir Mark Masterman Sykes, 3rd Bt., enhanced his father's book collection and in the early 19th century the extent of the Sledmere library was being compared to that at Chatsworth and Longleat. The bibliographer Thomas Dibdin noted in *Bibliomania* (1809) that it contained 'Editions Principes, tall copies, rare specimens and uniques.' The treasures included a perfect two-volume Gutenberg Bible of *circa* 1450 (from the collection of Cardinal Mazarin) and the only known specimen of Swaynham and Pannartz's *Livy* (Rome, 1469).

Unfortunately, however, these and some 2,690 other volumes from the Sledmere library were sold in 1824 by Sir Mark Masterman Sykes's brother and heir, Sir Tatton Sykes, 4th Bt., who found his favourite pack of hounds in desperate need of financial assistance. 'Old Tat' (as he was known) was a legendary sportsman, once described as one of the three sights of Yorkshire along with York Minster and Fountains Abbey, and treated the library as a place for exercise rather than study. He would rise at 5.30 a.m. and walk three or four miles – up and down, down and up, up and down – the length of the library before breakfasting off a basin of fresh milk and an apple or gooseberry tart, accompanied by lumps of mutton fat, occasionally supplemented by a glass of stout and cream.

Although Old Tat reigned at Sledmere until 1863, he retained a robust 18th-century outlook on life. His eight children were made to rise at dawn, take cold baths, endure spartan conditions (his six daughters all slept in one small room) and submit to frequent applications of the paternal whip. He devoted his energies to agriculture (completing the agricultural development of the Wolds), the breeding of racehorses and the discovery of bone manure.

As his descendant Christopher Simon Sykes put it in his anecdotal family history, *The Visitors Book*, Sir Tatton 'had an ability to treat all men as his equals, to make friends of servants, of farmers and cattle-drovers, stone-breakers and quaint rural or sporting characters, without in any way sacrificing his dignity'. When he died his groom observed: 'Aye, whya, there may be manny mair Sir Tatton Sykeses, the more the better, but there'll nivver be another Sir Tatton.'

Certainly the next Sir Tatton (the 5th Bt.) was of a very different stamp: a flower-hating hypochondriac addicted to milk puddings and prone to clad himself with half a dozen overcoats and two pairs of trouserings for good measure. Once when he wanted to cool down in a train, he removed his shoes and socks and stuck his feet out of the window. This Sir Tatton sold most of the horses from the family stud and advertised that he could not be responsible for his wife's debts.

Meanwhile, there had been few changes to the late Georgian house – apart from the sale of the books – until, in May 1911, a disastrous fire broke out early one morning and raged for nearly 18 hours. It destroyed the inside of the building, leaving only the four outer walls, the dairy and the laundry intact.

Sir Tatton was apprized of the conflagration as he was tucking into one of his beloved milk puddings. 'First', he said, 'I must finish my pudding, finish my pudding...'. Later, as he surveyed the scene of devastation, he was heard to observe: 'These things will happen, these things will happen...'.

What happened next was the most extraordinary aspect of the Sledmere story. From 1912 onwards the gutted building was splendidly restored by the York architect Walter Brierley (who had succeeded to Carr of York's practice) and Dobsons of Driffield, the local firm of builders.

Happily Rose's drawings for the decorative plasterwork, as well as a set of early Victorian watercolours of the interior, were rescued from the blaze and a brilliant re-creation was achieved. Furthermore the salvage team from the village were so successful in their efforts that almost all the contents were removed unharmed, even including such fixtures as doors and bannisters. The pattern of the destroyed carpet in the library was later, remarkably, to be reproduced in parquetry on the floor.

Faithful and sensitive though Brierley's late Georgian restoration work was, Sledmere also inevitably acquired an opulent feel of the Edwardian age – and it is emphatically none the worse for that. There is an intoxicating whiff of early 20th-century baroque to beef up the delicate Adam-Revival style. Sir Mark Sykes, 6th Bt., who succeeded his eccentric father in 1913, evidently took a close interest in the proceedings.

A man of delightful character and all-round brilliance, Sir Mark was a traveller in the Near East, an expert on the Ottoman Empire, a writer and a witty cartoonist. He was a Tory politician but had an equally strong sense of aristocratic duty, and a deep and practical concern for the under-privileged. During the First World War he exercised a decisive influence on Britain's Near Eastern policy, and seemed destined to become one of his country's leaders, when, at the age of 39, he fell victim to the influenza epidemic of 1919.

By way of a memorial to Sir Mark, there is a wonderfully exotic Turkish Room at Sledmere – one of the most unusual interiors in any great house. It was designed for him by an American artist, David Ohanessian, and is a copy of one of the Sultan's apartments in the Valideh Mosque in Istanbul. The tiles were made in Damascus, under Ohanessian's supervision.

Of Sir Mark's two elder sons, Richard succeeded to the baronetcy and maintained Sledmere in fine hospitable style, whereas Christopher became an author and biographer of Evelyn Waugh. Christopher's great-uncle and

The south front on a frosty Wolds morning, as seen from the Castle, a folly farmhouse on the estate.

namesake, a minor politician, had had the misfortune to become a butt of Albert Edward, Prince of Wales, who discovered, when he poured a glass of brandy over his friend's head, that Christopher would try to maintain his dignity when the target of royal 'practical jokes' – 'As Your Royal Highness pleases', was his only reaction.

Today Sledmere is open regularly to the public and the attractions include an exceptional series of portraits from Elizabethan times to the present day (with works by George Romney, Sir Thomas Lawrence and Sir Francis Grant among them), sets of 'Chinese Chippendale' chairs, Louis XVI furniture and a tea-table of Canton enamel. There is also a pipe organ which is played for the enjoyment of visitors.

27

HAREWOOD HOUSE

RICHARD Sykes of Sledmere was one of the 'Adepts' consulted by Edwin Lascelles of Harewood in the late 1750s, when he decided to build a palatial new seat on the Wharfedale estate in the West Riding that his father, Henry Lascelles, had bought in 1739 with his newly acquired fortune from the West Indies. 'The first step, I am told', wrote Edwin to his fellow Yorkshireman, 'is to provide the main materials; and wood and iron being of the number, I flatter myself I shall learn from you the lowest price of the latter.' Sykes advised him to lay in stocks of those materials in case they became scarce owing to the war with France.

Henry Lascelles, who came from a long-established Yorkshire family, had died in 1753, leaving his son the adjoining estates of Harewood and Gawthorpe, where he had made his home in the Old Hall (once owned by the ill-fated Earl of Strafford, executed in 1641). Edwin wanted a grander seat to match his plutocratic inheritance, and chose as its site the south-facing hill slope overlooking Gawthorpe Old Hall and the sweep of countryside beyond. He favoured a Palladian pile with a portico overlooking the valley, and eventually commissioned the local architect John Carr of York to draw up the plans, after considering the ideas of Sir William Chambers from London.

While Carr was engaged in building stables for the new house in 1759, Lascelles showed the York architect's drawings to Robert Adam, the ambitious young Scot, fresh from his neo-classical studies in Italy. Adam proposed various modifications without disturbing Carr's elevations. 'I have thrown in large, semi-circular back courts with columns betwixt the house and wings', he wrote to his brother James, also an architect. 'It affords me the greatest pleasure', replied James Adam, 'that you have tickled it up so as to dazzle the eyes of the squire.'

Lascelles, however, was not the sort of man to be easily dazzled, and compromised on the design of the exterior between Carr's and Adam's ideas.

The interior, though, was left largely to Adam and the results were indeed dazzling – all the more admirable in view of the restraints that the gritty Yorkshire tycoon placed on his designer. 'I would not exceed the limits of expense that I have always set myself', he admonished Adam. 'Let us do everything properly and well, *mais pas trop.*'

The exterior was finished in local yellow stone in 1765, the decoration by 1772, when 'Capability' Brown submitted plans for enlarging the lake and surrounding it with plantations artfully dotted around on the slopes. Gawthorpe Old Hall was duly demolished and Edwin Lascelles moved into the new house. To make his furniture, Lascelles chose another local man – by then established as an 'upholder' in London – the great Thomas Chippendale from Otley.

The combination of all these glittering talents – Carr of York, Adam, Chippendale and Brown – made Harewood into a great house *par excellence.* Watercolours by Thomas Girtin, Turner and John Varley record something of the original building's delightful charm. Josiah Wedgwood depicted it on an ice-pail made for Catherine the Great. Royalty – including Catherine's grandson, the future Tsar Nicholas I – flocked to admire it in the flesh.

Yet, alas, the Arcadian ideal did not appeal to early Victorian taste. In 1843 Sir Charles Barry, architect of the new Houses of Parliament, was commissioned to remodel the house in a rather heavy-handed Italianate style, which involved adding a storey for bedrooms and a massive balustrade, the loss of the portico and the installation of elaborate terraces with fountains.

Barry's clients were the 3rd Earl of Harewood and his redoubtable Countess, formerly Lady Louisa Thynne from Longleat. The builder of the house, Edwin Lascelles, had been created Lord Harewood in 1790 but as he was childless the barony died with him and the estate passed to a cousin, Edward Lascelles, who was elevated to an earldom. Edward's son, known as 'Beau' Lascelles, was the spitting image of the Prince Regent, who was not amused when somebody once tapped the royal shoulder with the hearty greeting, 'Ha, Lascelles, how is it?'

When Louisa took up residence in 1841 she found a house virtually unaltered since Edwin's day. She resolved to bring it up to date. Piped water and all manner of modern conveniences were introduced, including batteries of water closets, with mahogany seats for the quality and oak for the servants. A central heating system was installed whereby hot air emerged through stone grilles in the floors.

Louisa's husband, the 3rd Earl of Harewood, died from a fall out hunting in 1857. The 4th Earl, who married a daughter of the 1st Marquess of Clanricarde and installed gas at Harewood, and the 5th Earl, who married a Bridgeman and installed electricity, were also both ardent fox-hunters, and it was not until the time of the 6th Earl that there were further significant changes to the collections at Harewood.

The 6th Earl was able to make these changes largely because of a curious incident in a London club during the First World War. Then styled Viscount Lascelles and serving in the Grenadier Guards, he was on leave in 1916 and spotted his disreputable great-uncle, the 2nd Marquess of Clanricarde, skulking in a corner. As a rule Lord Clanricarde's relations gave the old boy a wide berth, not least because he stank to high heaven. A white-bearded, down-at-heel figure, he was frequently mistaken for a tramp and was reputed to dine off the dustbins of Piccadilly. Indeed he was a notorious miser and treated his Irish tenants disgracefully – though he was also a collector of fine paintings.

PRECEDING PAGES The newly restored, 77-foot-long gallery at Harewood, a triumphant combination of Adam, Chippendale and Old Masters. The mythological paintings in the ceiling are by Biagio Rebecca.

BELOW The garden front from across the park.

However, out of manners, Harry Lascelles went to sit with his great-uncle for half an hour before lunch. A few months later Lord Clanricarde died, and when his will was published it was discovered that he had bequeathed most of his £2.5 million fortune, the derelict Portamac Castle in Co. Galway and his collection of Italian and Flemish paintings to his great-nephew.

Suddenly young Lascelles was extremely rich. He shared his great-uncle's love of pictures and proceeded to put his legacy to magnificent use in buying a superb series of Italian masterpieces, including works of the Florentine Renaissance and from the Venetian school. There are Madonnas by Bellini and Catena, a St Jerome by Cima and portaits by Titian, Veronese and Tintoretto. The collection grew to be one of the finest in private hands in England and Wales.

ABOVE, ABOVE LEFT, BELOW LEFT & FAR RIGHT
Details of the gallery, as re-organized by Alec
Cobbe to show off the best things at Harewood
to their greatest advantage. The Chippendale
furniture here is probably the finest ever made in
England. Besides the exquisite marquetry and
gilding, he also made the pelmets, the pier
glasses and many of the picture frames.

In 1922 Harry Lascelles married Princess Mary, who was to become the Princess Royal, the only daughter of King George V; and seven years later succeeded to the earldom of Harewood and to the Harewood estate. The house, which had been a convalescent hospital during the First World War, needed extensive renovation and restoration, but the new Lord Harewood soon had it in fit shape for a princess.

The Princess Royal filled the rejuvenated gardens with new flowering trees and shrubs, and Harewood was entering a halcyon era when the Second World War broke out. The house again became a hospital, and the family moved into the east wing. The estate provided large amounts of timber and food for the war effort.

Soon after his return from the war – and a spell in the Nazis' prison fortress, Colditz Castle – the Harewoods' elder son, George, found himself faced with a daunting inheritance. On the death of his father in 1947 the estate had to be reduced from 20,000 to 7,000 acres in order to meet the exorbitant death duties, and shortly afterwards Harewood was obliged to

LEFT Adam's bold decoration of Carr's grand entrance hall. The plasterwork was by Joseph Rose.

RIGHT The Spanish Library, so named because of its wall-covering of Spanish leather, installed by the 6th Earl of Harewood to hide Victorian wall-paintings. The library steps are by Chippendale.

enter the 'stately home industry'. It did so to such good effect that soon upwards of 300,000 visitors a year were arriving to see not only the house and grounds but also such attractions as a bird garden, exhibitions and shops, and to avail themselves of restaurants and adventure playgrounds.

Lord Harewood is a great believer in the need to involve young people in the preservation and conservation of country houses and in 1972 established an education centre at Harewood. The number of school parties visiting the house and estate grows every year, and Harewood has won two Sandford Awards for Heritage Education from the Heritage Education Trust, which is now based in Yorkshire.

Somehow Lord Harewood has found the time, in addition to running Harewood and its estate, to be artistic director of the Edinburgh and Adelaide Festivals, and to manage the English National Opera. He developed his remarkable knowledge of music while incarcerated by the Germans as a prisoner of war.

'It's very odd about George and music', observed his uncle, the Duke of Windsor (formerly King Edward VIII). 'You know, his parents were quite normal – liked horses and dogs and the country.' In reality there is nothing abnormal about Lord Harewood; in the best traditions of the *uomo universale* he is equally happy in the world of opera as of sport and games (for example, he has been president of the Football Association).

He and his second wife, the former Patricia Tuckwell from Sydney, share a passionate commitment to the arts, and in the last few years they have carried out a sensational restoration at Harewood which has brought out the house's great qualities to the full. The aim has been to turn the clock back to the heyday of Edwin Lascelles, Adam and Chippendale.

Much as one admires Sir Charles Barry for his palazzo-style gentlemen's clubs in London, and for the Houses of Parliament and Highclere (see pages 384-95), some of his remodelling work at Harewood in the 1840s can only be regretted. The Harewoods have re-introduced a series of new wall coverings in keeping with the schemes devised by Adam and Chippendale; ceilings and mirrors have been cleaned or repainted; and pictures extensively rehung.

ABOVE The dining room, by Sir Charles Barry. The furniture is Chippendale; the chairs have unusual curved seats. The portrait over the fireplace is of the late Princess Royal, Countess of Harewood, by Sir Oswald Birley.

BELOW A detail of the dining room, showing an outstanding Chippendale sideboard and wine cooler.

Beginning with the repainting of the Music Room, with its roundels by Angelica Kauffmann, the Harewoods then brought in Alec Cobbe, whose phenomenal 'eye' has enlivened so many great houses in modern times, to re-hang what had been the Green Drawing Room but is now known as the Cinnamon Drawing Room. Silk for the walls was specially woven in France, the ceiling was cleaned, and the room now contains the work of major English artists such as Reynolds and Gainsborough. The Rose Drawing Room, which has a carpet by Adam, has also received the Cobbe treatment, but the climax of the interior is the Long Gallery.

This great room is now once again everything Adam dreamed of, and a good deal more besides. Adam's chimneypiece, which Barry had shifted to the dining room, surrounded by 19th-century portraits (the best being Sir Francis Grant's study of the 3rd Earl of Harewood and his determined Countess, Louisa), has been reinstated in the centre of the gallery's east wall. The main windows opposite are once more adorned by pillars and pilasters.

Yet this is far from being a merely academic 'Adamesque' revival. For the gloriously spacious gallery – which completely fills one pavilion of the house and almost attains the proportions of a triple cube, 77 feet long – also shows

RIGHT The Cinnamon Drawing Room is dominated by the two Reynolds portraits of Lady Worsley (left) and Edwin Lascelles, 1st Lord Harewood (above the fireplace), who is shown surveying his estate.

BELOW Detail of a console table, supported by four gilded goats' heads.

The terraces and the garden front,
showing Barry's heavy balustrade.

off to amazing advantage two of Harewood's most outstanding features: the Italian masterpieces collected by the 6th Earl and a veritable phalanx of Chippendale mirrors, two of them newly discovered and re-assembled.

The idea of concentrating the great collection of Italian pictures in one place came from Alec Cobbe, who has masterminded the complete renovation of the gallery. Certainly these walls were designed for pictures, and it makes excellent sense to hang the best ones in the best room under a lofty ceiling featuring mythological paintings by Biagio Rebecca.

As for Chippendale's furniture on display at Harewood, the superlatives are inadequate. Sufficient to say that here the visitor will find probably the finest furniture ever to be made in England – from pelmets and picture frames to marquetry and gilt side tables, rosewood and ormolu, inlaid satinwood and all the rest of it. The Younger Chippendale also chipped in with gilded side tables and 'Egyptian' tables.

The plasterwork throughout the house is the work of Joseph Rose of York and William Collins. And to enhance the decorative splendours there is Sèvres and Chinese porcelain.

Having so successfully answered the conflict of taste between Robert Adam and Sir Charles Barry in the gallery and elsewhere, Lord Harewood still poses a bold challenge to the visitor in the entrance hall, which is dominated by Jacob Epstein's massive naked *Adam* (from the Garden of Eden, rather than Scotland), carved from a single piece of alabaster. Whether or not this ape-like apparition contributes to Robert Adam's notions of unity or design must be left to the visitor's viewpoint – though the statue itself leaves little to the imagination.

28

KEDLESTON HALL

DERBYSHIRE

W HEN Doctor Johnson and James Boswell visited Kedleston Hall in Derbyshire in the autumn of 1777, the sage's biographer was struck by the magnificence of Robert Adam's building (finished a dozen years earlier for Sir Nathaniel Curzon, 1st Lord Scarsdale), delighted with the extensive park and filled with 'a sort of respectful admiration' for the number of old oaks. 'One should think', said Boswell, 'that the proprietor of this must be happy', to which Dr Johnson replied: 'Nay, Sir, all this excludes but one evil – poverty.'

In fact, the 1st Lord Scarsdale was not a particularly rich man (his income of about £9,000 a year only just placed him in the 'magnate' class above that of the squirearchy) and the building of the palatial Kedleston overtaxed his resources. Another contemporary observer, Horace Walpole, remarked that it was 'too expensive for Lord Scarsdale's estate'. Robert Adam's masterpiece is certainly worthy of a duke; indeed it was used as the seat of 'the Dukes of Broughton' in the BBC television series *Nanny*.

The Curzons have owned the Kedleston estate for nearly 900 years, the proud family motto being 'Let Curzon holde what Curzon helde'. In the closing years of the 17th century Sir Nathaniel Curzon, 2nd Bt., whose father had been created a baronet by King Charles I, pulled down the old manor house here and replaced it by a red-brick building to the design of Francis Smith of Warwick.

Sir Nathaniel's elder son, John, considered enlarging Kedleston shortly before his death in 1727 to the designs of James Gibbs, architect of All Saints, Derby (now the Cathedral) nearby, but the 4th Bt. did not proceed with the plans. It was left to the 5th Bt., another Sir Nathaniel, who inherited Kedleston in 1758, to aggrandize the family seat.

Young Nat, who had been on a somewhat truncated Grand Tour and collected paintings, wasted no time in putting his ideas into practice. A fervent admirer of Palladio and of the Earl of Leicester's monumental new pile at Holkham, he had Lord Leicester's architect and builder Matthew Brettingham up to Derbyshire within a month of coming into his patrimony.

The red-brick house, old stables and outbuildings were swept away, as was the village in front of them. The plans Brettingham drew up followed the familiar Palladian pattern: the *piano nobile* of the central block would be for state and parade and as a showcase for the owner's works of art; the pavilions would contain the family's living quarters and the kitchens and offices.

Brettingham and Curzon envisaged four pavilions, as at Holkham: the north-east for the family, the north-west for the kitchens, and the two southern ones for the chapel and the stables respectively. As it turned out, neither of the two southern pavilions was built.

Brettingham began work on the family pavilion – which remains the residence of the present Lord and Lady Scarsdale to this day – in 1759, but by this time Sir Nat was already having second thoughts about his choice of architect. Perhaps he was realizing that 'Brett's' own high opinion of himself – it was he who, quite unjustifiably, claimed all the credit for Holkham – did not measure up in reality.

PRECEDING PAGES Kedleston: the south front, illustrating Robert Adam's ideas of 'movement' in architecture.

RIGHT The promenade through the drawing room, where James Paine's alabaster Venetian window was 'improved' by Adam.

BELOW Adam's atrium: the Marble Hall, 67 feet by 42 feet and 40 feet high. The floor is of local Hopton Wood stone inlaid with Italian marble; the huge Corinthian columns (25 feet high) are of veined local alabaster. The plasterwork is by Joseph Rose and his team.

James Paine arrived on the scene to tackle the kitchen pavilion and also to start work on the two northern quadrants, and the eastern end of the main block, with its hexastyle portico reminiscent of Colen Campbell's Wanstead in Essex (demolished in the 1820s). Poor Paine, however, was overtaken by fashion, of which Sir Nat was a keen follower. Palladian architecture and rococo decoration were now being outstripped by neo-classicism.

First Sir Nat had toyed with the idea of interiors by James 'Athenian' Stuart, but then he was introduced to Robert Adam, an ardent enthusiast of the new style. Adam showed Curzon some of the drawings he had made in Rome, and reported back to his brother James how the potential client was

> struck all of a heap with wonder and amaze and every new drawing he saw made him grieve at his previous engagement with Brettingham. He carried me home in his chariot about three and kept me to four seeing said Brett's designs, and asking my opinion. I proposed alterations and desired he might call his own fanceys.

Initially, though, Adam was only brought in to design the buildings of the park – a ravishing collection including the cascade bridge over the lake, the boathouse and the fishing house. By the spring of 1760, however, the pushy young Scot had assumed control of the whole building operation.

On the north, or entrance, front, Adam had little option other than to retain the main features designed by Brettingham and Paine, but he managed to make the central portico more dramatic. As the Marble Hall within was to be top-lit, he arranged for the planned windows to be replaced by niches and medallions in the manner of a Greek or Roman temple.

Although this front has a monumental grandeur, it is the garden, or south, front that is much more exceptional. This, of course, is entirely Adam's work. As a central feature he drew on the inspiration of the Arch of Constantine in Rome, combined with the low, stepped dome of the Pantheon.

This brilliant design gives the south front an uncanny feeling of what Adam called 'movement'. As he put it in his *Works in Architecture*, here we see 'the rise and fall, the advance and recess with other diversity of form in the different parts of a building, so as to add greatly to the picturesque of the composition'. Even though Sir Nat's money ran out before the flanking corridors and southern pavilions could be added, Adam's garden front is a thrilling piece of architecture.

Inside, Adam's hand is detectable everywhere, right down to the design of the inkstands. The celebrated Marble Hall, however, is not as pure Adam as is popularly believed: the fluting of the alabaster columns was done against his advice and the stucco ceiling is not one of his own. Beyond the Marble Hall comes Adam's Saloon, a circular Roman temple with a lofty coffered dome. To the left are the three rooms devoted to music, painting and literature, the paintings inset into the walls as Sir Nat and Adam arranged them; and to the right the Great Apartment.

Of all the rooms at Kedleston, the dining room seems the purest Adam. Horace Walpole considered this, 'the Great Parlour', 'in the best taste of all'. The richly decorated ceiling is based on one in the Palace of Augustus in the Farnese Gardens, and the marble chimneypiece by the Danish sculptor Michael Spang has suitably festive figures of Ceres and Bacchus.

The delicacy of Adam's work at Kedleston is a joy to behold. What particularly lifts the spirits is that it seems all of a piece: house, contents, gardens and park combine to form a splendid Georgian ensemble, with the old parish church adding a reassuringly intimate touch.

ABOVE Detail of door furniture.

BELOW Detail of an abandoned mermaid, sporting herself on a sofa in the drawing room.

ABOVE The sofas in the drawing room were described by Horace Walpole as 'settees supported by gilt fishes and sea gods absurdly like the king's coach'. They were based on a design by Adam but altered in execution by the cabinet-maker John Linnell.

The central panel on the south front records, in Latin, the completion of the building in 1765 and the dedication of Lord Scarsdale (as he had become in 1761) 'for his friends and himself'. This nicely illustrates Sir Nat's hospitable nature, but his generosity and extravagance in building and furnishing such a great house within barely half a dozen years left his descendants a difficult inheritance to maintain.

In the 19th century the successive Lords Scarsdale, notwithstanding their title, their ancient name and their magnificent palace were really 'just ordinary country gentlemen', as their descendant, the great George Nathaniel Curzon, put it. Very few alterations were made to the house in that time and the Kedleston of George Nathaniel's childhood had the atmosphere not so much of a palace as of a parsonage, for his father, the 4th Lord Scarsdale, was in Holy Orders.

George Nathaniel – traditionally portrayed as a 'Most Superior Person' – grew up far from the great world of affairs which, through his own brilliance and his marriage to a rich American heiress, Mary Leiter, he afterwards attained. He became 1st Marquess Curzon of Kedleston, Viceroy of India and Foreign Secretary, and would actually claim, not without some truth, to be a self-made man.

When he went out to India as Viceroy, Lord Curzon is said to have had the remarkable resemblance between Government House, Calcutta, and Kedleston drawn to his attention. The story goes that Curzon replied –

making good use of his much-mimicked Derbyshire short '*a*' – that whereas the pillars at Government House were of lath and plaster, those at Kedleston were of *alabaster*.

Curzon was a connoisseur of art and antiques and added many exotic items to the Kedleston collections from his travels in the East. The Indian Museum in the old 'Tetrastyle Hall' at Kedleston includes a pair of Indian ivory thrones, Chinese bronzes and enamels, Tibetan and Nepalese metalwork, Burmese lacquer and memorabilia from the Delhi Coronation Durbar of 1903.

The very masculine Smoking Room is another interior evoking Lord Curzon's time at Kedleston. It was formed from three rooms previously under the sway of the housekeeper, Mrs Wilson, who was apparently most disgruntled at being shunted off to the kitchen pavilion.

A pioneering conservationist, Lord Curzon restored and redecorated his beloved family seat with exemplary care. However, he had little enough time to enjoy it as he only succeeded his father in the property in 1916 and died in 1925, broken by his inexplicable failure to become Prime Minister in succession to Bonar Law.

Curzon was a founder member of the National Trust and bequeathed Tattershall Castle in Lincolnshire and Bodiam Castle in Sussex, both of which he had bought and restored, to the Trust. He had also helped to restore the Elizabethan Montacute House in Somerset, which later passed to the Trust.

LEFT The top-lit Great Staircase, finally finished to Adam's designs by the great Lord Curzon in the 1920s. The plaster decoration was by Jackson & Co.

RIGHT The curving 'Family Corridor', hung with Curzon portraits.

The marquessate and an earldom became extinct on his death, but his nephew, Dick, a notable amateur boxer who inherited Kedleston and the Scarsdale barony, was also able to succeed to a viscountcy of Scarsdale which had been conferred on Lord Curzon with a remainder. The present Viscount Scarsdale, Francis, is another of the Viceroy's nephews and inherited the title and the estate in 1977.

It proved a difficult inheritance, for Kedleston was owned by a family trust, and Francis Scarsdale, who knew the place intimately (having been his predecessor's estate manager), did not have the complete say in what should happen to secure the house's future. The problem was an enormous tax bill incurred by the death of the 2nd Viscount.

Negotiations with the various heritage bodies dragged on into the 1980s, when there were real fears that this great Georgian ensemble might be dispersed. Lord Scarsdale wanted to offer the house and principal contents in lieu of the tax, 'with the special wish and hope that it would then be vested in the National Trust'. Other beneficiaries of the family trust wanted, in his words, for it 'to be sold up lock, stock and barrel to the highest bidder because they appear to have no feeling for the place at all'.

Lord Montagu of Beaulieu, chairman of the newly formed Historic Buildings and Monuments Commission ('English Heritage'), threw his hat in the ring, but Lord Scarsdale considered that the National Trust, of which his uncle had been such a major benefactor, was the right organization to take Kedleston on. Eventually, in 1987, an unprecedented grant of £13.5 million from the National Heritage Memorial Fund enabled the majority of the

ABOVE The birds may have flown but the Curzons are still there... looking across the bridge to the north (entrance) front.

FAR LEFT Adam's sober and masculine library, employing the Doric order and geometric patterns.

contents of the house to be purchased for the National Trust, and an endowment to be set up for future maintenance. The Trust also launched an appeal for a further £2 million to secure the remaining contents and to carry out repairs.

For his part, Lord Scarsdale generously gave the house and park to the Trust, and was able to stay on in the family pavilion with his wife, thus ensuring Kedleston's future and upholding the family motto – 'Let Curzon holde what Curzon helde.'

29

BELVOIR CASTLE

LEICESTERSHIRE

T HE GOLDEN vision of Camelot, on a wooded hill high above the Vale of Belvoir, that greets the visitor to Belvoir Castle in Leicestershire, seat of the Dukes of Rutland, might strike some as a little too good to be true. Indeed, on closer inspection, the castle turns out to be a Regency construction, yet the towers and bastions are somehow justified by the site's long and romantic history.

Belvoir, otherwise Belvedere, was granted to William the Conqueror's standard-bearer at the Battle of Hastings, one Robert de Todeni. It passed from his descendants, the Albinis, to the family of de Ros when the heiress of Belvoir, Isabel de Albini, married the 1st Lord de Ros in 1246.

Their son, the 2nd Lord de Ros, was an unsuccessful competitor for the Crown of Scotland; and two centuries later the 10th Lord de Ros, a Lancastrian supporter, was attainted and beheaded during the Wars of the Roses. His lands were forfeited and Belvoir was granted to Lord Hastings, but de Ros's friends disputed this and tried to take back the old castle with force. As a result it was left ruinous.

In Tudor times Belvoir reverted to the de Ros family and then passed down to the Manners family. Thomas Manners, 1st Earl of Rutland, rebuilt the castle from the 1520s onwards, the work being finished by his son, the 2nd Earl, in 1555. Later in the 16th century the 5th Earl was implicated in the Earl of Essex's plot against Queen Elizabeth I and was thrown into the Tower of London, but recovered his lands on the accession of King James I, whom he entertained at Belvoir.

The castle's vicissitudes continued during the Civil War when it was first held for the King, then besieged and surrendered, and finally demolished by the Cromwellians with the reluctant consent of the 8th Earl of Rutland, who was himself of mildly Parliamentarian sympathies. After the Restoration of

PRECEDING PAGES Belvoir Castle: Regency Camelot.

LEFT The Pre-Guard Room: blunderbusses, buckets and a bull.

BELOW A sabre star in the Guard Room.

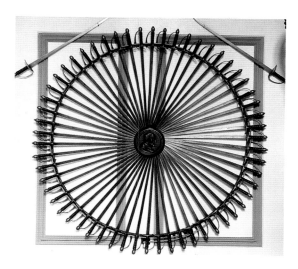

BELOW The Guard Room: Belvoir's overwhelming Gothic entrance hall, adorned with arms and armour.

King Charles II, Belvoir was rebuilt yet again, this time as a fairly plain house; the stables of the present castle are contemporary with this 17th-century rebuilding.

The 8th Earl's son, Lord Roos [*sic*], divorced his wife for adultery, which caused a great stir. John Evelyn noted in his diary for 22 March 1670: 'I went to Westminster, where in the House of Lords I saw his Majesty sit on his throne, but without his robes, all the peeres sitting with their hattes on; the business of the day being the divorce of my Lord Rosse. Such an occasion and sight had not been seene in England since the time of Henry VIII.'

The case evidently did Lord Roos no harm and after succeeding to the earldom of Rutland he was to the fore in rallying support for William of Orange and the 'Glorious Revolution'. Celebrated for his hospitality, he gave shelter to Princess Anne at Belvoir during these troubled times, and by way of reward she created him Duke of Rutland when she acceded to the throne.

His grandson, the 3rd Duke of Rutland ('a nobleman of great worth and goodness', according to the not usually charitable Horace Walpole), nurtured a special affection for Belvoir and was known as 'the Old Man of the Hill'. In about 1750 he carried out various improvements to the house, adding the Picture Room with cellars underneath.

The Old Man of the Hill's son and heir, the Marquess of Granby, was the most celebrated member of the Manners family. He distinguished himself at the Battle of Minden in 1759 and went on to command the British forces during the remainder of the Seven Years' War. Popular with his troops, he is commemorated by numerous public houses up and down the country, the signs bearing his benevolent bald-headed features. Such a memorial seems not inappropriate in view of the fact that he was a hard drinker.

From the Guard Room to the Grand Staircase: the cannon was captured during the First Sikh War; the armour is 16th-century.

Lord Granby never succeeded to the dukedom of Rutland, dying of 'gout in the stomach' when aged 49. His son, who became the 4th Duke, was a noted patron of the arts and a friend of Sir Joshua Reynolds. He contemplated various changes at Belvoir and invited 'Capability' Brown, who worked as an architect as well as a landscape gardener, to submit plans for a remodelling of the house; but the 4th Duke too died young and the scheme came to nothing.

The 4th Duke's widow, Duchess Isabella (a Somerset from Badminton) lived on until the 1830s and was nicknamed 'Duchess Was-a-bella' after she lost her looks. A story was told in the Vale of a country girl explaining the absence of a front tooth: 'Oh, the Duchess had lost one of hers, so she forced me to have mine taken out to replace it.'

In 1789, when the 5th Duke was still a boy, the diarist John Byng visited Belvoir and found 'everything... in neglect and Ruin'. A housekeeper 'of a very drunken dawdling appearance' took him round and he saw 'no Furniture

The Grand Staircase, rebuilt by the Gothic enthusiast Sir John Thoroton after the fire of 1816.

(Pictures excepted) that a Broker would think the worth carrying away; Nor one Chair, Table, Carpet or Curtain of use or comfort'.

The 5th Duke of Rutland's bride, Lady Elizabeth Howard from Castle Howard, was equally unimpressed when she came to Belvoir for the first time in 1799. This was not her idea of a castle.

The new century brought forth, at last, a new and fitting Belvoir Castle. The 5th Duke and his Duchess wanted a fairy-tale structure and promptly commissioned one from James Wyatt, who had by then switched from the neo-classical to the Gothic style and was engrossed in building William Beckford's fantastic and ill-fated Fonthill Abbey in Wiltshire. The Belvoir project was hardly less ambitious and almost as ill-starred.

Although progress was slow, by the time of Wyatt's death in 1813, two of the new fronts were finished, the crested and turreted chapel contrasting with a mammoth neo-Norman tower. In the same year the Prince Regent came to Belvoir and was presented with the key to the castle by the Reverend Dr

ABOVE & ABOVE RIGHT The elaborate Elizabeth Saloon is named after the castle's prime mover, Elizabeth, wife of the 5th Duke of Rutland. Her statue by M.C. Wyatt is seen in the detail, and (mirrored) standing over the highly Frenchified room. The carpet is Aubusson, the panelling partly genuine Louis XV.

LEFT The chapel, with the Manners family gallery above the altar. The picture over the altar is Murillo's *Holy Family*; above the family gallery hangs Gaspard Poussin's *Last Supper*. The recumbent marble figure (bottom left) is the nine-year-old Lord Haddon, sculpted from a model by his mother, Violet Duchess of Rutland; a copy is at Haddon (see pages 26-41).

Staunton of Staunton, in accordance with the tradition that this ancient Nottinghamshire family holds the manor of Staunton across the Vale by virtue of the feudal duty of 'castleguard'. To mark the royal visit, the best room in the new castle, a vast gallery hung with Gobelin tapestries, was named in the Prince Regent's honour.

Three years later, in October 1816, disaster struck. A terrible fire roared through the new castle early one morning, wrecking most of Wyatt's work. The north-east and north-west fronts were completely destroyed, and it is said that only the bricking-up of the doorway leading into the Regent's Gallery from the Grand Staircase prevented the fire from spreading further. The great staircase itself crumbled into powder with the heat.

The worst losses, though, as the 5th Duke of Rutland wrote sadly to the Prince Regent, were the pictures collected by his father. About half the collection, including works by Reynolds, Titian and Van Dyck, perished in the blaze. The Castle had been insured for £40,000 and the loss was conservatively estimated at £120,000.

The romantic vision of the 5th Duke and his Duchess, however, was not extinguished by the flames and they turned to the Duke's chaplain, the Reverend Sir John Thoroton (knighted at the time of the Prince Regent's visit to Belvoir), to pick up the pieces. A Gothic scholar, he did his best, but he was hardly an adequate substitute for James Wyatt. To help him, he had the services of Wyatt's sons, Benjamin, Philip and Matthew Cotes Wyatt.

Buttressed by the Rutlands' coal fortune and with the enthusiastic and knowledgable support of Duchess Elizabeth, the new team plugged gamely on until the enormous castle was finished about ten years later. Whatever its shortcomings, the final result was, as the diarist Charles Greville noted, 'so grand as to sink criticism in admiration'.

Sadly, Duchess Elizabeth died in 1825, aged 45, and never saw the fully completed article. Her presence lives on, though, in the lavish Elizabeth Saloon in Thoroton's eastern tower. Her life-size statue in marble by M.C.

Wyatt dominates the room, which has a ceiling depicting the amours of Jupiter and Juno, luxurious Louis XV white and gold panelling and furniture upholstered in rose-red damask silk.

The 5th Duke of Rutland lived on until 1857, when he was succeeded by his bachelor elder son. The second son, Lord John Manners, inherited the romanticism of his parents in full measure. A poet, he penned the celebrated couplet:

Let wealth and commerce, law and learning die
But leave us still our old nobilitie.

Lord John became a leader of 'Young England', a group of high-minded, youthful Tory politicians that was traditional and aristocratic in outlook while at the same time advocating social reform. The group included the young Benjamin Disraeli, who portrayed Manners in his novel *Coningsby* as 'Lord Henry Sydney', and Belvoir as 'Beaumanoir'.

Lord John went on to hold office in a series of Tory administrations but turned down the Viceroyalty of India. In recommending him to Queen Victoria his old friend Disraeli wrote that he was 'a man of many admirable

ABOVE Internal telephone 'below stairs'.

LEFT Backstairs spiral.

RIGHT The old kitchen, with its original open range and spit. There is a notable collection of copper and pewter.

The hilltop castle dominates the Vale of Belvoir.

qualities, and unjustly underrated by the public... an admirable administrator with a great capacity of labor; a facile pen; brave, firm, and a thorough gentleman'.

On succeeding his brother as 7th Duke of Rutland in 1888, he maintained what the old gossip Augustus Hare delighted to call 'mediaeval ways' at Belvoir. Trumpeters would parade the passages sounding the time to dress for dinner and watchmen would call the hours through the night – which must have made it hard to enjoy a good sleep.

The 7th Duke's granddaughter, the venerable beauty Lady Diana Cooper, who lived on into the 1980s, recalled in her autobiography how her grandfather would wrap himself in a thick black cape when walking along the chill corridors of Belvoir. She also recorded how much the 7th Duke enjoyed opening Belvoir to the public, and the 'look of pleasure and welcome on his delicate old face' as he watched the populace pouring in.

Lady Diana's parents, the 8th Duke of Rutland and his Duchess, a talented artist and sculptor, made various improvements to Belvoir when they took up residence there on the 7th Duke's death in 1906, including the installation of bathrooms and central heating. Their elder son, Lord Haddon, died aged nine and the Duchess sculpted the model for the marble memorial to the boy in the chapel at the family's Derbyshire seat, Haddon Hall.

Haddon was the dream home of the dead boy's younger brother, who became the 9th Duke of Rutland and realized his boyhood ambition of restoring this romantic old manor house. At the same time he continued to live in proper ducal style at Belvoir.

The 10th and present Duke of Rutland, who succeeded in 1940, continues to open Belvoir regularly to the public. The attractions include medieval jousting tournaments and the regimental museum of the 17th/21st Lancers (the 'Death or Glory Boys').

Thoroton's headily Gothic Guard Room has a high vaulted ceiling, vistas through a complex arrangement of arches and displays of weapons associated with the Leicestershire Militia. The vaulted ballroom, up the Grand Staircase, contains portraits of the first four Dukes of Rutland.

Despite the bad losses in the fire of 1816 much remains to be seen in the Picture Gallery, including works by Poussin, Gainsborough and the younger van de Velde. There is an outstanding David Teniers of *The Proverbs*, in which the artist manages to cram 43 different allegories, such as the flatterer blowing into his neighbour's ear with a pair of bellows. Not to be outdone by the earlier masters, J. Shannon, a 19th-century portrait painter, contributes a silkily narcissistic study of Lord John Manners, the 'Young England' politician.

Belvoir is popular as a location for films – *Little Lord Fauntleroy*, starring Sir Alec Guinness, was one of the many productions filmed there – and its air of romance has an irresistible appeal that has entranced artists from Turner onwards.

30

HIGHCLERE CASTLE

B ENJAMIN Disraeli may not have featured Highclere Castle in Hampshire in one of his novels, as he did Belvoir, but he was, according to his friend Lady Dorothy Nevill, no less impressed by this 'Jacobethan' seat of the Herberts, Earls of Carnarvon. In her *Reminiscences* (1906) she recalled him 'walking with some of us in front of the house, suddenly coming to a halt, and in impressive tones ejaculating: "How scenical! How scenical!"'

'Dizzy's' expression can be applied to many of the views of this extraordinary pile in its glorious park, whether it is the mass of towers and pinnacles that loom up out of the surrounding trees as you approach along the main drive from the north; or from high up on the Downs to the south, when it has the appearance of a vast Gothic liner steaming across the countryside. From a distance, one might even mistake it for a genuine Elizabethan house in the manner of Longleat or Hardwick, but on closer inspection it becomes clear that the strapwork parapets and pinnacles, the obelisks, the carved panels and mottoes are all Victorian tricks to disguise the fact that underneath this is an 18th-century house.

The Herberts inherited Highclere from the Sawyers. Sir Robert Sawyer, who was Attorney-General in the reign of King Charles II and a friend of Samuel Pepys, the diarist, bequeathed the estate to his only daughter, Margaret, who married the 8th Earl of Pembroke of Wilton. Their elder son, Henry, succeeded to Wilton, and Highclere passed to the second son, Robert Sawyer Herbert, and thence to his nephew Henry, who remodelled the old house into a restrained Georgian affair with an engaged central portico and groups of pilasters at the corners. He also called in 'Capability' Brown to embellish the naturally beautiful park, of which William Cobbett in his *Rural Rides* (1821) was to observe approvingly: 'This is, according to my fancy, the prettiest park that I have ever seen.'

PRECEDING PAGES 'How scenical! How scenical!' Highclere Castle in its idyllic Downland landscape.

LEFT A cast-iron mask of a wolf guards the front door and the entrance hall.

RIGHT The pseudo-Gothic saloon, with its strange use of stucco, soars up through three storeys. The walls are lined with Cordova leather.

Henry Herbert of Highclere was a Tory MP who drifted into the Whig camp and appears to have earned his peerage – he was created Lord Por-chester in 1780 – for his role in quelling the 'No Popery' riots incited by Lord George Gordon, who subsequently embraced Judaism and died in Newgate Gaol. Thirteen years later, Porchester was advanced to the earldom of Carnarvon.

The 2nd Earl of Carnarvon returned to the Tory fold, being violently opposed to the Reform Bill. His son, the 3rd Earl, who inherited Highclere in 1833, was described by Sir Walter Scott as 'A young man who lies on the carpet and looks poetical and dandyish... fine lad too.' He was indeed a poet of sorts and had a passion for travel. He roved through North Africa, Portugal, Greece and Spain in pursuit of Moorish culture and architecture.

The exotic Earl wrote travel books; a tragedy, *Don Pedro, King of Castile* (performed at the Theatre Royal, Drury Lane, in 1828); and *The Moor*, a poem in six cantos. The introduction to Canto V, about the Alhambra Palace in Granada, affords a clue as to his architectural tastes: 'The minute carving, the delicacy yet richness of detail produce an indescribable fascination for the traveller who beholds it for the first time; with little variation of surface, or

bold projection all is graceful and harmonious and like the regular features of perfect beauty, for a few minutes rivet his attention.'

It is hardly surprising that the 3rd Earl was not going to be content with his rather tame Georgian seat in Hampshire. In 1837 he called in Sir Charles Barry, then working on the new Houses of Parliament, to enliven Highclere. Barry initially underestimated his client's yearning for something sensational. His first design of 1838, while grand in its Italianate way, was not nearly extravagant enough for the exotic Earl.

The architect tried again. This time, in 1840, he came up with a style he called 'Anglo-Italian', basing his plans on the classically inspired great English Renaissance 'prodigy' houses which enabled him to load the exterior with eye-catching ornament and incident – turrets, towers, obelisks, strapwork, enriched pilasters and carved panels under the windows.

This was better, thought the 3rd Earl of Carnarvon, but another plan, produced early in 1842, was required, and even that did not include the final great tower, reminiscent of the Houses of Parliament. Finally, in the summer of 1842, the foundation stone was laid by Lord Carnarvon's son and heir, Lord Porchester, on his eleventh birthday. 'People crowded up from Newbury

LEFT The main staircase fills Sir Charles Barry's Italianate tower. The marble sculpture by Tenerani shows the future 4th Earl of Carnarvon and his sister Evelyn (later Countess of Portsmouth). The portrait on the wall is of the 18th-century actress Mrs Musters as Hebe, goddess of youth.

RIGHT Golden knowledge: library door.

and the country about it', wrote Lord Carnarvon in his journal, 'and what I did not expect, many people were a good deal affected by it and tears were standing in many eyes.'

Barry himself was moved enough, according to his son, to declare that the building thus transformed was one of his favourite works. Inside the elaborate stone crust, the shell of the original house remained fairly intact.

For the interior Barry planned a flamboyant Italianate central hall, but in the event nothing came of it and there is indeed little of Barry's proposed decoration inside Highclere, apart from the main staircase. The internal redecoration was far from complete when Lord Carnarvon died in 1849.

His son, the 4th Earl, who had laid the foundation stone as a boy, resumed building operations on his marriage in 1861 to Lady Evelyn Stanhope, daughter of the 6th Earl of Chesterfield. Barry had died in 1860 so the new Lord Carnarvon turned to Thomas Allom, a typographical illustrator and architectural draughtsman who had worked with Barry.

The result was a curious hotchpotch of styles. The chocolate-and-gold library, reminiscent of a London club, comes off splendidly, and the imposing Gothic Revival entrance hall boasts excellent rib vaulting and an encaustic-tiled floor by the mighty William Butterfield. Other rooms are less successful, such as the pseudo-Gothic saloon, with its strange use of stucco, and the Music Room, an odd 18th-century palimpsest, possibly a hangover from the pre-Victorian Highclere.

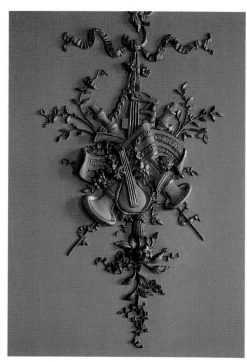

ABOVE The club-like library, Barry's most satisfying interior at Highclere.

ABOVE LEFT Napoleon's desk and chair in the library. The desk was made for his rooms on St Helena by George Bullock, and was acquired by the Herbert family from the exiled Emperor's chaplain. The chair came from Fontainebleau.

BELOW LEFT Detail of a gilded trophy in the Music Room.

The 4th Earl of Carnarvon and his Countess were an hospitable couple at Highclere. He became Secretary of State for the Colonies and Lord Lieutenant of Ireland, though some of his critics found that, in the words of one society chronicler, 'he has a manner too mincing to inspire confidence... he wants both grip and grit'. Lady St Helier, in her *Memories of Fifty Years* (1909) was more charitable: 'His deep affection for his wife, and her devotion to him, combined with the complete sympathy of their tastes and occupations, made them... an ideal couple, and in his own house and among his own people, no-one was more beloved. He was too chivalrous a man for the hurly-burly of public life.'

Lady Carnarvon enjoyed a universally good press. Lady Waterford thought she 'had everything, beauty, talent, charm and goodness' and Lord Ronald Gower, the sculptor and aesthete (model for 'Lord Henry Wotton' in Oscar Wilde's *The Picture of Dorian Gray*), deemed her 'Amiable, clever, accomplished, and kind, with a charm of voice and manner peculiar to herself, she was the most perfect hostess, and in her time no place was more delightful to stay at than Highclere.'

Their son, the 5th Earl of Carnarvon, inherited his grandfather's love of travel and formed a passion for Egyptology. He sponsored a series of excavations, led by Howard Carter in the 'Valley of the Kings', culminating in the discovery of the fabulous tomb of Tutankhamun in 1922. His death from an infected mosquito bite helped give rise to the legend of 'King Tut's Curse'.

LEFT The cupboard between the double doors of the smoking room and the drawing room where the butler, Robert Taylor, discovered 'the Egyptian stuff'.

BELOW The 'Stuart Revival' Victorian dining room. The equestrian portrait of Charles I is from the school of Van Dyck. The portrait above the fireplace is of the 1st Earl of Carnarvon.

The Egyptologist Earl was responsible for redecorating the drawing room at Highclere in a lavish Victorian-rococo manner and for establishing the Highclere Stud. Horse-racing became the obsession of his successors, beginning with his son 'Porchey', the irrepressible 6th Earl, who bred the 1930 Derby winner, Blenheim, for the Aga Khan ('the dear old fat boy', as the 6th Earl called him).

Racing parlance was 'Porchey's' preferred mode of speech and his most celebrated *bon mot* was addressed to his old Army friend, Sir 'Jock' Delves Broughton, when the Baronet was surprisingly acquitted of the murder in Kenya of his wife's lover, the 22nd Earl of Erroll – an incident that formed the subject of the book and film *White Mischief*. 'Congratulations', went Porchey's telegram (later framed at White's Club), 'on winning a neck cleverly.'

Porchey lived in Edwardian style – with house parties for race meetings and shooting, and a staff of nearly 20 – at Highclere into the 1980s. It is something of a mystery why he never opened the place to the public as he was a born showman – not to say an outrageous exhibitionist. He rejoiced in

RIGHT Service directory.

Westminster in Wessex.

his manifestation as a 'television personality' following the publication of his racy memoirs, *No Regrets* (1976), and would relentlessly regale chat-show audiences with salacious anecdotes about how he had been chased through the back gardens of Maidenhead by cuckolded husbands.

In the event it was left to his son, the 7th and present Earl of Carnarvon, to throw open the doors of Highclere in 1988. The grand opening received a helpful publicity boost when the long-serving butler, Robert Taylor, happened to mention during the compilation of an inventory of the castle's contents that everything seemed in order except that 'the Egyptian stuff was missing'.

When asked what he meant, Taylor explained that some years previously, while making arrangements for a party, he had discovered two cupboards set into the walls in the small gap between the door to the smoking room (Porchey's atmospheric den) and that of the drawing room. 'The drawing room', Taylor recalled, 'was closed during the war and there had always been a table across the door so nobody went in. On that rare occasion the two doors were open and I noticed these cupboards. I opened one and there was this sort of tin cigarette box or something and a lot of tissue paper.'

On finding a necklace inside, the butler assumed that it must be something to do with the 5th Earl of Carnarvon's Egyptian collection and that the family knew about it. He closed the cupboards and thought nothing of it until the inventory was being discussed.

When the cupboards were re-opened in 1988 they were found to contain various small antiquities from the Egyptologist Earl's excavations. More treasures turned up in the dark-room (the 5th Earl had been a keen photographer), the muniment room and even in a drawer used by the housekeeper. None of these items had been seen for more than 60 years.

Today they are all on view to the public, together with other memorabilia from the Egyptian adventures of the 5th Earl. There is also a horse-racing exhibition, a particular project of the present Earl, who is racing manager to the Queen, and his family, who are all involved in the Turf.

Unlike many great houses, the main bedrooms upstairs are also open to visitors, and there is an enticing collection of bathrooms – those most illuminating indexes of taste – with names such as 'Dyke', 'Steam' and the sinister-sounding 'Ray'. The library contains Napoleon's ornate desk and chair; the Stuart-revival dining room is hung with portraits by the school of Van Dyck.

'Downstairs' life is evoked by the steward's and housekeeper's rooms, now converted to tearooms. The other attractions include a Victorian tropical conservatory and a 'secret garden' with curving herbaceous borders, serpentine paths and ornamental trees and shrubs.

The present Earl lives in a stylish modern house on the estate, but the castle retains a lived-in atmosphere, recalling the opulent heyday of Victorian and Edwardian country house life on the grand scale.

31

CARLTON TOWERS

YORKSHIRE

*A*S AT Highclere Castle, the amazing Victorian appearance of Carlton Towers in the old East Riding of Yorkshire is, in fact, only skin deep. Beneath the fantastic embellishments of the 1870s, commissioned by the eccentric 9th Lord Beaumont and carried out by the even more eccentric architect Edward Welby Pugin – who ruined himself by trying to prove that his father, Augustus Welby Pugin, rather than Sir Charles Barry, had designed the Houses of Parliament – is an older house.

As you stand before the main facade of this sensational Gothic pile – surely the most spectacular of its kind in England and Wales – you will see that the three-storey square block on the left is the original Jacobean house of 1614, known as Carlton Hall. It may even retain some of the masonry of the medieval house of the Stapletons, which occupied the same site.

The property has passed down by inheritance since the Norman Conquest, first from the de Brus family to the Bellews, whose 13th-century heiress married into the Stapleton family, which was originally from Co. Durham. The first of the Stapletons to base himself at Carlton, in the 1390s, was Brian Stapleton, whose grandfather and namesake (Warden of Calais and a Knight of the Garter), had acquired the family crest, a saracen's head, by killing an infidel in the presence of the Kings of Scotland, England and France.

Brian married Joan, niece and co-heiress of the last Viscount Beaumont, a family descended from the princely house of Brienne, which had produced the last Christian King of Jerusalem. Such romantic medievalism was later to have a profound influence on Carlton's architecture and decoration.

During the 16th century the Stapletons remained loyal to the old faith of Catholicism and were penalized by the anti-recusancy laws. An air of Catholic piety still pervades Carlton to this day and when Elizabeth Stapleton, widow of a later Brian, rebuilt the house in 1614, a priest's hiding hole was constructed in the space between the chimney stacks in the middle of the building, with access from a concealed trap door in the base of a cupboard.

PRECEDING PAGES Carlton Towers: the outer hall, which was fitted up as a temporary chapel when Cardinal Manning visited Carlton in 1876. The marble bust in the window is of the 8th Lord Beaumont by Patrick McDowell.

LEFT A particularly ferocious gargoyle.

RIGHT The megalomaniac clock tower.

BELOW Time stands still at this Victorian extravaganza.

Elizabeth Stapleton was a great-granddaughter of Bess of Hardwick, and had something of her ancestress's passion for building. She constructed a compact three-storey house of decidedly Northern solidity.

Later in the 17th century, the family's unwavering Catholicism continued to land them in difficulties. Sir Miles Stapleton, 1st (and last) Bt., was tried for High Treason during the anti-Catholic hysteria whipped up by Titus Oates's 'Popish Plot', but sensibly acquitted by a jury of his Yorkshire neighbours. His chaplain, the Venerable Thomas Thwing, was not so lucky, being executed at York in 1680.

Early in the 18th century Carlton passed to Sir Miles's nephew, Nicholas Errington, who took the surname of Stapleton. His grandson, Thomas Stapleton, who succeeded to the estate in 1750, carried out major alterations to the house, adding the long east wing *circa* 1777 (the date on the clock), probably to the design of Thomas Atkinson of York.

This new wing contained a chapel and the stables, which loomed large in Thomas's life. Barred by his religion from entering politics or the services, he concentrated his energies on the Turf and twice won the St Leger at Doncaster. He also found time to lay claim to the dormant barony of Beaumont – a barony in fee, inheritable through the female line. The matter was referred to the Committee of Privileges in the House of Lords and the case dragged on for many years.

It was not until the reign of Queen Victoria, when it became fashionable, particularly among Catholic dynasties, to exhume medieval baronies, that the Stapletons achieved their romantic ambition. In 1840 Miles Stapleton, a great-nephew of Thomas of the Turf, was duly summoned to the Lords as the 8th Lord Beaumont, the peerage having been called out of abeyance by the Queen.

He celebrated his ennoblement by converting the long east wing into part of the main house, and adding what Mark Girouard has called 'anaemic Gothic trimmings' to the exterior, probably to his own, not very distinguished, design. The chapel was converted into an *enfilade* of state rooms, with bedrooms behind.

The figure of St George in the east window of the outer hall. The stained glass was designed by John Francis Bentley, the church architect responsible for Carlton Towers' scholarly interiors.

The reason for the abandonment of the chapel was that Lord Beaumont's wife, Isabella Browne, was an Irish Protestant, and their children were brought up as Anglicans. Lord Beaumont himself turned Anglican during the controversy over the 'Papal Aggression' of 1850, when Pope Pius XI restored the English Catholic hierarchy, replacing the previous Vicars-Apostolic with bishops of territorial sees. 'The late bold and clearly expressed edict of the Court of Rome', declared Lord Beaumont, in an open letter, 'cannot be received or accepted by English Roman Catholics without a violation of their duties as citizens.'

However, both his sons, Henry and Miles, reverted to Catholicism – and they were joined by their mother. Henry belonged to the generation of the great Catholic revival in England and was up at Oxford with the 3rd Marquess of Bute, whose conversion to Catholicism inspired Benjamin Disraeli's novel *Lothair*, about a rich young nobleman attracted to the Church of Rome.

An intensely romantic young man, Henry became a Knight of Justice in the Catholic Order of Malta, and was drawn to fight abroad for various traditional causes. In 1873 he went off to fight in the last Carlist War in Spain, as he was a passionate supporter of the claim of Don Carlos, who stood for a Catholic and conservative monarchy, to the Spanish throne.

Lord Beaumont apparently envisaged receiving Don Carlos at Carlton when the latter became King of Spain. In the more than slightly unbalanced peer's vision, the Most Catholic King would descend the grand staircase in state, to be greeted by the entire European nobility, assembled in the Hall of the Barons. Then His Catholic Majesty would ascend to the chapel for a solemn Mass of Thanksgiving, in the presence of all the Catholic bishops of Europe.

To fulfil this megalomaniac fantasy, of course, Lord Beaumont first needed to aggrandize his family seat on a monumental scale. Carlton Hall was to become Carlton Towers, and Edward Pugin was called in to draw up plans featuring a bizarre conglomeration of great towers. Even if not all these dreams were realized, the result is still one of the most extraordinary Victorian houses in England and Wales.

Pugin refaced the old house with cement to look like stone, and managed to add more than enough turrets, gargoyles, battlements and coats of arms to justify the change of name from 'Hall' to 'Towers'. Yet the remodelling of the old house was only half the plan. Lord Beaumont and Pugin's intention was to extend the house to twice its present size – a staggering concept – complete with a giant keep-like tower, a cathedral-like chapel and the mighty Hall of Barons.

Unfortunately, however, the money ran out and these loopy structures were never erected. Patron and architect made an odd couple: both obsessive Catholic romantics, both distinctly unsatisfactory characters and both hurtling down the headlong slope to bankruptcy. While Lord Beaumont dashed off on quixotic military adventures – he delighted in being decorated with the Orders of Military Merit by the King of Bavaria ('Mad Ludwig', another megalomaniac builder) and by the Grand Dukes of Baden and Mecklenburg – Pugin was seldom out of the law court. 'On my tomb', the architect observed, before his death in 1875, 'I should like written: "Here lies a man of many miseries."'

Earlier that year he and Lord Beaumont seem to have fallen out. In any event, for the interior decoration of Carlton Towers, Beaumont turned to another architect, John Francis Bentley. An infinitely more sympathetic figure,

LEFT Looking from the inner hall to the glitter of the Venetian Drawing Room beyond.

RIGHT The Venetian Drawing Room, the finest room at Carlton and one of the most complete Victorian interiors in existence.

BELOW 'Shylock, Boldlock and Padlock': N.H.J. Westlake's figures from *The Merchant of Venice* on the dado panels of the Venetian Drawing Room.

the Yorkshire-born Bentley specialized in ecclesiastical work (most notably Westminster Cathedral), and he gave Carlton a series of splendid interiors which, as the architectural historian John Martin Robinson has pointed out, 'are a complete contrast to Pugin's exterior, both in their sensitive scholarly design and also in quality of craftsmanship'. After seeing the outside the visitor expects to wallow in Victorian gloom within, but instead finds himself enchanted by light, airy rooms full of robust confidence and character.

Bentley had no easy task. In 1874, before starting work, he observed to a friend: 'Last week I was at Lord Beaumont's. The work he has done is a caution. Fancy, the fittings in the best bedrooms are the same as those in the servants' offices, stained and varnished and of the most miserable description. From what I saw I should think it will cost from £12,000 to £15,000 to complete the work which I am commissioned to do.'

In the series of state apartments which stretch away from the ecclesiastical outer hall (fitted up as a temporary chapel in 1876, when Cardinal Manning visited Carlton) for nearly 200 feet to the east, Bentley expended particular care on the detailing. He designed much of the furniture to match the architecture in his effort to achieve a unified effect.

The finest Victorian interior at Carlton – indeed almost anywhere – is the Venetian Drawing Room, where all the original colouring and textiles of the 1870s are dazzlingly preserved. There is a tremendous chimneypiece decorated with heraldry and panels of 'Flora' and 'The Four Seasons' by N.H.J. Westlake, who was also responsible for painting the figures from *The Merchant of Venice* on the dado panels, irreverently referred to by the artist as 'Shylock, Boldlock and Padlock.'

The riot of heraldry at Carlton Towers was under the control of the American-born John de Havilland, York Herald of Arms and a general in the Carlist army, whom Lord Beaumont had met in Spain. It was probably de Havilland who introduced the peer to Bentley. The satisfying oak heraldic newels on the staircase were carved by J. Erskine Knox.

In 1879 Lord Beaumont – then engaged in the Zulu War – was deeply in debt, and on his return from Africa was obliged to live abroad. Until he was nearly 40 he remained a bachelor, in accordance with his knightly rank in the Order of Malta. However, in 1888, in an attempt to recoup his finances, he decided to forswear celibacy and married Violet Isaacson, whose mother, 'Madame Elise', a fashionable milliner in the West End of London, is said to have settled £6,000 a year and the sum of £100,000 on her daughter.

This exercise in matrimony did not achieve the desired results, and shortly afterwards most of the Carlton estate had to be sold. The erratic 9th Lord Beaumont died in 1892, aged 43, and Carlton was inherited by his younger brother Miles, the 10th Lord Beaumont. Miles's wife, Ethel, a Tempest from Broughton Hall in the West Riding of Yorkshire, proved just the chatelaine Carlton needed to save it from disaster. She brought to the property many of the most interesting pictures, including the Old Masters in the Picture Gallery, collected by her father Sir Charles Tempest, Bt., in Paris and Rome.

Miles, though, had only three years to put things straight at Carlton. In 1895, while crossing a stile in the park, he accidentally discharged his gun, with fatal consequences. The heir to the barony of Beaumont was his one-year-old daughter, Mona, who was to own Carlton for 76 years.

Despite two World Wars (in the Second, Carlton was used as an auxiliary military hospital) and the social upheavals of the 20th century, the redoubtable Lady Beaumont managed to maintain Carlton Towers as a Victorian time capsule, which is perhaps now appreciated more than it ever has been in

ABOVE The Venetian Drawing Room: detail. The curtains were designed by Bentley in terracotta and green to match the green velvet upholstery. Here one is accompanied by a text from *The Merchant of Venice*.

LEFT The spectacular chimneypiece in the Venetian Drawing Room, decorated with heraldry and panels of 'Flora' and 'The Four Seasons' by Westlake, embossed fireplace tiles by William De Morgan and brass firedogs by Bentley. The large shield, supported by Beaumont talbots and surmounted by the crest of a saracen's head, carries 36 armorial quarterings.

the past. Mona married the 3rd Lord Howard of Glossop, a scion of the illustrious and ducal house of Norfolk, England's premier Catholic dynasty, and they had eight children, all of whose names begin with 'M' – including the eldest son, Major-General Miles Fitzalan-Howard, who not only succeeded his parents in their respective peerages but also his cousin Bernard in the dukedom of Norfolk.

Miles Norfolk opened Carlton Towers to the public in the 1970s, and in the 1980s the house played a starring role, looming ominously out of the mist, in Charles Sturridge's feature film of *A Handful of Dust*, adapted from Evelyn Waugh's novel about a Gothic monstrosity called 'Hetton Abbey'. The Duke himself, an engagingly modest and unaffected man, delighted in a cameo role as a gardener; he is seen briefly in the film, sweeping up leaves.

The Duke's elder son, the Earl of Arundel, has devoted himself to restoring the Fitzalan-Howards' principal seat of Arundel Castle, the family's unbeatably historic pile in Sussex, which dates back to the Norman Conquest. Carlton Towers is now the home of the Duke's second son, Lord Gerald Fitzalan-Howard, and his young family. Although no longer open regularly to the public, the house continues to be available for functions and group visits. Amid the Gothic glories, family life still goes on, and the tiny chapel – with the sash of Cardinal Hinsley, born in the village in 1865 – continues to express the true tradition of the Old Faith.

ABOVE The main staircase at Carlton, designed by E.W. Pugin to fit into the great staircase tower. The windows are filled with heraldic glass devised by General de Havilland, York Herald of Arms, and made by Lavers and Barraud.

ABOVE LEFT Detail of the heraldic newels on the staircase, designed by Bentley and splendidly carved in oak by J. Erskine Knox.

RIGHT From Victorian towers (and gargoyle) to
20th-century towers (and belching smoke): the
Goole power station across the park.

32

WADDESDON MANOR

BUCKINGHAMSHIRE

W ITH Waddesdon Manor in Buckinghamshire, completed barely a century ago and now being superbly restored, it is possible to end this chronicle of great houses with a very big bang. For this sumptuous treasure house of the Rothschilds, designed in the French Renaissance taste, is on the grandest scale, and the quality of craftsmanship and connoisseurship is nothing short of staggering.

All around the extensive estate and the great house itself the eye is caught by a distinctive symbol, five arrows bound in a sheaf. This heraldic device signifies the five sons of Mayer Amschel Rothschild (1744–1812), founder of the celebrated Frankfurt banking house, financial adviser to the Elector of Hesse-Cassel and patriarch of the Rothschild dynasty. His eldest son succeeded his father at Frankfurt, and the four younger sons were sent out, like arrows at bull's eyes, to found banking houses in London, Paris, Vienna and Naples.

Baron Ferdinand de Rothschild, a grandson of the founder of the Austrian branch of the family, settled in England in the 1860s and married his English cousin, Evelina, younger daughter of Baron Lionel de Rothschild, the first Jewish MP, who was seated at Tring Park in Hertfordshire.

The Rothschilds congregated around the borders of Hertfordshire and Buckinghamshire – indeed, at one stage they owned seven substantial country houses and 30,000 acres in the area – and one day, out hunting, Baron Ferdinand spotted a bare hilltop outside Aylesbury which he thought might have possibilities. Although by now, in the 1870s, a widower (his wife had died in childbirth), Baron Ferdinand was set on staying in England and keen to acquire an estate of his own.

He discovered that the Waddesdon estate belonged to the 7th Duke of Marlborough, of Blenheim, and duly acquired the property of some 2,700 acres. 'This much could be said in its favour', noted the methodical Baron

Ferdinand, 'it had a bracing and salubrious air, pleasant scenery, excellent hunting, and was untainted by factories and villadom.'

If his Buckinghamshire neighbours were surprised by such an unlikely purchase, they were astounded when the bare hillside suddenly acquired many hundreds of fully grown trees. Sometimes 16 horses were needed to haul up the larger trees; telegraph wires on the surrounding roads had to be lowered to allow them free passage. Similarly, after the hill had been levelled and planted, Bath stone and other building materials were brought halfway up the hill by a specially constructed steam tramway, and then hauled to the top by teams of Percheron mares, imported from Normandy.

It was not only the horses that came from across the Channel, but the architect, the landscape gardener, the architectural style and most of the contents too. As soon as Baron Ferdinand had signed the contract with the Duke of Marlborough he set out for Paris 'in quest of an architect'. He settled on Gabriel-Hippolyte Destailleur, whose father and grandfather had been architects of the Duc d'Orleans and who himself had recently restored the Château de Mouchy.

It was Destailleur who chose the site of the new house and drew up a plan of such grandeur that Baron Ferdinand begged him to reduce it. 'You will regret your decision', the architect told his client, 'one always builds too

PRECEDING PAGES Waddesdon roofscape.

RIGHT A corner of the Red Drawing Room, with its gilt armchairs covered in mid-18th-century Beauvais tapestry and a chest of drawers made by Jean-Henri Riesener for Louis XVI's sister, Madame Elisabeth, in 1778.

BELOW The Red Drawing Room. The table in the foreground, which has a top inlaid with pearls of *pietra dura,* was probably made in Florence in the 17th century; on top of it is a miniature spinning-wheel, probably French, of *circa* 1760.

small'. Sure enough, Baron Ferdinand later found himself compelled to add first one wing and then another.

In a fascinating account of the building of Waddesdon, written shortly before his death in 1898, Baron Ferdinand de Rothschild addressed himself to the question of why he employed foreign instead of native talent, of which there was no lack at hand: 'My reply is, that having been greatly impressed by the ancient Châteaux of the Valois during a tour I once made in Touraine, I determined to build my house in the same style, and considered it safer to get the design made by a French architect who was familiar with the work, than by an English one whose knowledge and experience of the architecture of that period could be less thoroughly trusted.'

Certainly anyone familiar with the châteaux of the Loire can detect echoes of Chambord and Blois (the external staircases, for instance) in Waddesdon's design. Baron Ferdinand admitted that the towers were borrowed from Maintenon, the château of the Duc de Noailles.

In Baron Ferdinand's view, the French 16th-century style ('on which I had long set my heart') was particularly suitable to the surroundings of the site he had selected. He felt it was 'more uncommon than the Tudor, Jacobean or Adam of which the country affords so many and such unique specimens'.

As for the landscape gardening, he was at pains to stress that Elie Lainé was called in only 'after Mr Thomas, the then most eminent English landscape gardener, had declined to lay out the grounds for reasons he did not deign to divulge'. With hindsight, though, Baron Ferdinand came to regret the phenomenal tree operations: 'If I may venture to proffer a word of advice to anyone who may feel inclined to follow my example – it is to abstain from transplanting old trees.... Young trees try your patience at first, but they soon catch up with the old ones, and make better timber and foliage.'

The interior of Waddesdon was lavishly fitted up in the French 18th-century taste. Most of the panelling Baron Ferdinand had installed came from historic Parisian houses destroyed in the traffic-widening schemes of the 1860s; this was no fancy 'repro' but the genuine article. As Baron Ferdinand recorded,

> [that] in the Billiard Room [came] from a château of the
> Montmorencies; that in the Breakfast Room and the Boudoir
> from the hotel of the Maréchal de Richelieu in the street
> which was named after his uncle the great Cardinal and which
> has now been transformed into shops and apartments;
> the Grey Drawing Room came from the convent of the
> Sacré Coeur, formerly the hotel of the Duc de Lauzun,
> who perished on the guillotine; and the Tower Room
> from a villa which was for some time the residence of
> the famous Fermier-Général Beaujon, to whom the
> Elysée also belonged.

Baron Ferdinand rejected what he called the 'bastard 19th-century style, graceless and tasteless, borrowing hardly a single feature from its predecessors' and, like the rest of the Rothschilds, was determined to revive the decoration of the 18th century in its purity. His aim at Waddesdon was to reconstruct rooms 'out of old material, reproducing them as they had been during the reigns of the Louis'.

These elegant rooms were the perfect setting for the Baron's marvellous collections of Savonnerie carpets, furniture by the great Jean-Henri Riesener (including an exquisite, jewel-like marquetry writing table, created for Marie Antoinette), Sèvres porcelain and *objets d'art* such as Madame de

ABOVE A political pamphlet by Beaumarchais, worked into the *trompe-l'oeil* marquetry of his desk in the Baron's Room.

RIGHT A corner of the Baron's Room, showing the cylinder-top desk of 1779 traditionally given by his friends to P.A. Caron de Beaumarchais, author of *The Marriage of Figaro* and *The Barber of Seville*, and music-master to the King of France's daughters. This masculine treasury is adorned with portraits of actresses; Lady Hamilton is on the left.

ABOVE & LEFT Two of the superb Sèvres vases in the Red Drawing Room.

Pompadour's gold snuffbox showing a poodle and spaniel frolicking on the lid. Two of the most remarkable items of furniture Baron Ferdinand acquired were P.A. Caron de Beaumarchais's cylinder-top desk, adorned with *trompe-l'oeil* documents, and a massive, owl-like structure in black and gold, surmounted by a clock and a gilt eagle.

Yet not everything is French at Waddesdon. There are collections of Chinese vases, Meissen porcelain, Dutch paintings, two enormous canvases of Venice by Francesco Guardi and a splendid set of English portraits by Reynolds, Gainsborough, Romney and Lawrence. Indeed one of the joys of Waddesdon is the way Baron Ferdinand, with his sure, perfectionist's eye, confidently mingled French pictures and furniture with 18th-century English portraits.

In the morning room, for example, the propinquity of Gainsborough's 'Pink Boy' (Master Nicholls) and Louis XVI's writing table, by the cabinet-makers Guillaume Benneman and Guillaume Kemp, is particularly pleasing. And in the opulent Red Drawing Room, Gainsborough's portrait of Lady Sheffield in a blue dress is set off by the neighbouring Savonnerie carpet and Riesener commodes. In his own very masculine sitting room (the 'Baron's Room') Baron Ferdinand surrounded himself with beguiling portraits of beautiful actresses and singers – Lady Hamilton (by Romney), Mrs Sheridan (Reynolds), *La Courtisane Amoureuse* (Boucher) and Mrs Robinson (by both Gainsborough and Reynolds).

Baron Ferdinand, who was in residence in the main part of the house by 1883, entertained on a princely scale. The guests ranged from Guy de Maupassant and Henry James to the Prince of Wales, who in 1889 palmed off the erratic Shah of Persia on the long-suffering 'Ferdy'. The Shah, on learning that the Prince of Wales himself had not turned up for the house party, sulked in his room, refusing to come down to dinner until Baron Ferdinand tempted him out with the promise of 'a most excellent conjuror'.

The next year Queen Victoria herself came out of her customary seclusion to inspect this exotic corner of France in Buckinghamshire. Her Majesty, Baron Ferdinand noted, 'partook of every dish, and twice of cold beef' at luncheon and 'took away three copies of the bill of fare'. Well-fed, the Queen, as Baron Ferdinand recalled with pride, then 'looked with interest on the old English portraits in my Green sitting room, and at some of the curiosities in the Tower Room; and was so struck with the decoration, furnishing and arrangement of the rooms that she afterwards sent the superintendent of the furniture from Windsor Castle to inspect them'.

The Queen toured the grounds in her pony carriage, but her pony shied at the sight of the cockatoos and macaws in the elegant aviary. Fortunately Her Majesty came to no harm, though her eldest son's visit to Waddesdon eight years later ended in disaster when His Royal Highness slipped on the spiral staircase and broke his leg. There was further indignity when at Aylesbury Station the chair carrying him collapsed under his weight and deposited him in the middle of the bridge, where his ample and immobile form was regularly engulfed by acrid smoke from trains passing by underneath.

A few months after this unhappy incident Baron Ferdinand died and Waddesdon passed to his sister, Alice, a formidable but kindly chatelaine who added to the works of art and improved the estate. On Alice's death in 1922 Waddesdon was inherited by her great-nephew, James de Rothschild, who had fought as a private in the French Army during the First World War and had recently become a British subject.

'Jimmy' de Rothschild went on to become an MP and a junior minister, but was probably best known as a racehorse owner. His wife, Dorothy ('Dollie')

Pinto, shared her husband's commitment to Zionism and to Waddesdon. Although Dollie shunned publicity – believing that the really decent individual only appeared in the newspapers on two occasions, birth and death – she was a tireless worker for charitable causes and wrote a delightful book, *The Rothschilds at Waddesdon Manor* (1979), about the beloved house which she and her husband did so much to preserve.

During the Second World War Waddesdon became a residential nursery for young London evacuees from the Blitz. On Jimmy's death in 1957 he bequeathed the house to the National Trust, but Dollie stayed on as chatelaine. She died in 1988, aged 93, and since then her heir, the present Lord Rothschild, Chairman of the National Heritage Memorial Fund, has masterminded a magnificent restoration programme to show the great Waddesdon treasures to their best advantage.

The idea is not only to bring the presentation up to museum standards but to make the house live, in the same way as Jacob Rothschild has achieved the triumphant restoration of Spencer House in London. Many more rooms are to be opened to the public once the restoration is complete, and the most sophisticated forms of scholarly conservation and lighting are being deployed.

In the grounds, too, the aviary has been restored; the parterre, with its Giuliano Mozani fountain of Pluto and Proserpine, from the ducal palace of Colorno, has been faithfully replanted in the original bright colours by Beth

ABOVE A corner of the Chilterns that is forever France.

LEFT Detail of Waddesdon's triumphal stonework.

Rothschild (Jacob Rothschild's second daughter); and the old dairy complex, complete with picturesque lake and rock garden, imaginatively re-created by Julian Bannerman.

Baron Ferdinand feared that Waddesdon would 'fall into decay' but hoped that 'the day yet be distant when weeds will spread over the garden, the terraces crumble into dust, the pictures and cabinets cross the Channel or the Atlantic, and the melancholy cry of the night-jar sound from the deserted towers'. A century on, his nightmares have not been realized, and Waddesdon – thanks to the National Trust and above all to the taste, imagination and munificence of Jacob Rothschild – has become a fantasy of substance that can be shared by everyone.

— Acknowledgements —

WE HAVE received wonderfully generous help, hospitality and advice from many owners, friends, administrators and experts, and we would particularly like to thank the following, all of whom have made significant contributions to the book and to our enjoyment in producing it: Julian Bannerman, the Marquess of Bath, the Duke and Duchess of Beaufort, Mark Bence-Jones, the Duke of Buccleuch, the Earl of Burlington, William and Sarah Bulwer-Long, the Earl of Carnarvon, John Chesshyre, John Chichester-Constable, the Marquess of Cholmondeley, Susan Cleaver, Alec Cobbe, Selina Coghlan, Viscount and Viscountess Coke, Sophie Collins, Jacky Colliss Harvey, Jon Culverhouse, Lady Victoria Cuthbert, Warren Davis, Viscount and Viscountess De L'Isle, the Duke and Duchess of Devonshire, Paul Duffie, Howard Eaton, Lord and Lady Egremont, Terry Empson, Lord Gerald Fitzalan-Howard, Gareth Fitzpatrick, David Freeman, Christopher Gilbert, the Knight of Glin, Rosamund Griffin, the Earl and Countess of Harewood, John Harris, the Marquess of Hertford, Min Hogg, Simon Howard, Norman Hudson, St Clair Hughes, Robert Innes-Smith, Gervase Jackson-Stops, John Kenworthy-Browne, the late John Langton, Lady Victoria Leatham, James Lees-Milne, Cynthia Lewis, Candida Lycett Green, the Duke and Duchess of Marlborough, Luke Massingberd, John Montgomery-Massingberd, Teresa Moore, the Marquess of Northampton, the Duke of Northumberland, Dr Diane Owen, the Earl of Pembroke, George Plumptre, Peter Reid, John Martin Robinson, Lord Rothschild, Christopher Rowell, Cosmo Russell, Graham Rust, the Duke of Rutland, Lord Sackville, Hugh and Bridget Sackville-West, Michael Sayer, Viscount and Viscountess Scarsdale, Selma Schwartz, Lady Scott, the Earl of Shelburne, Peter Sinclair, Lady Anne Somerset, Karen Stafford, Freddie Stockdale, Sir Tatton Sykes, Bt., the Marquess and Marchioness of Tavistock, the Reverend Miles Thomson, the Reverend Henry Thorold, Hugo Vickers, David Watkin, Lavinia Wellacombe, Lady Willoughby de Eresby, David Wrench and the Earl of Yarmouth.

HMM
CSS
London, December 1993

Select Bibliography

Antram, Nicholas, Jackson-Stops, Gervase, Harris, Leslie, Laing, Alistair *et al*, *Kedleston Hall*, London, 1988

Archer, Mildred, Rowell, Christopher and Skelton, Robert, *Treasures from India: the Clive Collection at Powis Castle*, London, 1987

Aslet, Clive, *The Last Country Houses*, New Haven and London, 1982

Bateman, John, *The Great Landowners of Great Britain and Ireland*, London, 1883 (4th edn)

Beard, Geoffrey, *The Work of Robert Adam*, Edinburgh, 1978

Bedford, John, Duke of, *A Silver-Plated Spoon*, London, 1959

Bence-Jones, Mark, *Ancestral Houses*, London, 1984

—— *The Catholic Families*, London, 1992

Bence-Jones, Mark and Montgomery-Massingberd, Hugh, *The British Aristocracy*, London, 1979

Blake, Robert, *Disraeli*, London, 1966

Bruyn Andrews, C. (ed.), *The Torrington Diaries*, London, 1934–8 (4 vols)

Buckle, Richard (ed.), Cecil Beaton, *Self-Portrait with Friends*, London, 1979

Burke, Sir Bernard, *Burke's Peerage, Baronetage and Knightage*, London, 1826–1970 (105 editions)

—— *Burke's Landed Gentry*, London, 1833–1972 (18 editions)

—— *A Visitation of the Seats and Arms of the Noblemen and Gentlemen of Great Britain and Ireland*, London, 1852–5 (4 vols)

—— *The Romance of the Aristocracy*, London, 1855 (3 vols)

—— *Family Romance*, London 1860

—— *Vicissitudes of Families*, London, 1883 (2 vols)

—— *Burke's Dormant and Extinct Peerages*, London, 1964 (reprint), London, 1969 (reprint)

Burnett, David, *Longleat*, 1978

Campbell, Colen, *Vitruvius Britannicus*, London, 1715–25 (3 vols)

Carnarvon, Earl of, *No Regrets*, London, 1976

—— *Ermine Tales*, London, 1979

Castle Howard, 1988 (guidebook)

Clemenson, Heather A., *English Country Houses and Landed Estates*, London, 1982

Coke, Viscount, *Holkham Hall*, Derby, 1990

Cole, G.D.H. (ed.), Daniel Defoe, *A Tour through England and Wales 1724–6*, London, 1928

Colvin, H.M., *A Biographical Dictionary of British Architects, 1600–1840*, London, 1978

Colvin, H.M.,(ed.), *The History of the King's Works*, London, 1963–81

G.E.C., *The Complete Baronetage*, Gloucester, 1983 (introduction by Hugh Montgomery-Massingberd)

G.E.C. and others (eds), *The Complete Peerage*, London, 1910–59 (13 vols)

Cooper, Lady Diana, *Autobiography*, Wilton, 1978

Cornforth, John *et al*, *Sledmere House*, Norwich, 1988

Country Life: Various articles on houses by Christopher Hussey, Arthur Oswald, Gordon Nares, Mark Girouard, John Cornforth, Marcus Binney, James Lees-Milne, Gervase Jackson-Stops, John Martin Robinson, Giles Worsley, Clive Aslet *et al*

Devonshire, 6th Duke of, *Handbook to Chatsworth and Hardwick*, London, 1844

Devonshire, Duchess of, *The House*, London, 1982

—— *The Estate*, London, 1990

—— *Treasures of Chatsworth*, London, 1991

—— *Chatsworth*, Derby, 1992

Dictionary of National Biography

Downes, Kerry, *English Baroque Architecture*, London, 1966

—— *Hawksmoor*,London, 1970

—— *Vanbrugh*, London, 1979

Egremont, Lord, *Wyndham and Children First*, London, 1968

Fedden, Robert and Kenworthy-Browne, John, *The Country House Guide*, London, 1979

Fielding, Daphne, *Mercury Presides*, London, 1954

Foss, Arthur, *Country House Treasures*, London, 1980

Freeman, David, *Tredegar House*, Newport, 1989

Girouard, Mark, *The Victorian Country House*, Oxford, 1971, and New Haven and London, 1979

—— *Life in the English Country House*, New Haven and London, 1978

—— *Historic Houses of Britain*, London, 1979

—— *Robert Smythson and the Elizabethan Country House*, New Haven and London 1983

—— *A Country House Companion*, London, 1987

—— *Hardwick Hall*, London, 1989

Green, David, *Blenheim Palace*, London, 1951

—— *Grinling Gibbons*, London, 1964

—— *Sarah Duchess of Marlborough*, London, 1967

—— *The Churchills of Blenheim*, London, 1984

Greenwood, Sarah, *Highclere Castle*, Banbury, 1988

Greeves, Lydia and Trinick, Michael, *The National Trust Guide*, London, 1989 (4th edn)

Greville, Charles, *Journals of the Reign of Queen Victoria 1837–52*, London, 1885 (3 vols)

A Short History of Grimsthorpe, St Ives, n.d.

Gronow, Captain Rees Howell, *Reminiscences and Recollections 1810–60*, London, 1900 (2 vols)

Guedalla, Philip (ed.), Benjamin Disraeli, *Novels and Tales*, London, 1926–7 (12 vols)

Hall, Ivan and Hall, Elizabeth, *Burton Constable Hall*, Beverley, 1991

Halsband, R. (ed.), Lady Mary Wortley Montagu, *Complete Letters* , Oxford, 1965–7 (3 vols)

Hare, Augustus, *Memoirs of a Quiet Life*, London, 1872–6 (3 vols)

—— *The Story of Two Noble Lives*, London, 1893 (3 vols)

—— *The Story of My Life*, London, 1896–1900 (6 vols)

Harris, John, *Sir William Chambers*, London, 1970

Herbert, David, *Second Son*, London, 1972

Hertford, Marquess of, *Ragley Hall*, Derby, 1984

Hill, Oliver and Cornforth, John, *English Country Houses: Caroline*, London, 1966 (also other titles in this series)

Hussey, Christopher, *English Country Houses Open to the Public*, London, 1951

—— *English Country Houses: Early Georgian, 1715–60*, London, 1955

—— *English Country Houses: Mid-Georgian, 1760–1800*, London, 1956

—— *English Country Houses: Late Georgian, 1800–40*, London, 1958

Jackson-Stops, Gervase, *The English Country House: A Grand Tour*, London, 1985

—— *The Country House in Perspective*, London, 1990

—— *Knole*, London, 1993

Jackson-Stops, Gervase (ed.), *Treasure Houses of Britain*, New Haven and London, 1985

James, Robert Rhodes (ed.), Sir Henry Channon, *Chips: The Diaries of Sir Henry Channon*, London, 1967

Ketton-Cremer, R.W., *Horace Walpole*, London, 1964

Lamington, Lord, *In the Days of the Dandies*, London, 1890

Leatham, Lady Victoria, Culverhouse, Jon and Till, Dr Eric, *Burghley House*, Derby, 1989

Leslie, Anita, *Edwardians in Love*, London, 1972

Mantell, Keith H., *Haddon Hall*, Derby, 1990

Markham, Sarah, *John Loveday of Caversham*, Wilton, 1984

Montgomery-Massingberd, Hugh, *Blenheim Revisted*, London, 1985

—— *Great British Families*, London and Exeter, 1988

Montgomery-Massingberd, Hugh (ed.), *Guide to Country Houses*, London, 1978–91 (4 vols)

Morris, Christopher (ed.), Celia Fiennes, *Illustrated Journeys*, Exeter, 1982

Masters, Brian, *The Dukes*, London, 1975 and 1980

Lees-Milne, James, *The Age of Adam*, London, 1947

—— *National Trust Guide: Buildings*, London, 1948

—— *Tudor Renaissance*, London, 1951

—— *The Age of Inigo Jones*, London, 1953

—— *English Country Houses: Baroque, 1685–1714*, London, 1970

—— *Ancestral Voices*, London, 1975

—— *The Country House*, Oxford, 1982 (anthology)

—— *Caves of Ice*, London, 1983

—— *Midway on the Waves*, London, 1985

—— *Some Cotswold Country Houses*, Wimbourne, 1987

—— *The Bachelor Duke*, London, 1991

—— *People and Places*, London, 1992

Newman, John, Fuggles, John, Clabburn, Pamela *et al*, *Blickling Hall*, London, 1987

Nicolson, Nigel, *Great Houses of Britain*, London, 1965 and 1978

Nicolson, Nigel (ed.), Harold Nicolson, *Diaries and Letters 1930–62*, London, 1966–8 (3 vols)

Oliphant, Jane, *Penshurst Place and Gardens*, Tonbridge, 1993

Pembroke, Earl of, *Wilton House*, London, 1974

Pevsner, Sir Nikolaus *et al*, *The Buildings of England*, London, 1950 (various vols and edns)

Powell, Anthony (ed.), John Aubrey, *Brief Lives and other Selected Writings*, London, 1949

Robinson, John Martin, *The Wyatts*, Oxford, 1979

—— *The Dukes of Norfolk*, Oxford, 1983

—— *The Latest Country Houses*, London, 1984

—— *The Architecture of Northern England*, London, 1986

—— *The English Country Estate*, London, 1988

—— *The Country House at War*, London, 1989

—— *A Guide to the Country Houses of the North-West*, London, 1991

Rose, Kenneth, *Superior Person*, London, 1969

Rothschild, Mrs James de, *The Rothschilds at Waddesdon Manor*, London, 1979

Rowell, Christopher, *Powis Castle*, London, 1986

—— 'The North Gallery at Petworth,' *Apollo*, July, 1993

Rowse, A.L., *The Later Churchills*, London, 1958

Rutland, Duke of, *Belvoir Castle*, Derby, 1987

Sackville-West, V., *The Edwardians*, London, 1922

—— *Knole and the Sackvilles*, London, 1922

—— *English Country Houses*, London, 1946

Sayer, Michael, and Montgomery-Massingberd, Hugh, *The Disintegration of A Heritage*, Wilby, 1993

Sedgwick, Romney (ed.), Lord Hervey, *Memoirs*, London, 1952

Sitwell, Sacheverell, *British Architects and Craftsmen*, London, 1964

Stewart, A.F., (ed.), Horace Walpole, *Last Journals*, London, 1910

Strong, Roy, Binney, Marcus, Harris, Jon *et al*, *The Destruction of the Country House*, London, 1974

Stroud, Dorothy, *Humphry Repton*, London, 1962

—— *Henry Holland*, London, 1966

—— *Capability Brown*, London, 1975

Sykes, Christopher Simon, *The Visitors Book*, London, 1978

—— *Black Sheep*, London, 1982

—— *Ancient English Houses*, 1988

Syon, Derby, 1992 (guidebook)

Tavistock, Marquess and Marchioness of, *Woburn Abbey*, Norwich, 1987

Toynbee, Mrs Paget and Toynbee, Paget (eds), *Letters of Horace Walpole*, Oxford, 1908–8, and 1918–25; (Yale edn, ed. W.S. Lewis, London, 1937–)

Vickers, Hugo, *Gladys, Duchess of Marlborough*, London, 1979

—— *Cecil Beaton*, London, 1985

Walpole, Horace, *Memoirs of the Reign of King George III*, London, 1894 (4 vols)

Waugh, Evelyn, *Brideshead Revisited*, London, 1945 and 1959

Whibley, Charles, *Lord John Manners and Friends*, Edinburgh, 1925 (2 vols)

Whistler, Laurence, *Sir John Vanbrugh*, London, 1938

—— *The Imagination of Vanbrugh*, London, 1954

Yarwood, Doreen, *Robert Adam*, London, 1970

Accres, Thomas *171, 174*

Adam, Robert 13, *15,* 19, 20, *20,* 23, 71, 75, 77, *77, 78,* 150, 294, *301,* 312, 351, 351, *352, 357,* 359, 361, 363, *364,* 366, *367, 368, 371*

Alnwick Castle, Northumberland 10, **17-25,** *18, 23, 24;* anteroom 24; chapel 23, *24;* dining room 24; Guard Chamber *18;* library *22;* museums 25; Music Room *20,* 24; Prudhoe Tower *22, 23, 24;* Red Drawing Room *19,* 24

Ancaster, Countesses of: Eloise 111-12; 'Wissy' 112, *112,* 115; Dukes of: 1st 107; 2nd 107; 3rd *112;* Earls of: 1st 111; 2nd 222; 3rd 110, 112, 115

Anne, Queen 269, 285, 305, 308, 311, 375

Archer, Thomas *246,* 250

Artari, Giuseppe 241, 323

Arthur, Prince of Wales 32, 35

Atkinson, Thomas (of York) 150, *150,* 151, 398

Aubrey, John 118, 119, 120

Badminton House, Gloucestershire 10, 12, 15, **219-31;** dining room 220, *229;* east front *220;* entrance hall 222, *222, 223;* Great Drawing Room (ballroom) 224-5; Horse Trials 219, *231;* inner hall *227;* library 224, *224;* Master's sitting room *225;* north front 220, *220;* Oak Room 228; parkland 224; staircase *220;* Worcester Lodge 220, 222

Barry, Sir Charles 205, *273,* 352, 358, *358,* 359, *360,* 361, 389, *389,* 390, *391,* 397

Bath, Marquesses of: 2nd 161; 4th *160,* 161-2; 5th 164; 6th 15, 155-6, 164-5; 7th 155, 165

Batoni, Pompeo *339,* 339-40

Beaton, Cecil 128, 131

Beaufort, Dukes of: 1st ('Mr Herbert') 46, *49,* 219, 220-21; 3rd 221, 224, 225; 4th 222; 5th 224; 6th 224; 7th 225; 8th 219, *222,* 225, 228; 10th ('Master') 219, 220, 228, 230; 11th (David Somerset) 15, 230

Beaumont, Lords: 8th 398, *398,* 401; 9th 397, 401, 405; 10th 401, 405

Bedford, Earls of: 1st 192, 194; 4th 195, 196; Dukes of: 1st (William Russell) 197; 2nd 209; 4th *192,* 197, 199, *202;* 5th 199, 200, *201;* 6th 200, *201;* 7th 200; 9th 200, 202; 12th ('Spinach' Tavistock) 191, 202; 13th 15, 191, 192, 202

Belvoir Castle, Leicestershire 10, 13, 28, **373-83,**

375, 382; Elizabeth Saloon *379,* 379-80; Grand Staircase *377;* Guard Room *375,* 383; kitchen *380;* Pre-Guard Room *375*

Bentley, John Francis 401, *401,* 405, *405, 406*

Birley, Sir Oswald 143, *358*

Blandings Castle (TV series) 67

Blenheim Palace, Oxfordshire 12, 95, **305-15,** *309;* front door key and lock *306;* Grand Bridge 312, 314, 315; Great Hall 305, *306,* 308; Green Writing Room 308, 309, 311, 312; Long Library 305, 312, *312;* park and gardens *314,* 315; saloon *311;* Blenheim Tapestry 309; Water Terraces *314,* 315; Willis organ *312*

Blickling Hall, Norfolk 9, 12, 14, **181-9,** *182;* clock tower 189; east front *188;* Great Staircase *182;* Long Gallery 184, *184,* 189; north front *182;* Peter the Great Room *186;* State Bedroom *187;* Stone Court *182*

Boleyn, Anne 58, 182

Boughton House, Northamptonshire 12, 264, **277-91,** *278;* ceilings *281,* 284, *284;* entrance and colonnade *289;* Great Hall *281;* Little Hall *281,* 284; north front *290;* panelling *278, 281;* parkland 285; staircases *282, 285, 286*

Bourchier, Thomas, Archbishop of Canterbury 84, *89*

Brakespeare, Sir Harold 32, *35*

Brettingham, Matthew, the Elder 266, 332, *364,* 366

Brettingham, Matthew, the Younger 270

Brown, Lancelot 'Capability' 12, 17, 71, 140, 150, 155, 160, 224, 233, 250, 261, 306, 315, 344, 346, 352, 376, 385

Buccleuch, Dukes of: 3rd 286, 289; 9th 291

Buccleuch, Mollie Duchess of (*née* Lascelles) 289-91

Buckingham, 3rd Duke of 58

Buckinghamshire, Earls of: 1st 186, 187; 2nd (John Hobart) *186,* 186-9; 3rd (George Hobart) 189; 9th 189

Buckinghamshire, Mary Countess of *186,* 189

Burghley, Lord *see* Exeter, 6th Marquess of

Burghley, William Cecil, Lord 136, 139

Burghley House, Cambridgeshire 12, 15, 133-43, *135;* Blue Silk Dressing Room *136;* Bottle Lodges 143; courtyard and clock tower *143;* gardens 140; Great Hall 135-6, 139; Heaven

Room *136,* 140; Hell Staircase *135,* 140,143; Jewel Closet ceiling *135;* kitchen 136, *139;* Roman Staircase 140; roofscape 140; Second George Room *139,* 140; state bed *139*

Burke, Sir Bernard 98, 104, 327

Burlington, Richard Boyle, 3rd Earl of 123, 294, 318, 324, 331, 335

Burton Constable, East Yorkshire 12, **145-53;** Blue Drawing Room 151; Chinese Room 153, *153;* dining room *150;* east front *153;* facade *146,* 147; Great Drawing Room (ballroom) 151, *151;* Great Hall *146, 147,* 149, 151; Lamp Room 153; Long Gallery 149, *149,* 150, 153; stables *153;* Staircase Hall 150

Byng, John 28, 50, *50,* 51, 167, 376

Byron, George Gordon, Lord 91, *294,* 301

Camden, Sir William 61, 101

Campbell, Colen 318, 322, 323, 329, 366

Canaletto, Antonio 24, 192, 199, *202,* 222

Canina, Commendatore Luigi *20, 22*

Canova, Antonio: *Sleeping Endymion With His Dog* 258; *The Three Graces* 200

Carlisle, Earls of: 3rd 293, 294, 299, 300; 5th 301-2; 8th 302; 9th 302

Carlisle, Rosalind Countess of 301, *302*

Carlton Towers, Yorkshire 9, 10, 14, **397-406,** *407;* clock tower 398; gargoyle 398; outer hall 398, *401,* 405; staircase *406;* Venetian Drawing Room 402, 405, *405*

Carnarvon, Earls of: 1st (Henry Herbert) 385-6, *392;* 2nd 386; 3rd 386, 389-90; 4th 389, *389,* 390, 391; 5th 391-2, 395; 6th ('Porchey') 392, 395; 7th 395

Carnarvon, Evelyn Countess of 390, 391

Carr, John (of York) 150, *247,* 346, 348, 351, 352

Casali, Andrea 75, 150

Castle Ashby, Northamptonshire 98, 101, 103, 104, 105

Castle Howard, Yorkshire 10, 12, 15, **293-303;** Antique Passage *299;* Atlas Fountain *302;* Carrmirr Gate 293; chapel 302; dome 294, *294, 299;* east wing (burnt out) *301;* Garden Hall 302, 303; gardens *302;* gatehouse 293; Great Hall *8, 295,* 303; Long Gallery *296,* 302; north front 294; Obelisk 293, 299; Orleans Room 301, *301;* south front 294; Temple of the Four Winds 299; waterfall and bridge *294*

Catherine II, of Russia, Empress (the Great) *186*, 189, 317, *321*, 327, 352
Cavendish family *see* Devonshire, Dukes of
Cavendish, Sir William 168, 169, 249
Cecil family 12, 136
Cecil, William *see* Burghley, Lord; Exeter, Earls of
Chambers, Sir William 123, *128*, 315, 351
Charles I, King 119, 196, 207
Charles II, King 45, 46, 49, *92*, 120, *124*, 184, 220, 282, 286, 309
Chatsworth, Derbyshire 10, 12, 15, 78, 95, 168, 169, 178, **245-59**, *252*; Blue Drawing Room *247*; Duke's Sitting Room *246*; Emperor Fountain 255; *enfilade* of state rooms *255*; Flora's Temple 256; gardens 246, 250, 255; giant foot *247*; library 250; Mercury (bronze) *255*; Painted Hall 249; Sabine Bedroom *255*; Sculpture Gallery *258*; south front *246*; stair-cases *249*, *255*; Tapestry Gallery 250; Violin Door 250; west entrance hall *256*; west front *13*
Cheere, Sir Henry *53*, 109
Chéron, Louis *281*, *282*, 284
Chichester-Constable, John 145, 146
Chippendale, Thomas *124*, 146, 151, *151*, 153, 243, 352, *352*, *354*, *357*, 358, *358*, 361
Chippendale, Thomas, the Younger 361
Cholmondeley, Marquesses of: 1st 327; 5th 317, 318, 329; 6th 329; 7th 329
Cholmondeley, Sybil Marchioness of 289, 317-18, 329
Churchill family *see* Marlborough, Dukes of
Churchill, Sir Winston 291, 305-6, 311
Cipriani, G. B. 75, *77*
Claude (Lorraine) 192, 335
Clive, Robert Clive, Baron 50, 51, 53
Clive, 2nd Lord *see* Powis, 1st Earl of
Cobbe, Alec *51*, 53, 270, 343, *354*, 359, 361
Coke, Sir Edward 331-2
Coke, Viscount Edward 15, 340
Coke, Thomas *see* Leicester, 1st Earl of
Coke, Thomas (*né* Roberts) ('Coke of Norfolk') 336, *339*, 339-40
Collins of London, William *150*, 361
Compton, Sir William 98, 100, 101
Compton Wynyates, Warwickshire 11, **97-105**; Big Hall 98, *98*, 100, 105; chimneystacks *98*; Council Chamber 100, *102*; dining rooms 105; fishponds *100*; Priest's Room 100-1, *102*, *103*; west front *104*
Constable, William 147, *149*, 149-50, 151
Conway, Edward, 1st Earl of 238, 241
Cooper, Lady Diana 31, 383
Cornforth, John 212, 347
Crace, John 160, 161, 162, *246*
Cucci, Domenico *19*, 24
Cuer, Cornelius 85, *89*
Curzon, George Nathaniel Curzon, 1st Marquess 367-8, 370
Curzon, Sir Nathaniel, 2nd Bt. 363; 5th Bt. *see* Scarsdale, 1st Lord

de Caus, Isaac 119, 123, 196

de Havilland, General John 405, *406*
De L'Isle and Dudley; Lords: 1st 64, 66; 2nd 66; 4th 66; Viscounts: 1st 57, 66; 2nd 15, 58; Viscountess Isobel 15, 58
Devonshire: 1st Earl of (William Cavendish) *169*, 172, 249; Duchesses of: Deborah 15, 245-6, *247*, 255, 256; Evelyn 178; Georgiana 250, 255; Dukes of: 1st *246*, *249*, 250; 2nd 209; 4th 250; 5th 250; 6th 178, *247*, 255, *255*, 256 (*Handbook to Chatsworth and Hardwick* 178, *246*, 255, 256); 8th *247*; 9th *249*; 11th 15, 245-6, *246*, 249
Disraeli, Benjamin (Lord Beaconsfield) 55, 209, 228, 380, 385; *Coningsby* 243, 380; *Lothair* 401
Dobson & Sons of Driffield 343, 348
Dorset: Earls of: 1st (Thomas Sackville) 85, 87, *89*, *90*; 3rd 87; 6th 87, 89, *92*; Dukes of: 1st 89; 3rd 89, 91; 4th 91
Duchêne, Achille *314*, 315
Dungan, Richard 85, *89*, *90*

Edward VI, King 58, *58*, 71-2, 192, 194
Edward VII: as Prince of Wales 349, 415
Egremont, Earls of: 2nd 266; 3rd 261, 264, 270, 273; Lords: 1st 274-5; 2nd 275
Elizabeth I, Queen 11, 61, 84, 101, 131, 136, 139, 157, 169, 174, 195, 331, 373
Exeter, Earls of: 1st (William Cecil) 139; 5th 139, 140; 9th 139, 140; Marquesses of: 1st 140, 143; 2nd 143; 3rd 143; 6th 133, 135, 143

Fastolfe, Sir John 182
Fiennes, Celia 221, 250
Flaxman, John 261; *St Michael and Satan* 273
Flitcroft, Henry 12, *192*, 197, 199, *202*
Fowler, John 112, *112*, 115
Freud, Lucian 246, *247*

Gainsborough, Thomas 89, 133, 255, 261, *294*, 339, 359, 383, 415
George I, 109, 327
George II, King 18, 186
George III, King 150, 188, 241, 305, 339
George IV (as Prince Regent) 241, 243, 339, 377, 379
Gheeraerts, Marcus, the Younger 64, 149
Gibbons, Grinling 140, 220, 224, *229*, 261, 264, *264*, 306, 322
Gibbs, James 219, 221-2, *222*, 235, 241, 323, 363
Girouard, Mark 9, 158, 303, 398
Gould, Sir Charles: 1st Bt. 209; 2nd Bt. 209; 3rd Bt. *see* Tredegar, Lord
Granby, Marquess of 375-6
Grant, Sir Francis 349, 359
Greville, Charles 20, 200, 243, 379
Grey, Lady Jane 71, 168
Grimsthorpe Castle, Lincolnshire 12, 14, **107-15**; ceilings 109; chapel *14*, 109, *112*, 115; Chinese Drawing Room 109, 115, *115*; dining room 109; Great Hall ('Vanbrugh Hall') 107, 109, *110*, *111*; King James's Drawing Room 109; King John's Tower

108, 115; north front 108, *108*; staircase balustrades 109, *111*; State Drawing Room 112; west front *115*
Gwydir, Lord *see* Willoughby, 21st Lord

Haddon, Lord 31, 383; marble effigy *30*, *379*
Haddon Hall, Derbyshire 10, 11, **27- 41**, *40*, 383; Banqueting Hall 32, *35*; chapel 28, *30*, 31, *31*; courtyard *28*, *33*; dining room 32, 35, *35*; 'Dorothy Vernon's Steps' *33*; gargoyle *33*; gardens 40-41; kitchens 32; Long Gallery 27, 28, 32, 36, *36*, *38*; north-west tower *28*; south front *28*; State Bedroom 36; tapestries 35-6; terrace *32*
Handful of Dust, A (film) 406
'Hardwick, Bess of' *see* Shrewsbury, Lady Elizabeth
Hardwick Hall, Derbyshire 10, 12, 14, 36, 157, **167-78**, 245, *250*; doorways *171*, *177*; Green Velvet Room *171*; High Great Chamber 172, 174, *176*; Long Gallery 174, *174*, 178; sea dog walnut table *173*; staircases *168*, 173
Hare, Augustus 143, 383
Harewood, Earls of: 2nd (Beau Lascelles) 352; 3rd 352, 359; 4th 352; 5th 352; 6th (Harry Lascelles) 352-3, 355, *357*, 361; 7th (George Lascelles) 15, 355, 357-9, 361
Harewood, Edwin Lascelles, Lord 351-2, *359*
Harewood, Mary, Princess Royal, Countess of 355, *358*
Harewood, Patricia Countess of 15, 358
Harewood House, Yorkshire 13, 15, *15*, **351-61**; Adam's library 15; Cinnamon Drawing Room 359, *359*; dining room *358*; entrance hall *357*, 361; garden front 352, *360*; Long Gallery 352, *354*, 359, 361; Music Room 359; Rose Drawing Room 359; Spanish Library *357*; terraces *360*
Hatton, Sir Christopher 174, *174*
Hawksmoor, Nicholas *14*, 109, *112*, 293, 294, 299, 300-301, 305, 312, *312*
Henry VII, King 109, 207
Henry VIII, King 43, 58, 71, 80, 84, 98, 100, 101, 107, 108, 109, 156, 194, *250*, 278
Herbert family *see* Pembroke, Earls of
Herbert, David 128, 131; *Second Son* 128
Herbert, Sir Edward 43, 45, *50*
Herbert, Henry *see* Carnarvon, Earl of; Pembroke, 17th Earl
Hertford, Lady Isabella ('the Sultana') 241, 243
Hertford, Marquesses of: 1st 241; 2nd 241; 3rd 243; 4th 243; 8th (Hugh Seymour) 15, 233, 235, 241
Hervey, Lord 323, 327, 332
Highclere Castle, Hampshire 10, 14, **385-95**, *386*; bathrooms 395; dining room *392*; entrance hall 390; library *389*, 390, *391*, 395; Music Room 390, *391*, saloon *386*; tower *389*;
Historic Houses Association 14, 317, 340
Hobart family *see* Buckinghamshire, Earls of
Hobart, Sir Henry 182, 184
Holkham Hall, Norfolk 12, 15, 266, **331-41**; *enfilade* 335, *335*; Green State Bedroom *339*; Long Library 332, *335*; Marble Hall 332,

332, 335, 339; North Dining Room 335, *336*; north front *341*; saloon *336*; south front 332, *332*; Statue Gallery *332*, 335
Holland, Henry 199, *200*, 202
Hooke, Robert 238, 241
Houghton Hall, Norfolk 9, 12, 187, 290, **317-29**, 331; east front *318*; Great Staircase *324*; Green Velvet Bedchamber 324, *327*; library *323*; Marble Parlour *322*, 323, 324; parkland 329; saloon *321*; staircase *318*; Stone Hall *318*, 323, *323*; west front *328*
Howard family *see* Carlisle, Earls of
Howard, Lady Elizabeth *see* Rutland, Elizabeth Duchess of
Howard of Henderskelfe, George Howard, Lord 15, *299*, 302-3
Hussey, Christopher 9, 182

Jackson-Stops, Gervase 12, 94
James I, King 104, 108, 139, 182, 184, 332
James II, King 45, *92*, 286, 309
Johnson, Francis 343, *345*
Jones, Inigo 12, *112*, 117, *118*, 119-20, 196, 205, 312
Jonson, Ben: on Penshurst Place 57, 67

Kedleston Hall, Derbyshire 9, 13, 14, **363-71**; dining room 366; door furniture *366*; drawing room 364, *366*, *367*; 'Family Corridor' *368*; Great Staircase *368*; Indian Museum 368; library *371*; Marble Hall *364*, 366; north front 366, *371*; Smoking Room 368; south front *364*, 366, 367
Ken, Bishop 160; library *158*, 160, *164*
Kent, William 12, 89, *118*, 119-20, 123, *124*, 219, *220*, 222, *222*, 255, *299*, *321*, *322*, 324, *324*, 329, 331, 332, 335, *335*, *336*, *339*, 340
Kerr, Philip *see* Lothian, 11th Marquess of
Kneller, Sir Godfrey 133, *262*, *269*, 311
Knole, Kent 12, 14, **83-95**, *84*, *94*; ballroom 89; bed (in Venetian Ambassador's Room) *92*; Brown Gallery *90*, 92; Cartoon Gallery 85, *90*, 92; Great Staircase 89, *91*; Jacobean arcade *11*; King's Room silver furniture 92, *92*, 94; parkland *11*; wooden screen 85, *86*; wooden soldier *87*
Knox, J. Erskine 405, *406*

Laguerre, Louis *249*, *273*, *308*, *311*
Landseer, Sir Edwin 222, 225
Lanscroon, Gerard *46*, 49
Lascelles family *see* Harewood, Earls of
Lascelles, Edwin *see* Harewood, Lord
Lawrence, Sir Thomas 133, 349, 415
Leatham, Lady Victoria 15, 133, 135, 140, 143
Leconfield, 2nd Lord 273, 274; 3rd Lord 261, 275
Lees-Milne, James 11, 92, 189, 219, 255, 275
Leicester, Earls of: 1st (Sir Robert Sidney) 64; 7th 64; 1st (2nd creation) (Thomas Coke) 331, 332, 335, 336; 2nd 340; 3rd 340; 4th 340; 5th 340

Lely, Sir Peter *124*, 128, 133, 149
Lightoler, Thomas *146*, 150, *150*, 151, *153*
Lightoler, Timothy *146*, 150, *150*, 151
Lindsey, Earls of: 1st (Robert Bertie) 108; 3rd 108
Liotard, Jean-Etienne: *William Constable* 149, *149*
Little Lord Fauntleroy (film) 383
Longleat, Wiltshire 12, 15, **155-65**; Bishop Ken's Library *158*, 160, *164*; Brown Stairs *162*; door *160*; gallery *163*; gardens and parkland 155, 160; Great Hall *158*, 160; library table *162*; Red Library 160; Roman busts *157*; roofscape *156*; saloon *162*; State Dining Room *162*; State Drawing Room *160*
Lothian, Marquesses of: 8th 189; 11th (Philip Kerr) 181, 189
Louise of Stolberg, Princess *339*, 340
Louis XVIII, King of France 151
Loveday of Caversham, John *98*, 105
Lucas van Leyden 121
Lyminge, Robert 12, 184

Manners family 10; *see* Rutland, Earls and Dukes of
Manners, Lady Dorothy (née Vernon) 27-8, *33*
Manners, Sir George 27-8
Manners, Lord John *see* Rutland, 7th Duke of
Manners, Sir John 27, 28
Manners, Sir John (grandson of the above) *see* Rutland, Earls and Dukes of
Manning, Cardinal Henry 398, 405
Marie Antoinette 91, 412
Marlborough, Duchesses of: Consuelo *312*, 315; Gladys *312*; Laura 306; Rosita 315; Sarah 197, 308, 311, *311*, 312, 314-15; Dukes of: 1st 305, *308*, 308-9, 311, 312, 314-15; 4th *308*, 315; 5th *308*; 9th *312*, *314*, 315; 10th 306, 315; 11th 315
Marot, Daniel 264, 277
Mary Queen of Scots 101, 169, 176
Massingberd, Burrell 324, 327, 331
Maynard, Allen 157, 160
Medd, Scott *299*, 303
Monnoyer, Jean-Baptiste *249*, 284
Montagu, Dukes of: 1st (Ralph Montagu) 264, 277, 282, 284, 285, 286; 2nd (John) 285-6
Montagu, Sir Edward 278, 281
Montagu, Lady Elizabeth (née Wriothesley) 285
Montagu of Beaulieu, Lord 145, 370
Montagu of Boughton, Edward Montagu, Lord 281-2
Morgan family 205, 207; *see* Tredegar, Viscounts
Morgan, Sir William (1) 207; (2) 207; (3) 209
Morris, Roger *118*, *119*, 123, *128*
Mortlake tapestries 35, 284, 335, *339*
Murillo, Bartolomé 192; *Holy Family 379*

Napoleon Bonaparte, desk and chair of *391*, 395
National Heritage Memorial Fund 145, 146, 370
National Trust 14, 15, 55, 81, 83, 91, 92, 94, 95, 98, 178, 181, 189, 261, 270, 275, 368, 370, 371, 416, 417

Norfolk, Miles Fitzalan-Howard, Duke of 406
Northampton, Elizabeth Countess of 103-4
Northampton, Earls of: 1st 103-4; 2nd 104; 3rd 104; 8th 105; Marquesses of: 3rd 105; 5th 97
Northumberland, Earls of (Percy family): 17; 9th 17, 72, 262; 10th 262; Duchesses of: Elizabeth (née Seymour) 18-19, 20, 71, 75; Elizabeth (formerly Montagu Douglas Scott) 25; Dukes of: 1st (Hugh Smithson) 18-19, 71; 2nd 20, 77; 3rd 20, 24, *72*, 78; 4th 20, *22*, 23-4, 78; 6th 80; 10th 25, 81; 11th 25, 71, 81
Nost, John van 45, *53*

Ohanessian, David *346*, 348
Orford, Earls of: 1st *see* Walpole, Robert; 3rd 317, *321*, 327; 4th *see* Walpole, Horace

Paine, James 250, *364*, 366
Palladianism 12, 95, *119*, 123, 318, 323, 324, 331, 340, 364, 366
Paxton, Sir Joseph 78, 255
Pellegrini, Carlo *299*, 302, 303
Pembroke, Earls of: 1st (Sir William Herbert) 43, 117-18; 2nd 118; 3rd 117, 119; 4th 12, 117, 119; 7th 120, *124*; 8th 121, 124; 9th ('Architect Earl') *119*, 121, 123, 315, 324; 10th 123; 11th 123, *123*, 124; 15th 124; 16th 128, 131; 17th 131
Pembroke, Mary Countess of (née Sidney) 62, 118
Penshurst Place, Kent 8, 11, 15, **57-67**; Baron's or Great Hall 58, *58*, 61, *61*, 62, 64; cabinet 62; chapel *61*; courtyard 66; gardens 57-8, 66; gargoyle *61*; Long Gallery 64, *64*, 66; north front *59*, 68; Queen Elizabeth Room 64; south front 66; west front 68
Percy family *see* Northumberland, Earls of
Percy, Sir Henry ('Hotspur') 17, *18*
Petworth House, Sussex 10, 12, 14, 75, **261-75**, *262*, *274*, 277; Beauty Room *269*; Carved Room 264, *264*, 270; door furniture *263*; enfilade *263*; Grand Staircase *273*; Marble Hall *270*; North Gallery 266, 270, *270*; parkland *261*; Red Library *269*; sculpture gallery 270; staircase hall *270*; west front 264, *275*; White and Gold Room *269*; White Library 266
Pollen, John Hungerford 184, 189
Portinton, William 85, *86*, 89
Poussin, Nicolas 192, 335, 383
Powis, Violet Countess of (Lady Darcy de Knayth) 55
Powis, Earls of: 1st (Henry Herbert) 49-50; 2nd 50-51; 1st (3rd creation) (2nd Lord Clive) 51, 53; 2nd (Edward Herbert, né Clive) 51, 53; 3rd 55; 4th 55; Marquesses of: 1st 45, 46, 49, *49*, 53; 2nd 49
Powis Castle, Powys 8, 10, 14, **43-55**, *45*; Aviary Terrace 53, *54*; Clive Museum 51, *51*, 53; gardens 53, 55; Grand Staircase 46, *46*, 49, *49*; inner courtyard *45*; Long Gallery 45, 50, *50*; State Bedroom 45-6, *49*; west front *45*
Pritchard, T. F. 46, 50, 51
Puget, Pierre 264

Pugin, Edward Welby 397, 401, *406*
Ragley Hall, Warwickshire 12, 15, 205, **233-43**; dining room *240*; Great Hall *235*, 241; Music Room 238, 241; Red Saloon *237*, 238, 241
Rebecca, Biagio *352*, 361
Rembrandt van Rijn 121, 192
Reynolds, Sir Joshua 19, 89, 128, 192, 243, 255, 261, *301*, *308*, 359, 376, 379, 415
Richardson, Sir Albert 202, *202*
Riesener, Jean-Henri *410*, 412
Ripley, Thomas 322-3, 329
Robinson, Sir Thomas 300-301
Romney, George 261, 349; *Lady Hamilton 412*, 415
Rose, Joseph (of York) *72*, 75, *75*, 347, 348, *357*, 361, *364*
Rothschild, Baron Ferdinand de 409-10, 412, 415, 417
Rothschild, Baron Jacob 15, 416, 417
Rothschild, Baron James de 415-16
Rubens, Peter Paul 121; *Holy Family* 335
Russell family 191, 192, 194, *195*; *see* Bedford, Dukes of
Rust, Graham: *The Temptation* 235, 237-8, *238*
Rutland, Earls of: 1st (Sir Thomas Manners) 27, 373, 2nd 373; (Sir John Manners) 28; 5th 373; Duchesses of: Elizabeth 377, 379, *379*; Isabella 376; Violet *30*, *31*, *379*, 383; Dukes of: 1st (Lord Roos) 375; 3rd 375; 4th 376; 5th 376-7, 379, 380; 7th 380, 383; 8th 31, 383; 9th 27, 28, 31, 36, 40, 383; 10th 27, 40, 383
Rysbrack, John Michael 224, *318*, *322*, 323

Sackville, Lords 84; 3rd 83; 4th 91
Sackville-West, Vita 83, 91-2, 95; *The Edwardians* 84
Salvin, Anthony 20, 23, 273-4
Sargent, John Singer *160*, *247*, 317
Scarsdale, Lords: 1st 363-4, 366, *367*; 4th 367; Viscounts: 2nd 370; 3rd 370, 371
Scott, Sir Walter 20, 23, 386
Seymour family *see* Hertford, Marquesses of; Somerset, Dukes of
Shakespeare, William 117, 118, *121*, 182
Shrewsbury, 6th Earl of 169, 249
Shrewsbury, Elizabeth Countess of ('Bess of Hardwick') 167-9, *169*, *171*, 172, 174, 176, 178, 249, 398
Sidney, Sir Henry 58, 61
Sidney, Sir Philip 61-2, 64; *Arcadia* 62, 118, 120
Sidney, Sir Robert *see* 1st Earl of Leicester
Sidney, Sir William 58, *58*
Sitwell, Sir Osbert 8, 228
Sitwell, Sir Sacheverell 174, 299, 315
Sledmere House, Yorkshire 15, **343-9**; library 343, *344*, *345*, 347; south front *348*; Turkish Room *346*, 348; west elevation *344*
Smith, Francis (of Warwick) 221, 363
Smithson, James 18-19
Smythson, Robert 157, 158, 172-3
Somerset, Lord Arthur 219, 228
Somerset, Dukes of (Seymours) 80, 205, 220; 1st

(Lord Protector) 71-2, 156-7, 241; 6th ('Proud Duke') 17, 72, 75, 262, 264; 7th 18
Somerset, Elizabeth, Duchess of (*née* Percy) 17, 72, 158, 262
Somerset, Lord Henry 219, 228
Stanyon, Edward 184, *184*
Stapleton, Elizabeth 397-8
Stapleton, Miles *see* Beaumont, 8th Lord
Staunton, Rev. Dr 377, 379
Stothard, Thomas *135*, 143
Stuart, Arabella 169, 174
Suffolk, Henrietta, Countess of 186, 187
Swift, Jonathan, Dean 107, 293
Sykes, Sir Christopher, 2nd Bt. 343, 346, 347
Sykes, Christopher Simon 347-8
Sykes, Sir Mark ('Parson Sykes'), 1st Bt. 346
Sykes, Richard 344, 351
Sykes, Sir Richard, 7th Bt. 348
Sykes, Sir Tatton: 4th Bt. 347-8; 5th Bt. 348; 8th Bt. 15, 343, *345*
Syon House, Middlesex 9, 10, 11, 13, **71-81**, 157; anteroom 75, *75*; bedroom *81*; conservatory 78; dining room 75; drawing room (private) *78*, *80*; *The Dying Gaul* (bronze) *72*, 75; gardens *9*, 71, 72, 75, 81; Great Hall *72*, 75; lion statue *72*, 78, 80; Long Gallery 75, *77*, *78*; pavilion boathouse *77*, 78; Print Room *77*, 78; Red Drawing Room 75, *76*, *77*; river front *72*

Talman, William *246*, 250, 264, 293, 294
Tatham, C. H. *296*, 302
Tavistock, Marquess and Marchioness of *200*, 202
Taylor, Robert (butler to Earls of Carnarvon) *392*, 395
Teniers, David, the Younger 192, *250*; *The Proverbs* 383
Tennyson, Alfred, Lord: *The Lord of Burghley* 7, 140
Thornhill, Sir James 109, *110*, *308*, *311*; *The Rape of the Sabines* 255
Thoroton, Rev. Sir John *377*, 379, 383
Thynn(e) family *see* Bath, Marquesses of
Thynne, Sir John 156, 157, 158
Thynne, Thomas 17, 72, 158, 262
Tijou, Jean 140, *249*, 303
Tintoretto, Jacopo 24, *160*, 192, 353
Titian *160*, 261, 353, 379; *The Bishop of Armagnac...* 24; *Rest on the Flight into Egypt* 162
Tredegar, Viscounts: 2nd (Godfrey Morgan) 209; 3rd (Evan Morgan) 209, 212
Tredegar House, Gwent 12, **205-17**, *206*; Brown Room 206, *208*; corridor *217*; 'Cow Bathroom' 212; entrance front *217*; Gilt Room 206, *206*, *207*, 217; Great Staircase 206, *211*; kitchens *214*, 217; Master's Bedchamber *211*; New Hall *211*; service bells 212
Turner, J. M. W. 261-2, 352; *A Stag Drinking* 261; *The Temple of Jupiter Panhellenios* 19

Vanbrugh, Sir John 12, 107, 108, *108*, 109, *110*, 293-4, *294*, 299, *299*, 300, 301, 305, 306, 308, 311-12, *312*, 314-15, 323

Van Dyck, Sir Anthony 12, 24, *118*, 119, 133, 164, 192, 261, *282*, 335, 379
Vernon, Sir George 27-8
Veronese, Paolo 140, 353
Verrio, Antonio 46, 49, 133, *135*, *136*, 140, 250
Victoria, Queen 35, *139*, 143, *197*, 200, 286, 339, *339*, 398, 415
Victorian Kitchen (TV series) 217

Waddesdon Manor, Buckinghamshire 14, 15, **409-17**, *416*; Baron's Room *412*, 415; gardens 412, 416-17; morning room 415; panelling 412; Red Drawing Room *410*, 415, *415*; roofscape *410*
Walpole, Horace 18, 19, 36, 94, 186, 187, 189, 264, 299, 301, 305, 327, 363, 366, *367*, 375
Walpole, Sir Robert 317, 318, 322, 323, *323*, 324, 327, 331
Waugh, Evelyn 7, 348; *Brideshead Revisited* 7-8, 14-15, 84, 233, 291, 303; *A Handful of Dust* 406
Webb, John 120, 205, 220
Westlake, N. H. J. *402*, 405, *405*
Weymouth, Viscounts: 1st 158, 160; 2nd *158*; 3rd 161
William III, King 49, 87, 109, 250, 277, 285, 375
Willoughby de Eresby, Lady Jane 107, 115
Willoughby de Eresby, Lords: 10th 107-8; 21st (Lord Gwydir) 110, 111; 24th *see* Ancaster, 1st Earl of
Wilson, Richard 128, 261
Wilton House, Wiltshire 10, 43, 62, **117-31**; Chambers' arch 123, 124, *128*; doorcase *12*; door furniture *120*; Double Cube Room 12, *118*, 119; drawing room (private) *127*; east front *10*, *118*; gardens 118, 119, 132, 131; Holbein Porch 118, 123; Palladian bridge *118*, *119*, 123, *128*; sculpture 121, 124; Single Cube Room 119, 120, *124*; south front *130*; statue of Shakespeare *121*; west front *130*
Winde, Captain William 46, 49, 108
Woburn Abbey, Bedfordshire 12, 15, **191-202**; Blue Drawing Room *194*, *195*; Canaletto Room *202*; Great Staircase 192; Grotto *196*, *196*; hall (ground floor) *192*; Long Library 199, *200*; parkland 200; Queen Victoria's Bedroom *197*; state apartments *199*; State Dining Room 199, *199*; west front *192*
Wodehouse, P. G.: *Blandings Castle* 7, 43, 67
Wootton, John *158*, 219, *222*, *262*, *323*
Worcester, 2nd Marquess of 219-20
Wren, Sir Christopher 238, 311, 312
Wyatt, James 13, 28, *123*, 123-4, 128, 150, 151, *151*, *237*, 241, 377, 379
Wyatt, Matthew Cotes 379-80
Wyatt, Samuel 188, 346
Wyatville, Sir Jeffry 160, 161, 200, 224, *224*, *249*, *250*, 255, *256*
Wyndham family 261; *see* Egremont

Yarmouth, Earl of 237, 243
Young, Arthur 305, 335